Pulse

Steve Rudd was born in East Yorkshire, England, in 1980. He is a music journalist, an experimental musician, an acclaimed poet, and a footloose vagabond. His travel writing has appeared in *Time Out, The Guardian* and *TravelMag,* and in 2010 he was a runner-up in the *Travellers' Digest* Young Writer of The Year Award.

Steve has explored more than seventy countries on his travels, and written enough material to fill five full-length books, much of which has been published online and devoured by a loyal following of more than 4000 readers. *Pulse* describes his latest journey, and marks the first time these articles have been collected in print.

Pulse

STEVE RUDD

Steve Rudd

VALLEY

PULSE

First published in 2011
by Valley Press
www.valleypressuk.com

Printed in England by Imprint Digital,
Upton Pyne, Exeter

ISBN: 978-0-9568904-5-0
IPN: VP0017

A catalogue record for this book
is available from the British Library

www.valleypressuk.com/authors/steverudd

9 8 7 6 5 4 3 2 1

Dedicated to Chris McCandless (1968 – 1992),
for seeing the world a different way,
and for providing a reason.

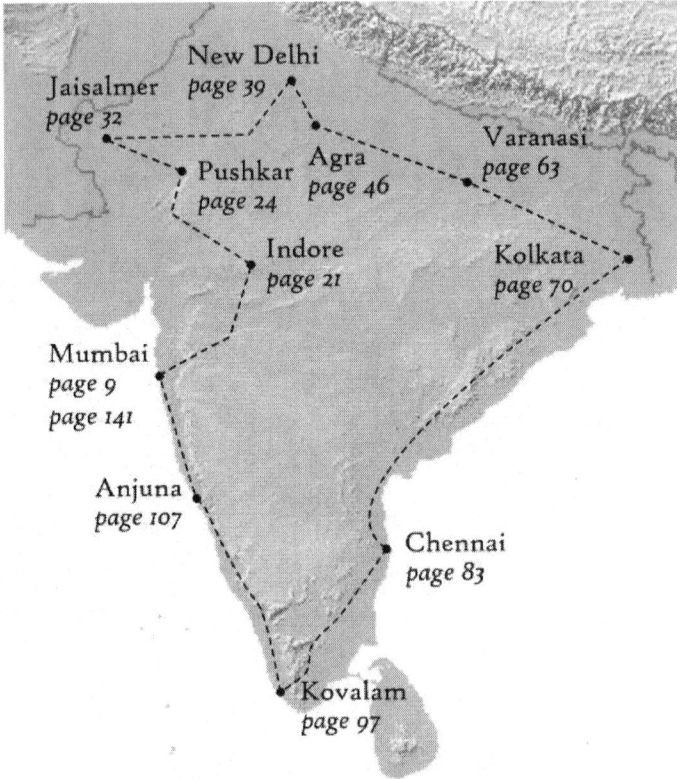

– The *Pulse* Journey –
India

Penang
page 288

Kuala Lumpur
page 295

Melaka
page 288

Singapore
page 253

Jakarta
page 253

Surabaya
page 156

Bali
page 161

– The *Pulse* Journey –
Malaysia / Singapore / Indonesia

IT SHOULD HAVE BEEN SO SIMPLE.

I'd bought a voucher for a taxi from the airport to the Colaba district of Mumbai, a drive rumoured to take approximately forty-five minutes after dark. The flight from London had been a sophisticated lark of nerve-calming proportions, during the course of which I'd devoured *The Celestine Prophecy* whilst listening to Bon Jovi's latest record on loop. It was *The Circle* by no coincidence. Ever tormented by words and all their possibilities, I took things personally if they didn't work in my favour, subtly manipulating such controllable entities since they're so partial to artsy malleability. Feeling as relaxed as could be for three o'clock in the morning, I half-expected my backpack to have gone missing in transit. When it reared its frayed head on the luggage carousel, I began to count my blessings. Shame I counted them too early. Hardwired to blaze through a life less blinkered as a beatnik seeker of truth, I was tempted to kowtow to the *Diceman*'s revolutionary logic, prone to tinker with the conservative notion of conformity. But how is it possible to cultivate self-respect if you're soul-dead? In times of distress, you must take yourself to new places, and then take such places with you.

Once shot of the airport, the taxi driver bolted down a potholed alley that couldn't have been any more ill-lit if a city-wide power-cut had struck. Bumping the Ambassador's chassis into submission whilst impatiently grinding its gears, my driver lurched to a halt beside some shacks. Four guys emerged. 'I'll be back,' the driver promised. Although his tone lacked the authority with which *The Terminator* had first delivered the same line back in 1984, I had no reason to doubt for a second that he'd return. I had no idea where he was going, though. In his absence, the guys surrounded the cab. Conveniently for them, but inconveniently for me, the rear windows had been rolled down, hence why they were able to paw at my shirt, begging for rupees. Given that it was the dead of night and I had literally been abandoned, it was an unsavoury set-up to say the least. Fortunately, the driver stuck to his word, hopping back into the cab five minutes later when the pimped-out beggars, evidently in league with him, realised I wasn't going to buckle in terms of buying my way out.

'You go to Colaba?' he barked, slamming shut the door before opening a bottle of rum he'd procured from beneath his seat. 'Yes,' I concurred. 'To the Red Shield Guesthouse near The Gateway of India.' Without uttering another word, he left the beggars for dust, angrily bouncing onto the main expressway with the wrong kind of spirit coursing through a body that camouflaged its soul with terrible stealth.

~

ALTHOUGH CERTAIN CITIES IN INDIA may be deemed 'expensive' by some people's standards, the bulk of the subcontinent is exceedingly cheap. Furthermore, certain areas of the most expensive conurbations have their value-for-money quirks. Take the ancient Colaba district of South Mumbai, for instance. While Mumbai at large is liable to drain a backpacker's budget within a very short period of time, Colaba seeks to aid those on tight budgets by offering a broad range of accommodation and grazing options.

Rising tall and proud behind the iconic Gateway of India, 'The Taj Mahal Hotel' is by far and away the most breathtaking hotel in the area, yet even its cheapest rooms threaten to send many potential 'residents' running for 'The Salvation Army' just around the corner. For fresh-off-the-plane newbies to the city, 'The Salvation Army' guesthouse cannot be faulted in terms of its pricing structure. For those unperturbed by the thought of roughing-it amongst like-minded individuals, a dormitory bed can and should be snapped up for approximately two-hundred and twenty-five rupees. A double room, meanwhile, shouldn't set you back more than eight-hundred rupees.

In the wake of my paranoia-inducing taxi ride to Colaba on the darkest side of midnight, I booked into 'The Salvation Army' without hesitation, hollering through the shuttered entrance to the guy snoozing on reception. Despite feeling guilty for waking him up, I was glad to be rewarded with a bed. Pity I had to trudge up to the third floor and negotiate a debris-flooded corridor which shouldered the room I'd been assigned. Out of respect for those backpackers already asleep, I crept into the room with silent courtesy, only to trip over a backpack and fall into bed with a guy who really didn't appreciate my accidental wake-up call. Above him, my upper bunk awaited. Consisting of nothing more than a spinally challenging mattress, there was neither pillow nor sheet in sight. Menaced by the subversive heat and flippant nightcrawlers, I slid my backpack into the nearest corner before hoisting my weary body up and into a woefully uncomfortable state of repose. Breathing a deep sigh of relief, only now could I appreciate the fact that I'd arrived in the most cosmopolitan city in India. More importantly, I was safe.

Breakfast greeted me with multiple surprises. Expecting a mouth-watering tray of myriad curries to be thrust in my direction, I hastened to display utmost gratitude for the plate of bread I was handed through the service hatch in the so-called dining hall. The mere thought of succumbing to 'Delhi Belly' on my first day in India was enough to make me hesitant. The three slices of bread were tempting, but the sliver of accompanying butter sent a subtle shiver of trepidation through me. Complementing the carbohydrates, a banana and an egg dared me to pick them up and gulp them down. Having no rupees with which to buy food anywhere else, I realised that to shun such sustenance would be foolish, hence why I found a seat and devoured everything to hand. At the foot of the crumbling stairwell, a Bollywood casting agent scouted for suitable extras to star in a commercial being shot on the edge of the city. Had I trusted the man, I would have followed him and milked the opportunity for all it was worth.

I finally hit the streets of Mumbai at ten. Given that it's a city spread over seven islands, I wasn't sure where to begin my forays on foot, so I lassoed logic by heading straight to the waterfront's Gateway, through which the last British troops marched when India embraced independence.

The act of seeking shelter and shade beneath The Gateway's heaven-bound arch proved to be frustratingly difficult. Not only did an army of touts stall my progress, but an intimidating wall of military personnel also sought to prevent me from standing where I wanted to set foot. I soon learnt that such personnel were preparing for Barack Obama's historic visit to Mumbai later in the week. Extricating myself from the area, I ventured deeper into Colaba, uncharacteristically stumbling upon 'Leopold's Cafe' in due course. One of the oldest and most popular haunts for backpackers wary of sampling food and drink from the barrage of stalls flanking Colaba Causeway, the joint's homely vibes are legendary. While it's certainly not the cheapest place to indulge (in fact, it is probably the most expensive place in all of Colaba to eat, drink and be merry),

Leopold's is most definitely a fabulous place to meet fellow travellers. The only reason I ducked inside boiled down to my desire to escape the heat. I flicked open my copy of *The People's Act of Love* and ordered a chicken omelette in tandem. In the past, I'd never been renowned for my ability to multi-task, but India had already forced me to focus on the bare necessities if nothing else. I left thirty minutes later, bound for the nearest vendor of fresh sugar cane juice. It's impossible not to notice the huge number of roadside stands sabotaging street corners. They come complete with a crushing device so devastating that to trap one's hand in the mechanism could give rise to a scream so piercing it might be heard over on Chowpatty Beach. At first, I suspected that the guys running such stands were in the throes of furiously liquidising bamboo. Questioning my own assumption, I asked a passer-by if it really was bamboo being crushed. 'No… it's sugar cane,' volleyed the no-nonsense, time-saving response. For just ten rupees, I promptly got to grips with the scandalously sweet elixir. A further twenty minutes and three glasses down the line, I was hopelessly addicted to such an extent that I couldn't resist stopping at every stand I passed, sheepishly handing over a ten-rupee note to each vendor. However, my addiction to sugar cane juice proved to be nothing more than a fad. Upon reaching CST, the biggest and busiest railway station in Mumbai, my attention was deflected towards the cheap tea and coffee available within its built-to-last walls. For five rupees, a scolding hot serving of Nescafe hit my throat where it hurt. For one rupee less, I was able to swish a few mouthfuls of Nestea down the hatch.

As diligently as I tried to save money in Mumbai, I wound up spending far more than anticipated simply because everything seemed so cheap. A sucker for sampling local culinary delights, I became progressively more daring when it came to sampling street food.

I ultimately dubbed the day 'a miracle'. Twelve hours in, and I'd never felt better. Jet-lag still hadn't caught up with me, and my digestive system was thankfully being responsive in a wholly positive manner. The last thing I wanted was a night on the tiles. Fortunately, it was the last thing I got.

~

'WHAT DO YOU MEAN THERE'S NO WATER?' I didn't mean to interrogate Israeli tycoon Eliran, but I desperately craved an answer. Longing for a shower of any description, I'd waited patiently for him to finish in the communal bathroom. Only Ganesh knew what he'd been doing in there. 'Hey, you'll be lucky to tease a drop out of that shower,' Eli taunted. 'And guess who's to blame?' I felt like throwing in the towel, literally. Three whole days had passed without a single drop of water hitting my back. 'I suppose it's the plumber's fault,' I ventured, my smile taking a slide. 'The plumber?' pondered Eli, a shock of puzzlement raising his brows. 'I don't think there is one. I'm talking about Obama!' Two guys from London hustled between us, rushing downstairs to greet a Bollywood agent. Twenty-four hours beforehand, an agent had thrown his flash car across a busy thoroughfare to ask my friends and I if we fancied starring in an all-singing, all-dancing movie. 'Today's your day!' he'd promised in vain. But it wasn't our day at all, for every day belongs to everyone. 'It's Barack who's using all the water!' Eli loudly disclosed, raping my reverie. 'Not only that, but his entourage has secured the monopoly on electricity usage for the next two days!' For a moment, I wondered if the most powerful man in the world had relocated from his palatial hotel to our joke of a guesthouse. 'Which dorm's he in?' I asked Eli. 'Stop joking with me, man... he's not here! He's still in the flash digs over the road, but there's not enough water or power to be shared, so the authorities have cut our supply,' Eli continued, visibly amused by our infuriating state of deprivation.

Listening whilst thinking, I reset my stance, peering behind Eli. A plastic vessel of water sat unattended in the corner of the bathroom. Intermittently, it served to flush the toilet, a bucket within the barrel contributing to efficiency when it came to conveying stagnant water across the void. Daubed in hair shed by a hundred travellers of mixed nationalities, the floor's cracked tiles had seen it all. Eli excused himself, slipping around the corner into a room beset by six rusty bunk-beds and three walls of sick graffiti. Did I possess the courage to undress and pour the barrel's contents over my head? The cold wave of water would undeniably liberate me from fatigue. I stepped over the threshold, towards the barrel. My toothbrush mutely voiced its distrust by leaping from a back pocket. Was I really vying to brush my teeth before attempting to cleanse my skin without considering what waterborne evil may have been present and suspect? The brush bristled at my feet, urging me to think again. Thrusting my arms forward, statuesque images of America's most revered men and women plagued my mind's eye. They were watching wasted water spin down their drains. Clean water, might I add. 'Don't do it, Steve. It's not worth the risk!' Eli had sloped back to check on me, perhaps expecting a random act of stupidity to befall balanced judgement. 'Step away from the barrel,' he instructed. 'But I feel dirtier than a nymph in mud,' I pleaded. 'Get out while you can,' responded Eli, brushing imaginary dust from his shirt in anticipation of a meeting with a property developer. 'Okay, okay – I give up!' I balled, spinning on my soles.

In spite of feeling wretched, I retreated from the bathroom to the dining recess. A window presented a sight to resent: claustrophobic lockdown on the street below. Yellow barriers spoke of restricted mobility for those not affiliated with the presidential convoy. Obama was poised to leave his hotel in a bulletproof vehicle that could only be described as a 'beast' in every respect. Armed military personnel nervously tapped rifle butts against burning stretches of tarmac, waggling their heads whenever stranded residents of 'The Salvation Army' sought to batter the barricades in order to gain access to the building. The President was scheduled to gain cultural insights into various projects raging in favour of disadvantaged women and children. Based in Colaba for the weekend, he was due to walk next to nowhere. His security aides would see to that. Thus, the roads were closed to civilian traffic, allowing Barack & Co. to be funnelled across Colaba Causeway without waiting for a single red light to turn green. Flashing my camera in the direction of his temporary abode, I prayed I wasn't mistaken for a sniper. Dizzy with boredom, I itched to look upon the streets with the reverence they deserved.

~

LOUDER THAN WAR, fireworks corrupted the otherwise quiet nook of Chowpatty Beach. Diwali, the Festival of Light, had reached a crescendo of raucous madness, an assortment of short-fused bangers throwing the promenade into turmoil. Marine Drive was dangerous enough as it was after dark without having to worry about stray fireworks striking shins or charring chests. Returning to Colaba from the airy heights of Malabar Hill, I had little choice but to use Marine Drive as a means to an end. Crushing the sand, lines of boats pointed their noses inland, resting up prior to being re-employed at dawn. Wedged between the sand and the main road, an army of brightly-lit food stands beckoned those tired of larking, saluting a vast range of appetites with everything from delicately decorated sweets to 'samosas' and 'pakoras'. Steam from cauldrons billowed as I wound a course through the gasping melee, nibbling at a mouth-watering variety of deep fried vegetables topped with chutney.

A crowd of onlookers gathered as I tucked into 'chaat' with a grin. In spite of its north Indian origin, vendors in Mumbai have long curried favour with the potato-based snack. Patting my stomach, I left the beach to lope back onto Marine Drive, ducking for cover as a potentially deadly firework whistled through traffic from the other side of the road, slamming into the wall to which I'd unconsciously clung. A gaggle of young boys chomping on grilled cobs keeled over, not in fear, but in hysterics. I'd over-reacted in their apparently fearless eyes. A split-second later, a follow-up missile indiscriminately whooshed in our direction. Its landing point represented nothing personal. It had to earth its pointed head somewhere, so why not near me?

Along with religious rituals, fireworks are all part and parcel of the five-day festival. Observed by Hindus, Jains and Sikhs, Diwali rejoices in the victory of good over evil on an annual basis. As expected, few - if any - laws govern folk with a penchant for fuelling explosions by lighting fuses. Proof was in the proverbial pudding when two policemen walked past. Neither batted an eyelid as a slew of firecrackers provoked me to slam my hands upon my sorely offended ears. Taking refuge atop the sea wall, I stepped aside to allow a couple of happy-clapping transvestites gain a square metre of sanctuary. It transpired that they weren't clapping as a result of being joyful, but in hope that a selection of promenaders might contribute a few rupees towards further surgery. Aggressive in demeanour, they looked down their noses at those who ignored them, continuing to clap until money was either relayed into their hands or tossed at their heads. Marginalised beyond redemption, Indian transvestites don't have it easy in terms of securing work. Routinely ridiculed by society, they literally beg to be accepted by relying on other people's cash to keep them in clothes. A courting couple of teenagers saw fit to leer at them, going so far as to fling a firecracker their way. Screaming colour-blind murder in retaliation, the transvestites understandably didn't take too kindly to such an inhumane assault. The tallest chased after the cops, pleading not to be ignored, yet there was to be no comeback, no repercussions, no justice. The duo on patrol simply walked on, callously laughing as they strode into an inferno of social animosity, ironically branding themselves sexist pigs with a difference.

~

'AFTER YOU!' My friend was too kind; our taxi driver was too wired. 'Okay, I'll take a look,' I promised, shunting open the door of the cab, hopping onto the pavement. Hanging over the club's door, a sign attached colourful significance to the building. It read: 'THE WHITE PALACE'. We were supposed to be drinking in one of the bars on Khar Road, but our driver preferred to propel his vehicle in elongated circles. I recognised the periphery of Colaba as soon as we wheeled past Churchgate Station. 'If you won't take us to Khar Road, how about Bandra?' I challenged. 'No! Too far! It would take an hour just to reach Mahim Bay,' he curtly complained. Incredibly, opulent high-rise malls helped to define the skyline just a few miles away from Dharavi: Asia's largest slum.

My friend gazed at me expectantly. Acknowledging the hint, I stretched my legs towards the ominous venue. The neon lights which defaced the bar-cum-club's entranceway inspired a dizzy spell of trepidation, pinning my feet to the far kerb. The two bouncers saw me coming a yard off, throwing punches at their own gloved hands. The guy nearest the handle turned to fling open the door. 'Whoah, whoah, whoah,' I blurted. 'What's inside, and how much does it cost to get in?' It looked shadier than a supermodel on holiday. 'Come in and have fun,' the man smirked. All we desired was a drink, yet our driver had convinced his seedy psyche that we youthfully lusted after more. 'Can I just have a look through the door,' I asked, faking a smile, a nauseating flashback catapulting me through time and space to the ski resort of Borovets, Bulgaria. There, along with a friend, I'd been lured into a dodgy bar by a detestable bunch of locals. Expecting a cheap dab of 'après-ski' mitigation, I was shocked to discover that the chirpy façade shielded an underground brothel. Accidentally spluttering an extortionately priced and unforgivably lukewarm can of 'Kamenitza' into the face of the aggressive barman, I froze in motion as four scantily-clad women began to circle, animalistically licking purple lips. Feeling distinctly uncomfortable, we abandoned the rest of our drinks and shot for the door, only to find it barred. Buying ourselves out in local currency, we vowed to be more careful in future when scouting for watering holes.

Dropped back into the present, I asked the Mumbian 'Guardians of Secrets' if I could confer with my shoulder-shrugging buddy before stepping any further. Daggers could be seen twirling in their opaque eyes. Petting an outburst of common sense, I returned to the cab with an unwarranted assertion. 'Drive!' I told the meter-smearing smoker up front. Fearing further linguistical reprisals, the man engaged something that resembled first gear, shakily conveying us to the next 'bar'.

~

'I'M LOOKING FOR A MURDERER.'

Unprepared to make the transition from warehouse operative to contract killer, I tried to stifle my gulp of dread. Trapped on a train somewhere between Aurangabad and Indore, I wondered if the man sat opposite sought to indoctrinate me into a world bursting with sawn-off shotguns, craftily concealed knives, and gang-orientated loyalty. Spiriting myself away, I peered between the bent bars guarding the window. Escape wasn't an option. 'Sorry, but I already have a job in England,' I fibbed. In truth, I'd resigned on grounds of boredom. I doubted the man would wish to hear about my ambition to make a living from writing full-time, especially not when he sounded to be in the business of cold-bloodedly terminating lives. 'I don't want you to become a murderer if that's what you think,' the man announced. 'I'm a policeman.' Subconsciously, I modified my posture, aiming to sit straighter. Suddenly, I was all ears. 'Yes, that's what I thought!' I haughtily laughed, unveiling my unease. His eyes noticeably shrunk in contemplation. 'I've been looking for the man - the murderer - for years. He's so far evaded capture, but my partner and I know where he is,' he stated, gesturing over to his scarily overweight sidekick. Constituting a couple of undercover cops, the mismatched pair divulged more details than the scope of professionalism would normally allow. Far from doing things by halves, they'd travelled hundreds of miles by train, vying to initiate closure on a cross-country manhunt which harboured the capacity to gain refined promotions for them both.

As the most talkative of the duo dug into a comparison study, desperate to see how the police force operated in the UK, a blind boy neared on his knees, his right arm instinctively creeping towards my lap, primed to pat me down. He couldn't have been older than six or seven. Wearing a soiled white shirt and partly ripped shorts, he turned his ear to the strangeness of my accent, the strength of his hearing making up for his compromised sight. Pushing a bowl along the gangway, he begged for rupees, stealing my sympathy. 'Food! If anything, give the urchin food!' spat the cop. 'But I don't have any,' I pleaded, struggling to liberate leftover coins from my pocket. 'Money will do the kid no good,' the man insisted. 'Forgive me if you think I'm being harsh, but a lot of children begging on trains are pimped out. Any money you give them will be collected by the men who have enslaved them. Sad, but true.' I looked down at the boy, wondering if his eyes had been gouged out as per *Slumdog Millionaire*.

What's become of humanity when desperation forces a deranged minority to commit acts of evil against innocent and vulnerable members of society? It required an enormous amount of resolve to resist giving the boy a financial boost. If the cop was right, my selfless nature would be exploited, in turn fuelling even more begging. But what if the kid returned to his pimp without anything to show for his humiliating crawl along the length of the train? Would he be beaten, or raped, or worse? I didn't know what I could do to help. Had poetic justice proved to be a reality, the cop would have intervened by asking the boy about his circumstances, to ascertain if he was 'working' on somebody's money-hungry behalf. I stared at the cop, desperate to telepathically convey my thoughts. 'I know what you're thinking, but I'm sorry – I'm powerless.' Futility collided with reality, hurtfully hurtling above and beyond my control.

~

THE BLOOD WAS MINE. That much I can reveal. The shave had been a long while in coming; it felt inclined to nick my neck. The spit, however, came courtesy of the man sat in front of me on the bus ride between Udaipur and Pushkar, both settlements which reside in India's diverse state of Rajasthan.

Three days spent in Udaipur had been enough for me to recharge my batteries. *Slumdog Millionaire* star Dev Patel had also been staying in the city, but he'd been busy shooting scenes with director John Madden for a new movie. Alas, our paths had failed to cross. At a loose end, I'd compared travel notes with Marina Maier, a road-savvy Swiss girl who'd been gadding about India's Golden Triangle alone.

As the dubiously 'deluxe' bus bumped out of Udaipur, a barrage of medical schools, dental surgeries and blood banks snared my attention, reminding me of the subcontinent's commitment to making advances in various scientific and technological fields. Out of such institutions gushed gaggles of girls wearing white uniforms and shawls, somehow managing to keep their garments immaculately clean in spite of the plumes of acrid smoke billowing from the hundreds of auto-rickshaws, buses and taxis bolting past them.

It's difficult to gain a sense of Udaipur's size from its Lal Ghat ghetto of tourists and travellers. It's only when you're driven to distraction on the roads leading to the city's outskirts that you realise how large the place really is.

Although the monsoon season had dematerialised, a shock downpour of biblical proportions wasted no time in flooding many of the city's streets, leaving businesses high and dry until the water was able to seize passage underground through the detritus-clogged drains. Such water had fortunately begun to recede as our bus eased out of the city, into the hills. I was sad to leave, but I couldn't wait to reach Pushkar, for I'd struck it lucky in the sense that the world's largest camel fair was due to reach its climax there in the morning. Unfortunately, the rickety bus had seen better days. Infested with inquisitive flies, its dank and dirty interior failed to inspire a single ounce of confidence. A bus of the double-decker variety, the upper section of the vehicle consisted of two lines of 'dens' in which four people could secrete themselves upon mattresses, privy to sliding doors.

The scenery immediately persuaded me to pay less attention to Adiga's Booker Prize-winning *White Tiger* novel and more to the epic vistas opening up to the east. A taut tapestry of hardy vegetation smothered the rocky hills in every direction. At ground level, yard after yard after yard of marble and granite ran parallel with the road on both sides, paying testament to the fact that such minerals are sourced and quarried in the vicinity. If they weren't being quarried, they were surely being curried.

The ingloriously overcast and cold afternoon rarely surrendered to random shafts of sunlight, but the succession of landscapes looked beautiful once the depressing cloud cover lifted. At one point I even fancied that I could smell the soil's fertility, until I realised that such an earthy fragrance had emanated from the man chewing 'paan' in front. He spat its red residue through the window in due course.

The gears of the bus changed with less regularity as we ploughed further into the hills. Nine hours later, with fatigue on my back, we rolled into Ajmer, a considerable distance short of my desired destination. Shouldering my backpack with a mixture of trepidation and excitement, it was time to re-negotiate my plans in stride with Irish vagabonder Paul Keelan.

~

DUMBSTRUCK BY A DUST-STRICKEN OCEAN OF CAMELS on the edge of Pushkar, I saw no way out. Jagged mountains laced the horizon, near and far. A tent of Indian men fancied themselves as Asian cowboys, whooping their way out from beneath their ill-erected shelter with a view to buying and selling horses. While the scene proved to be timeless, the sound of whining creatures proved to be unbearable, maltreated horses and camels crying to be released from ropes binding their spindly legs to metal pegs buried deep in the earth. Struggling feverishly in hope of escaping, a line of camels snorted as I passed. I like to think it had little to do with the length of raw sugar cane clamped between my jaws. Having been instructed to peel the tough skin with my incisors, I tried to access the sticky bounty to no avail. My teeth couldn't cut it. I traipsed on, careful to dodge out of the way of a horse galloping beneath the unbalanced weight of a man 'test-riding' the towering Appaloosa, a possible descendant of Genghis Khan's feted family of warhorses. Reining in nothing but a belated acknowledgement of his own inexperience, the man straddling the beauty shouted at the horse as though it understood Hindi. Its tail was short, its mane upright. It instinctively knew where it wanted to go: home... to Mongolia. In spite of almost been bucked off as he succeeded in slowing the horse to a halt, encouraging it to turn, the rider then summoned the nerve to whip it towards the fairground, challenging its agility, sullying its innocence. I looked away, unable to accept that the animals were being treated with such cruel intent.

The parade ground crawled with as many animals as people. Beyond it, three men rallied to a seemingly impossible cause, failing to recognise the futility anchoring their attempt to cram four camels into the back of a truck via a slatted ramp of insanely steep proportions. Sick of the charade, the driver decided to prod the hind legs of the last camel to be loaded. It was the worst thing he could have done, the camel reacting as expected by kicking the token fool in the stomach. Needless to say, he fell like a waterfall of breeze blocks - but not before flying ten yards. The rogue camel was eventually dragged onto the truck, only for it to subsequently tumble over the side, landing in a leggy heap in front of a wayward snake charmer.

Desiring a high altitude dose of perspective, I energetically slid out of the frame. Hoping karma would duly descend upon the heavy-handed men shouting at the heart of such contemptible darkness, I was exhausted by the onslaught waged between species. Snake Mountain was temptingly close, yet I opted to ascend a less intimidating peak in the footsteps of faithful Hindus. The path was clear; pilgrims were abundant. Taking their time, they paused after every few steps to catch breath that had been snatched by the humbling scope of the view. Pushkar Lake glistened in the near distance, sacred glimpses of its 'ghats' reminding me that an important religious festival was underway at arm's length from the ancient settlement's camel-dominated counterpart. I could also see Brahma Temple, the only temple in the world where Lord Brahma - Creator of the Universe - is worshipped. The sight of the summit proved more elusive.

~

WISELY, NOT ALL OF US CRAVE CHANGE. Before I departed on this voyage, 'Facebook' began to morph into a cesspit of broken dreams, and I broke free. I could no longer read papers or watch the news on TV. Both mediums depressed my upbeat attitude. I couldn't help but wonder if society had limped past the point of no return on grounds of decency. The promotion of moral degradation seemed to be all the rage. Extortion, rape, ruin, murder: they all had a part to play as products of a self-obsessed epoch. We needed to return to where we came from as a race. I, for one, felt like an alien on my own planet. Around me, robotised humans dashed hither and thither without once looking up to see what was in front of them. Enslaved by their mobile phones, they launched inconsequential missives dogged by purposefully misspelt text-speak. Back in Britain, on a train, I had asked a middle-aged commuter what he thought of the book in his hand. His frigid 'what are you talking to me for?' glare told me to shut up. Laughing in the face of emotional adversity, I wondered if I'd been wrong to ask the stranger an innocent question. One day in the distant future, vocal cords will be rendered redundant. It's true: more and more people are talking less and less. A whole host of abbv.'d apps have already seen to it that there's next to no room for old souls who prefer to live like they always have. Knowing that the media machine will stop at nothing to nail a headline, I vowed to stay strong, conscious that anybody's reputation can blossom, explode, then burn.

Proudly speaking her mind, my grandma had passionately voiced a complaint about the uncivil automisation of libraries a week before I absconded. The ability to scan one's own books in and out didn't impress her in the least. She cared not for increased efficiency. More than saving a few seconds, she wanted to converse with staff about what she'd been reading, and which titles they recommended. 'You can't speak to a machine,' she argued. Good on her, I say. Engineers may retaliate by insisting that you *can* speak to a machine and make it understand, but that's not the point. Unless such machines are capable of generating emotional responses, then it's not the same. It's all too much. And there's no need for any of it.

~

EMERGING FROM SPIRITUAL SLUMBER, I COULDN'T BELIEVE MY EYES. Having pushed and shoved my way up the steps, I looked down to be greeted by the sight of three cars encircled by a near-vertical wall of rotten wood. I'd stumbled upon an Indian version of a 'Wall of Death' in the midst of Pushkar Fair. People began to congregate on the steel walkway surrounding the 'pit' with stunning ferocity as soon as one of the motorcyclists took it upon himself to rev his bike as loudly as possible in order to attract surplus attention. Overshadowing the ill-erected structure, a provocative range of mountains sought to rise above the heat haze. Even though it was early in the morning, it was getting hot long before its time.

Sited in a truly beautiful neck of Rajasthan, Pushkar has it made in terms of being the perfect place to visit for folk eager to rebuild their spiritual foundations. Teeming with yoga centres and music schools, along with an imposing ashram on the edge of the conveniently compact town, it's easy to understand why Pushkar features so highly on people's 'Must Visit' lists. Its annual fair constitutes the main reason why people hone in on the area with such festive glee, the sprawling city of Ajmer providing an ideal hub for connecting bus and train services.

The allure of 'The Wall of Death' is a curious thing. It wields the power to inspire awe and terror in equal measure. In spite of the unnerving way in which the structure continued to sway whenever more people crowded onto the circular walkway, adrenaline surged in anticipation of the drama poised to unfold. In a last-ditch bid to attract a final flurry of paying punters, a young man jumped on one of the bikes to fling up sand with his back tyre, noisily skidding into the proverbial ring of doom via a set of Jurassic Park-esque gates. It was time - or so it would seem. A minute later, another motorcyclist entered the fray, followed by yet another. The scene was set... but nobody had seen anything yet. Two other guys then emerged, shutting the gates behind them before getting into two of the cars parked at the centre of the ring. I'd suspected that such cars had been strategically parked there so the tyre company with adverts on their roofs attained maximum exposure. In reality, they were rigged to take part in the spectacle as well.

Evil Knievel would have covered his eyes. Even some of the stunts performed by the 'Jackass' boys failed to compare in scope once two motorcycles and two cars took to the wall in quick succession, the skilled riders and drivers gunning their respective engines to the hilt in order that their vehicles defied physics and propelled them around the wall with enough speed to prevent them from spectacularly tumbling in a sorry heap. As speed and confidence increased in perfect synchronicity, one of the car drivers positioned himself directly below his comrade whilst rattling around the wall, conspiring to reach out and hold hands with him. As they both perched on the rims of their windows, it was unbelievable to think that they were still steering and accelerating as if born-contortionists.

The thrilled crowd stared on in rapt wonder. How were the stuntmen performing such feats? In truth, their five-minute run-around was arguably the most exhilarating show I'd ever seen. It had been a sight to behold. Four hours later, as I scoured the red horizon for a rickshaw, my legs were still trembling in the wake of witnessing the team's unquestionably dangerous heroics.

It was time to hang some distance between Pushkar and inflamed awe. The ancient, desert-shouldering city of Jaisalmer awaited in a rough westerly direction, so I sought to sign off, pay up, and make haste.

~

'THERE'S SOMEBODY SLEEPING IN MY BED!' The scenario was akin to something out of 'Goldilocks'. But it was true: there really was somebody tossing and turning upon the mattress with which I was desperate to acquaint myself.

I'd just stepped onto a bus bound for the fortified desert town of Jaisalmer. The preceding two days had been spent exploring Pushkar's world-famous Camel & Horse Fair. No long-distance buses departed direct from Pushkar, so it was necessary to take a slow local bus along the hairpin bend-anchored road through the mountains to Ajmer, the nearest city of repute. Given that it was the final night of the annual Camel Fair, the firework-fuelled feast of a climax meant the traffic flow in and out of Pushkar had been altered. The only way out was by what had to be dubbed 'the scenic route' - not that it was very scenic in the dark. The downside was that the detour was due to consume almost ninety minutes.

The 'luxury' bus to Jaisalmer was scheduled to leave Ajmer at ten. We rolled into the middle of the back of beyond at nine. Hope of reaching our connecting bus on time significantly diminished by the minute. Pausing at a random check-point, everybody including the driver hurriedly de-bussed for a ten-minute huddle. I remained seated near the back, staring through the window at the piercing constellations hung above the profile of the nearest mountain range. I wondered what my girlfriend, Sarah, might have been doing in England, wholeheartedly trusting that the distance between us would strengthen our relationship. I also wondered what had led me to be animatedly suspended in the Indian wilderness with little more than a few hundred rupees to my name. Unfairly cursing the truth expounded by my watch, I willed the driver to return to his seat in order to engage forward motion once more. Confident that my psychic abilities had been improving, I was woefully disappointed when the driver loped further away... in search of a toilet. I considered such a respectable course of action to be extremely strange, especially when most Indian men simply unzip or drop their trousers at the side of the road, in full view of anybody and everybody. In no respect are they shy.

We hit the road again ten minutes later, when - in fact - it was the potholed road that hit us. As we coyly bounced around a corkscrew of corners, the freaky creak of the vehicle's suspension heralded nothing but bad news. Wedged between my backpack and a handrail, my arm came to hate my funny bone. In turn, my funny bone lost its sense of humour, demanding a dictionary in order to redefine the meaning of 'patience'. In the wake of groaning up a mild gradient, we crested a hill. Below us lay what could only be described as Utopia: a dense patchwork of linear lights criss-crossing an expansive valley. Dropping into Ajmer reminded me of my approach to Salt Lake City in 2006 after a tortuous journey that had swept me clean across the canyon-contoured glory of Utah, a state beautified yet isolated by heavy snowfall. Ecstatic to see the city, I could have kissed the driver were he not wrestling the steering shaft to snapping point. I had twenty minutes to spare: ample time to score and devour a cracked bowl of cold rice.

The ecstasy inspired by eating was short-lived. Hating waiting, a friend demonstrated the most efficient choke hold known to Mixed Martial Artists, much to the astonishment of sweet-scoffing locals. They thought I was being beat up. Incidentally, I'd clocked a suitable place to test one's abilities in Pushkar, though it was uncertain if the training centre would attract the kind of numbers expected owing to a spelling mistake on the sign. Having said that, there may have been just as much demand for 'Marital Arts', depending on one's religion. Behind us, as we grappled, a lonesome cow kicked around a weed-encrusted yard, chewing on cardboard, gagging for fibre.

A deluxe bus had been promised; it had been depicted on posters in the travel agency's paperwork-heaped bureau; the balding agent had personally assured me that the bus to

Jaisalmer would be the very best to be seen peeling along Indian roads. Encouragingly, the agent had been at the departure point when I'd arrived, but fled amidst a dust storm of suspicion just five minutes before the dented wreck honked its repulsive arrival. I couldn't believe my eyes. 'Jaisalmer! Jaisalmer!' hollered a man hanging out of the door as the glorified shed shuddered to a halt. Sensing that I'd be joining him for the ride, the guy beckoned me over. 'Hurry! Hurry!' he spat. I might have been in a position to gain a tad more momentum had I not been weighed down by a backpack.

As I attempted to make headway along the gangway to my designated sleeper berth, a jamboree of passengers hustled towards me, elbowing for an inch, ushering me backwards. The bus was clearly no place for a backpacker: space was at a premium. I looked around, first at the decrepit state of the bus, then at the passengers. Almost all of them were Indian men. Judging by their wide-eyed expressions, they seemed surprised to see a foreigner on-board. Squeezing to the far end of the gangway, I literally searched high and low for my berth. The numbers were hard to find. My berth for the journey was right in the corner. Shame there was no floor space upon which I could drop my gear. Even worse, the berth was thrumming to a man's snoring. Shaking the man's elbow, I urged him to wake up. He was out cold, feasibly flat-lining. His buddies on the back seat laughed at my apparently futile plight. 'Excuse me – you're in my berth,' I said as softly as I could, yet loud enough for him to hear. His nostrils twitched, but only in response to a fly that had settled upon his beak. It was time to hail the cavalry: the so-called conductor. In spite of initially laughing along with the backseat reprobates, he roused the man by dead-arming him. The doe-eyed imposter might have taken half a minute to recover from the shock, but he soon got the message and descended. With all eyes on me, I flung my backpack through the gap between the sliding doors, seeking suitable footholds on neighbouring berths to aid my ascent. Once ensconced within what can best be described as a mobile grave, I shuffled my bones into what approximated to a horizontal position, keen to sleep for as much of the overnight ride as I could. The excitement of the camel fair had wiped me out.

I'd supposed that a comfortable state of repose would be easy to attain. I had, however, failed to factor in the disquieting stares emanating from the gangway-crowding men, not to mention a window which refused to stay shut for longer than thirty seconds at a time. I was cocooned in an unapologetic state of hell worse than sedated society ruled by routine. Disturbingly, there could be no chance of escape until the breathtaking fortifications of Jaisalmer hove into view. The journey had just begun, yet I already wanted to stagger down the gangway and plead for salvation. Cat Stevens might have once believed that 'the first cut is the deepest,' but that's not the case at all, for the never-ending bus ride between Ajmer and the edge of the Thar Desert went a long way to prove that every nick, knock and cut can be as deep as the one that precedes – if not deeper.

~

WE WERE DESERTERS. Every single one of us. Bouncing along the arrow-straight and surprisingly smooth road between Jaisalmer (a spectacular fortress city that couldn't fail to remind of Carcassonne in southern France) and the poverty-swept village of Kadoi, it was hard to believe we were driving through the heart of the Thar Desert in the rough direction of the India-Pakistan border. 'Five years ago,' mumbled our driver, 'all of what you see was desert in the truest sense, though recent rains have helped vegetation find a way.' Indeed, the desert-scape at our disposal failed to represent the type of scene we'd expected. While far-off sand dunes promised a certain degree of photogenic romanticism, much of the terrain over which we sped consisted of unattractive scrubland and rock.

I'd booked myself onto a safari tour through 'Sahara' - an ironic name for a company if ever there was one. We were in northern India, for Lord Kali's sake... not northern Africa. Owned and operated by 'Mr. Desert' himself, the company has been escorting travellers through the Thar for the best part of twenty years. 'Mr. Desert' was awarded his prestigious title as a direct result of winning the 'Mr. Desert Competition' for four successive years. Essentially a male beauty pageant in which competitors buckle up in all their Rajasthani finery, the competition continues to this day.

Poised to spend two days and one night in the desert, I'd brought enough layers of clothing to keep me warm through what could potentially be an extremely cold evening beneath the stars. Three Welsh brothers and a charming Dutch couple, Freek and Anna, had also slammed their rupees where saddle sores threatened to surface.

We stopped a few kilometres beyond Kadoi, in front of a school. Every child in the village sprinted towards our jeep, thrusting out their hands in unison, praying for pens and sweets. Lessons were scheduled to begin at ten every morning, but their teacher was late. He bounced into frame on a motorbike come a quarter to eleven, a chequered scarf wrapped tightly around his neck and over his mouth in order to stave off the throat-attacking evils of dust. We soon found ourselves waving back at the children as we made our first tentative steps on camel-back. Tears welled in my eyes. The poverty was extreme, yet every child appeared to be incredibly happy and confident, totally unafraid to run after us, waving and calling out as though the conditions in which they were living didn't bother them one bit. At the end of the day, they'd probably never known anything else to the extent that they couldn't compare their lives to those lived by other people elsewhere in the region, let alone elsewhere in the wider world.

On we clomped. Not a single oasis reared its head. At just after midday, the camels were reined in and laid to rest, thankfully failing in their collective effort to throw us off their backs before we'd had chance to climb down with as much dignity as could be mustered given our lack of experience in the saddle. Dinner came in the mouth-watering form of a plate of potato-based curry and rice, served with a freshly-made 'chapatti' that helped to mop up every last trace of sauce within a matter of minutes.

Our guides were happy to chat amongst themselves as they led us to our camp for the night. En-route, we alighted in a village where one of the youngest guides lived. It transpired that he was desperate for a shower. Perhaps he'd been away from home for longer than he dared to admit. The bright and cheer-filled village behind us, we struck out for the alluring contours of the golden dunes on the far horizon, finally stamping upon them an hour later. We'd timed it perfectly: the sun was slated to set, the sky threatening to turn pink then red before succumbing to black. In the shadow of a dune, our guides set a fire raging in order to cook as we raced up and over the dunes, sheer excitement manifesting itself on our faces. Knowing there's nothing more inane than wishing away one's time, I vowed to take not a single grain for granted. In the distance, a lone dog howled as stars began to brighten above. The UK couldn't have felt any further away. We were in the middle of the timeless Thar, and its tranquil essence couldn't help but make it feel like a suitable home from home until such a time that we felt inclined to return to civilisation... if indeed we ever did.

~

'FLY, LITTLE BIRD, FLY!' Balancing with the disciplined poise of a Russian ballet dancer, I readied my clasped hands. 'Ready when you are!' I confirmed, tilting my head back, figuratively chewing the sky. A friend positioned herself directly above me, an injured bird chirping upon her caring palms. Cocooned inside Mehrangarh Fort, the fluffy bundle of fear appeared helpless: edible putty in the paws of devilish cats. Afraid to let go, my friend's kind nature caved beneath second thoughts. 'What if it doesn't even try to flap its wings?' she hollered. On my heels, an invisible conveyor of visitors climbed a flight of steps, animatedly chatting about The Hall of Mirrors. 'We'll just have to hope it uses its intuition,' I called, my voice pinging off the sheer wall of burnished red sandstone. 'Are you sure you're ready?' my friend stressed. 'Release; be at peace!' I urged. At my philosophical insistence, she collapsed her supportive hand-bridge. The tiny bird plunged into a graceless spin, its gummy eyes still closed. Calling upon the inherited clown within, I fairy-stepped forwards then backwards, then side to side, gravity prematurely shoving me into a guilt-trip as I entertained a heartbreaking vision. 'Catch it!' she yelled. 'Its wings haven't opened!' Gritting my teeth, I thrust my cupped hands into the air, expertly cushioning the beautiful bullet. Five minutes later, we gave it another chance - from an even greater height. Four-hundred feet below the fort, founded in the fifteenth century, Jodhpur's patchwork of blue buildings looked surreal, the overcast day lending a downbeat mask to the city's naturally striking face. Second time around, the bird was on its own. We knew that if we rested it on a ledge, the fort's cats would take advantage within minutes. Sickened by the distance to the closest patch of concrete in the form of a blisteringly steep incline, we thought better than to watch what happened next. Suffice to say, we never saw the bird again.

~

IT WAS INSISTENT FROM THE MOMENT IT BEGAN. It was three in the morning, I was in the modern Rajasthani city of Jaipur, and sleep was proving more elusive than a snow leopard in the Himalayas. And then it began, emanating from the train station with such ferocity that it sounded like hell had burst through the ground. The cause of the noise? A stationary engine's drone calling potential passengers toward it in the same manner that a muezzin's call persuades Muslims to gather and pray at the nearest mosque.

I needed a wake-up call, sure... but not so early. I'd booked a train ticket from Jaipur to Delhi for five in the morning, so I slammed my head back against the pillow, brimming with hope. Alas, further sleep escaped me. I dragged myself out of bed at four. Out on the streets, auto-rickshaws were difficult to find. A staggering proportion of drivers sleep in their three-wheeled manifestation of pride, so I wasted no time in attempting to rouse a couple of bed-starved guys, bartering down their quotes of one-hundred rupees. I was exhausted, but I wasn't stupid, hence why I settled for nothing less than a thirty rupee ride to the station via the eerily deserted Ajmer Road. At least it appeared deserted on the physical and metaphorical surface until I glanced to my right. There, beneath a long-running overpass, hundreds of homeless men and women disturbingly lay spread-eagled, wrapped in blankets, their heads under cover of darkness, not to overlook their meagre means of comfort. The driver simply snorted his derision, both at them and the increasingly busy streets clipping our collective tail. Meanwhile, tatty posters of Bollywood stars Aamir Khan and Kareena Kapoor fluttered on the breeze, threatening to tear away from their shoddily tacked anchor-points on the roof.

Jaipur's train station appeared to be a drop-in centre for the hopelessly dispossessed. Almost every spare inch of floor space had been adopted by transients who were either homeless or waiting on trains out of the city. Knowing how efficient train services in India can be (I still couldn't believe that a Jodhpur to Jaipur service I'd taken had departed and arrived literally on the dot in both instances), I'd been wise enough to plant myself on the relevant platform a wholesome ten minutes before the train to Delhi was due in. Fortunately, it was easy to locate the required platform: overhead screens proudly displayed the train number and destination of the next service due to stop before steaming ever onward. As I waited, I collared a cup of 'chai' out of habit. Never had tea seemed so inexpensive. For just three rupees, one hundred and fifty millilitres of the sweet stuff found its way into my hands and down my throat. Though I'm rarely one to quarrel if short-changed, I had to ask the 'chai'-wallah for my change twice before he reluctantly handed over the two rupees I was owed in exchange for the five-rupee note I'd proffered. It said as clear as day on the front of his cart that 'chai' cost three rupees. On principle alone, I hated being ripped off, especially when every rupee genuinely does count if you're travelling on a budget tighter than a recession-ravaged miser.

Appropriately comforted by the tea's warmth and the vendor's belated show of honesty, I opened the latest Lee Child novel, half-hoping that the train might be a few minutes late so I could peel through the final few chapters. The train, however, eased to a stop not a second later than scheduled. I stood and stared, lost for words. If only British Rail would take a leaf out of Indian Rail's book. Ironically, it was the British who implemented the breathtakingly extensive rail network in India in the first place.

Having booked a sleeper berth, I was relieved to be able to score more rest. The layout of most sleeper carriages sees the gangway flanked by a linear run of two-tiered berths and zones in which three-tiered berths face one another. Often, people who shouldn't be in such berths 'play dare' by sleeping in them until they're dragged out by the folk who should rightfully be using them.

I missed Jaipur even before the train pulled out. The divine beauty and epic grandeur of Amber Fort, a few miles away from the city centre, had captivated my imagination more than the forts at Jodhpur and Jaisalmer combined. A sucker for forts with a view, I loved how the far-ranging vistas and lush mountains surrounding Amber Fort slogged home the fact that India really is achingly beautiful when it wants to be.

Guys serving 'masala chai' (a fiendishly addictive blend of tea, cardamom, cinnamon and ginger, along with copious amounts of sugar) and breakfast omelettes slid up and down the gangway with timely regularity. As hungry as I was, I conspired to sleep. The next thing I knew, it was eight in the morning. Outside, trackside fires helped to burn an even bigger hole in the sky as homeless men hunkered around playful flames to keep warm, even though the heat of the morning was intensifying by the second. A little while later, a group of four men slouched on the delectably cushioned seat beneath me. Within minutes of sitting, they started a fierce game of cards, aided and abetted by a battered old briefcase, slapping their hands upon it with such passion that it seemed as though their lives depended on winning. I didn't recognise the type of game in which they were engaged, partly because I'd never been much of a card-shark, and partly because they were slamming down their cards with such fury that it became increasingly difficult for my eyes to keep up. I felt a headache coming on, but I was entranced, so I continued to discreetly peer down from above, trying to decipher the unvoiced protocol. Through it all, not one paisa coin or rupee note changed hands; it was purely for fun.

At just after eleven, the train casually rolled to a halt, inspiring the majority of the remaining passengers to barge their way towards the nearest door. Patiently waiting until the crush of people had alighted, I shouldered my backpack and followed suit, my risen heart bloating my mouth.

Deep breaths. Deep breaths. Even from the sanctuary of the train carriage, Delhi dared to make demands. I forced a smile in tribute.

~

THE INDIAN CAPITAL is definitely a city of two halves: Old and New. Fresh into the city for the very first time, stress immediately engulfed me as I forged a track out of Old Delhi Train Station into the midday sun. I was travelling with two friends from London, Simon and Sheetha. Having first met them on a bus in 2006 whilst steaming through southeast Asia, I'd wound up attending their wedding on the Thai island of Koh Samui three years later. They'd courted Delhi four years previously (just before I'd run into them), but they still weren't sure how to reach New Delhi. Owing to the congested traffic levels, every rickshaw driver we flagged down seemed reluctant to venture anywhere near the 'New' part of the vast conurbation in which the heart-rending gulf between rich and poor makes itself immediately obvious.

We started walking. It wasn't the most inspired decision we'd ever made as a travelling trio, but our options were cruelly limited. A battalion of rickshaw drivers 'on the tout' offered to take us where we wanted to go, but the ride would cost us dearly: not one driver would budge for less than two-hundred rupees. Unprepared to be fleeced, we declined their offers and marched on, aiming for Qutab Road. In the wake of taking what I feared might be a wrong turn, we wound up walking down what was arguably the busiest street in the city. The traffic was going nowhere. Absolute gridlock prevented movement in all directions. As expected, impatient drivers hammered the stuffing out of their respective horns, many of which were musical if such drivers were at the helm of a truck or taxi. If anything, such horns sounded comical given the intensity of the situation. Smiling, we tramped on, weaving in and out of the crowds in a rough southerly direction, aspiring to reach New Delhi's Main Bazaar before we collectively collapsed through heat exhaustion. Above us, heavyweight power cables cleaved the blue sky into tiny portions. A Welshman we'd befriended in the Thar Desert wouldn't have known what to make of the twisted sight overhead. A linesman by trade, he knew when danger lurked. It was clear to see that if a person touched such cables, death would greet them swiftly. To our left, at our feet, three men huddled in a trench, each of them manhandling a jumble of colour-coded wires. With cable-ties and scissors to hand, they seemed prepared to take the type of risks that most electrical engineers would sprint a marathon to avoid. At the end of their shifts, they were professionals, and if a job needed doing, it needed doing.

Beyond the workmen, smatterings of tiny and ridiculously dingy restaurants advertised vegetarian dishes galore. Thankfully, a large proportion of the city's restaurants also served meat-based dishes, much to Simon's delight since he craved mutton curry more than anything as we cautiously rounded a corner and waded headlong into yet more traffic.

The act of asking for directions proved troublesome. The only language that most people spoke was Hindi. Vying to meet the locals halfway, Si valiantly attempted to converse by falling back on the basic Hindi he'd learnt before flying out to Mumbai. In response, many of the men shook their heads: a response which implied that they didn't understand. To confuse matters, a shake of the head in India means 'yes', a fact which encouraged us to continue nurturing our faith, hoping that such head-shakers understood what we were spouting in English after all. A couple of ill-pointed arms later, we hailed a bicycle rickshaw out of sheer desperation. We felt no shame in admitting that we were floundering. Our heavy backpacks were getting us down in every sense. Our specific whereabouts remained to be ascertained, so we pinned our hopes on the rickshaw driver to take us a little closer to New Delhi. He did so for just thirty rupees. To be brutally honest, it proved to be a herculean struggle for the young man to propel us forward once we'd hauled our excess baggage into our laps. The seat behind the driver was so narrow that Si opted to share the driver's seat, thereby facing Sheetha and I, a cheeky smirk brightening his burning visage as we slowly but surely made headway towards Ajmeri Gate.

Deposited beside a cluster of stalls, we picked a mixture of fruit, resting for a couple of minutes prior to battling on through the mass of humanity swarming around us. A metaphorical island of calm, we coolly peeled sour orange after sweet apple, savouring the refreshing extremes in taste. As my body convulsed with a fusion of exhaustion and exhilaration, half of my orange segments plummeted to the ground upon being peeled. Abiding by the fabled 'Two-Second Rule', I retrieved such segments in less than a second, scooping them into my mouth in one fell swoop. I was adamant that no food of any kind was going to be wasted.

We'd been in Delhi for over an hour, and we were still no closer to finding suitable lodgings. A nearby building set us free. Plastered with old posters promoting the Commonwealth Games that had taken place in the city a few months previously, the building housed one of many Metro stations serving the metropolis. For once, good fortune had descended at precisely the right moment, saving us the money we'd have splurged on successive rickshaw fees. Delhi's Metro pounds proud as a spectacular feat of engineering. Consisting of a multitude of lines radiating out from the city 'centre', it naturally cost a fortune to construct. In spite of the cost, it's bound to pay for itself sooner rather than later: approximately nine-hundred thousand people use it on a daily basis.

The station's clean and spacious interior was at odds with the dirty and overcrowded streets on its doorstep. Heavily policed, no loiterers were allowed inside. Vigilant security checks were in place. As a matter of course, it's necessary to step through metal detectors prior to passing one's luggage through X-ray machines. CCTV is also operational at every station for obvious reasons. Since the city is prone to receiving intimidating terror threats, the authorities take no chances, especially since the Metro system potentially makes such a high-profile target. Thus, it's extremely reassuring to know that such security measures have been implemented to help ensure that everybody feels as safe as they deserve to when travelling around the Greater Delhi area.

Metro prices are exceedingly cheap. Eight rupees lighter, we attempted to board a train bound for the station beneath New Delhi's overground edifice. Our attempts didn't come without error: no sooner had Si, Sheetha and I sprinted into the front carriage of the first appropriate service, we were shouted at by a platform guard. The man promptly jumped into the carriage after us, dragging us out with authoritative calm. Momentarily clueless to our apparent misdemeanour, we subsequently learnt that dedicated 'ladies coaches' are readily available for women who feel uncomfortable in the same carriages as men, not least because the male population has the opportunity to harass or even grope them. Sexual harassment on Indian public transport has long been an issue, so it's encouraging to witness steps to reduce it. We'd unwittingly bundled ourselves and our backpacks into a 'ladies coach' without realising we were essentially committing a crime in doing so. No wonder the guard wasted no time in highlighting our folly. It was surely more than his job was worth to turn a blind eye and let us ride on regardless. We apologised profusely so as not to be deemed criminals. The last thing we wanted was to get on the wrong side of anybody in authority, whether they were security guards, military personnel, or police officers.

Ironically exhilarated by the rush of being thrown off a train before we'd even settled ourselves on it, we couldn't help but laugh at the comedic nature of our mistake. It was our first day in Delhi. Our education had begun.

~

IT WASN'T LONG BEFORE WE WANTED OUT. The allure of Agra down the rail was too much to resist, yet our attempt to flee Delhi was initially thwarted in every respect. First of all, a tout pacing in front of New Delhi Station took it upon himself to direct us away from the reservation hall, claiming we needed to head down the road in order to find the place. The moment Sheetha butted in with a question, the man raised his voice, shooting her query down as though it wasn't important. But it was. As soon as he tried to change the subject, we sensed he was fobbing us off with a despicable pack of lies. Turning our backs on him, we marched back into the station foyer, only to spot a sign for the 'Tourist Information Desk' inconspicuously nestling at the foot of a stairwell. Up we climbed, to be greeted by a long corridor. Trusting our instincts, we followed a succession of signs into a spacious room teeming with foreigners. We seized a ticket reservation form and sat down.

Although the task of purchasing train tickets in India is easy, the painstaking process can test one's patience. If only it were possible to queue and buy a ticket without filling in any paperwork. Instead, all foreigners wishing to travel by train must fill in a detailed form, nailing specifics about where they've been and where they're bound, along with their name, age, passport number and contact telephone number. Luckily for us, the queue was relatively short, and we were brimming with patience after a hearty breakfast that had been anchored by fish curry.

The dishevelled man in front readily confessed that he'd been 'on the road' for three years. Only once had he returned home to Wales, at which point he'd lavished five months on a reconnaissance mission. Judging by his dilated pupils, not to mention the way he kept falling asleep, he was either stupendously tired, hung-over, or as high as a 747. Given that he hoped to be on his way to Kerala in the morning, he was fortunate: it was a three-day journey, during which time he'd be able to sleep all he wanted. Failing that, a good book would surely come in handy. I would have recommended *Don Quixote* had he not fallen back asleep before I plucked it from my pack.

Inching around the reservation hall a seat at a time, we began to entertain second thoughts about travelling to Agra by train. Having set ourselves tight daily budgets, the three-hundred and seventy rupees we needed for the ticket would render us near-penniless for the remainder of the day. It had just gone eleven. Still, we'd already filled in the form, and we were next in line to be seen by one of six men clamped behind a long desk. Sheetha had earlier remarked that the feel of the place reminded her of a doctor's surgery. For a start, silence reigned, resulting in a feeling of unease. The fact that the railway employees were wearing white overcoats further fuelled our imaginations, leading us to wonder if we had in fact stumbled upon some kind of research facility randomly embedded in the first floor of the station. Saying nothing, we stared ahead as protocol subliminally dictated.

Once summoned, Si slid the form over to the unsmiling man. We didn't expect any enthusiasm about our request on his part, and we certainly didn't receive any. 'How would you like to travel?' he asked. Stunned by such a seemingly stupid question, I replied: 'By train. We'd like to travel by train.' I felt the need to re-iterate the point just in case he thought that flying might be a more viable option for us. 'Yes, but would you like to travel in a compartment with air-conditioning or without?' Si had been consumed by juvenile laughter by this point, yet I had no idea what had tickled him. Seeing my confusion, he nodded at the man's name-tag. It read 'Dixit': a name that can be pronounced one of two ways depending on how much common courtesy emanates from its possessor. Stifling a smirk, I requested three seats blessed by the beauty of AC all the way. Secretly, we were hoping to pay less than three-hundred and seventy rupees for the privilege, but the man claimed that there were no cheaper tickets available. The speedy nature of the train reflected the high price. Allegedly, it was almost as expensive to cover the same ground by bus. Nevertheless, in a wild fit of scepticism, we told the ticket-vendor that we couldn't afford the price, glancing at one another to confirm such a harsh reality to ourselves. 'Let's see if we can score a better deal on a bus,' Sheetha piped up whilst standing. Simon and I nodded, then followed.

Opposite the station, a parade of diminutive travel agencies pined for our trade. Dodging the usual assault of touts, rickshaws and motorcycles on the way, we collated quotes from each. The news wasn't good. The cheapest ticket to Agra by bus would sting us for three-hundred and fifty rupees. Each of the five agencies we visited quoted the same price, toiling together as a money-making co-operative that took pride in fleecing travellers for every last rupee. Agra was practically so close to Delhi that it would feasibly be possible to catapult oneself there, so why did train and bus tickets cost so much? Knowing that almost all visitors to India will strive to see the Taj Mahal at Agra, travel agencies seem naturally inclined to charge as much as they feel they can get away with. That in mind, we were stuck between six socks and a sad face. Favouring train travel (if only for the early morning servings of 'chai' and delicious omelettes served by mobile vendors on-board), we bolted back over the road in order to pay Mr. Dixit another visit. Suffice to say, he was even less happy to see us the second time around.

Five minutes later we were booked up, pensively cradling the noticeable lack of change from our five-hundred rupee notes. With precisely one-hundred and thirty rupees left on which to survive for the rest of the day, it was time to fast… fast.

~

'WHY ARE YOU FOLLOWING US?' It was an honest question fully deserving of an honest response. We'd just arrived in Agra and we were scouting for a suitable guesthouse, a marble block's throw from the timeless Taj Mahal. The wily rickshaw driver who'd driven us to the Taj Ganj area of the city refused to let us be. We'd paid the fifty rupees we'd agreed to pay him for the ride, but he wanted more in the form of commission from a guesthouse. Here's the way it works: if a driver drops you at a guesthouse, they score commission. Such commission has to come from somewhere, so room prices are bunked up in order to accommodate the cut that the driver expects. It's the way of the world in the ugly guise of contemporary cut-throat business. Because we'd decided to look for a guesthouse under our own steam, the driver knew he wouldn't be in line for any commission whatsoever, hence why he pursued us. It's common for drivers to pretend that they've brought travellers to certain guesthouses in order to slyly make themselves money on the side. However, freshly attuned to the scam, we darted into the nearest café to fortify our thoughts, to reclaim our front. We were in no mood to be duped or pressured into staying somewhere we didn't want to. As a result, we cunningly formulated a foolproof plan.

Desperate to undermine the dogged persistence exerted by the driver, Si and I decided to check out a variety of guesthouses in the vicinity whilst leaving our backpacks in the café with Sheetha. So as not to appear rude, we ordered and downed a drink before ducking out of the café and skirting around the perimeter of the Taj Mahal to its East Gate. 'The Sheela Guesthouse' sounded a dream on paper; it looked even more of a dream in reality with its attractively shaded and lovingly landscaped garden. Such beauty was reflected in the price of the rooms, the cheapest chamber of repose costing seven-hundred rupees per night. As it was, the ignorant receptionist showed no interest in us, continuing to chat on his mobile phone without acknowledging our presence via sincere eye contact. To him, we were invisible. Curiously, we'd been greeted by the same level of apparent ignorance in Delhi whilst searching for accommodation. We could tell by the way that some of the hoteliers spoke to or looked at us that they immediately assumed us to be a couple, thereby limiting talking-space on those grounds alone due to their views on homosexuality. When all sneers had been aired and defused, Simon and Sheetha remained husband and wife, and my girlfriend was in the midst of winging her way to Kathmandu.

Coincidentally, the third annual 'Queer Pride Day' was taking place in Delhi. In spite of the day's working title offensively reeking of political incorrectness, the event was positive in the way that the three and a half thousand supporters who showed up were helping to raise awareness about the number of gays and lesbians in India who are effectively cast out of society due to an outdated melting pot of traditional cultural values.

Undeterred by the ignorance expounded at Sheela's place, we backtracked to the simple but effectively named 'Taj Guesthouse'. The place certainly wasn't primed to win any awards in recognition of its hopelessly unoriginal name, but it seemed set to serve us well enough. Si and Sheetha were happy to pay four-hundred rupees for a double room on the first floor, leaving me downstairs with a two-hundred rupee cell. It came without a toilet, but it felt as homely as things could for the price. Conscious that a visit to the Taj Mahal the following morning was poised to set me back seven-hundred rupees, I was prepared to entertain frugality in all its modest glory.

As we checked in, the rickshaw driver flashed his face, hoping to convince the proprietors that he'd brought us. We told them straight that we'd found the place ourselves, but the driver continued to loiter in the lobby, spouting a spiel designed to make us feel guilty for stealing his commission-guaranteeing thunder. He then began to converse with the receptionist in Hindi before sloping away, defeated. We weren't going to feel bad for inspiring such anger in him. We'd done nothing wrong. Anger just happened to consume many of Agra's touts. Even before 'our man' had persuaded us to go with him, a different tout had projected serious designs on us, going so far as to surround us with fellow henchmen to try and stop us from defecting with a driver who didn't work for him. Indeed, drivers often work in gangs, facilitating the fine art of networking. Furthermore, they see no shame in conveying unsuspecting travellers to guesthouses of their own choosing. In places like Agra, touts have the potential to make an astronomical amount of money through being ruthless. Not all drivers are out to exploit visitors, though. Far from it. Over the course of the previous few weeks, we'd encountered a handful of genuine drivers who were less bothered about making money and more concerned with doing their jobs properly by taking us exactly where we stipulated. Abiding by such principles is good for business. If only the dishonest touts in the proverbial pack would acknowledge as much.

In defence of rickshaw and taxi drivers, it has to be said that their jobs aren't easy by any stretch of the imagination. Since the Metro has become such an integral cog in Delhi's transport network, it's even harder for drivers to make a living since it's so quick, easy and cheap for people to go underground. It makes little sense to trap oneself in gridlocked scenarios when, for as little as eight rupees, you can travel a few miles beneath the city within minutes. It's safe to say that Delhi's Metro has totally transformed how people move around the city. With the stop beneath New Delhi Railway Station acting as the network's epicentre, the network operates between six in the morning and eleven in the evening, the maximum fare rolling in at the thirty-rupee mark for the most far-flung suburban stops. In spite of the high volume of people cramming onto the Metro, it's a joy to use. On our third and final day in the capital, we'd travelled to Nehru Place by Metro, a thirty-minute trip which necessitated a change at Central Secretariat. One of the busiest hubs, Central Secretariat can be a relative nightmare to negotiate, but we coped. The stretch of line between Central Secretariat and Nehru Place was far quieter. We were finally able to bag a seat each. The addictive thrill of hopping on and off different trains reminded me of when I lived in Mexico City and used its Metro every day without fail. From Nehru Place, a glorious panorama of Delhi can be gained from the station platform, the architecturally arresting design of the Lotus Temple spearing one's attention from afar. Construction work raged on in various nooks and crannies. In one corner, half-used tins of paint precariously rested atop wooden platforms; in another, live wires hung from the ceiling, pointing to earth in anticipation of being safely connected.

The high and mighty Eros Corporate Tower dominates the cityscape upon emerging at Nehru Place. Housing Barclays Bank, the ECT represents the tip of Delhi's financial interests. The adjacent complex - consisting of a cinema and innumerable fast-food restaurants - lured us in to launch us through a bustling courtyard bordered by dozens upon dozens of shops selling computer hardware. You could say we'd hit the pay dirt. Our ambition had been to find a computer store so Sheetha and I could buy a 'Netbook' each. Indeed, if not for a savvy retailer of 'Samsung' products on the first floor of the bazaar, you wouldn't be reading these words. More to the point, I wouldn't have written them in the first place.

~

I'D BEEN ITCHING TO BECOME PROPERLY ACQUAINTED with the real Agra, yet I'd failed miserably. The Taj Ganj quarter surrounding India's most beloved tourist attraction had thrown up minimal surprises. All I'd found had been a thousand and one touts desperate to offload anything and everything from a dozen rickshaw rides and a lorry-load of replica tat, to a handful of hashish and a lion-tamer's whip. I desired just one thing: to see Agra as it should be, away from the madness manifesting outside the mighty gates of the blinding monument. Buying cheap souvenirs didn't interest me in the least, so I hastened to extricate myself from the pressure of the touts by heading to Agra Fort. Both buildings overlook a wide arc of the Yamuna River, and both were constructed at the behest of Emperor Shah Jahan. The gently curving road separating them was near-deserted to an unsettling extent. I later learnt there is restricted access for certain vehicles around the Taj (which means 'crown'), not least because fumes blacken the polished marble. To be brutally honest, it made an agreeable change to be able to walk unhindered and without fear of being mown down.

Spying a metal bridge spanning the river north of the fort, I hoped to walk over the structure in order to admire Shah Jahan's testament to eternal love from a peculiar vantage point not usually enjoyed by visitors. Alas, the bridge entertained trains exclusively, so I sloped back to the fort, prior to returning to Taj Ganj.

After dark, Agra unveiled an altogether more exciting facade. Following my instincts, I slipped down a menacingly inconspicuous alley in search of street-food. Fearing the worst, I surprisingly became enamoured with the alley. I likened what had occurred to the point at which the children in *The Lion, The Witch and The Wardrobe* award an old hunk of furniture the benefit of the doubt and step into Narnia. A whole new world opened before my eyes, honing in on each sense. Judging by the high quantity of stares intercepted as I sauntered along the maze of alleys that so boldly broke free from the city's touristy facets, I surmised that few Westerners delved as deep as I did by default. As things stand, it's only a small proportion of Taj visitors who actually stay in Agra in any case; the vast majority of Mahal-devotees visit on a day-trip, or are part of a tour group that moves on to stay elsewhere once their time at the magnificent marble edifice has ebbed into history. It's often noted how Agra lacks nightlife for those who do hang back. Bars might be few and far between, but candlelit dinners on starry-eyed terraces never go amiss. What could be more romantic than dining opposite the person you love with the Taj Mahal as the backdrop?

Absconding down as many alleys as I could, I hunted high and low for Indian food I'd never tried before. If only Simon and Sheetha had been with me. Self-confessed food junkies, they were eternally on the lookout for new nosh. As a result of spending so much time in their company, I was developing my own taste for Indian cuisine. Astonished at the range of local delicacies available in different areas of the subcontinent, I was thrilled to discover that Indian food in Rajasthan contrasted sharply with the type of food found in Uttar Pradesh. Meat was often difficult to find, too, depending on whether or not the area was Hindu or Muslim-dominated.

Craving fresh fruit, I scoped stall after stall for mangoes. A sucker for their mouth-watering taste in the wake of having downed an exquisite mango-flavoured 'lassi' in Mumbai, I'd been looking forward to consuming the raw fruit as and when it revealed its curves. Alas, the fruit was out of season. Thus, I turned my attention to the wealth of equally-as-refreshing alternatives. First and foremost, bananas were abundant around every corner. Accompanying ripe bunches of the yellow beauties were guavas, pineapples, watermelons and pomegranates. Vegetable stalls, meanwhile, exploded in a riot of colour, overflowing with cauliflowers, tomatoes, potatoes and cucumbers.

Ravenous, I could have eaten a horse. Failing that, a cow would have done. However, given that cows are considered holier than thou, I would have been hunted down were I to realise my dream by such selfish means. Eating as though I was a vegetarian didn't bother me. Meat cravings had diminished. More than a sizzling steak, I wanted a genuine taste sensation of local origin, so I continued walking, searching, hoping. Picking up a curry-drenched 'samosa' for luck, I admired the bowl in which it had been served. Consisting of two dried leaves that had been fused together, the design of the biodegradable bowl was simple yet ingenious, helping to cut the amount of non-biodegradable waste plaguing India's urban and rural arteries. Further down the same street, a tempting proposition surged up my nostrils. As ever, they were on high alert. It took but a millisecond to realise that something extraordinary was cooking on the next stall. I asked the vendor what he was selling, but he didn't understand. His substandard level of English inspired catastrophic misinterpretation. Upon deducing that whatever he was selling cost just ten rupees per bowl, I nodded. Doing so could have implied anything. Cooking to order, he slapped a hunk of meat in a wok and placed it on what resembled a school Bunsen burner. The intensity of the heat did the job nicely. He subsequently crushed a potato-filled pastry in my bowl. Upon it, he lavished lashings of sweet sauce in which pieces of fruit appeared to languish. The meat was then placed atop the strange fusion of food: essentially the icing on the savoury cake. The textured taste could only be described as divine. Thumbing my satisfaction across to the cook from a perch beside a one-legged onlooker, I chuckled at the incongruity of the situation. Eating any kind of food in the realm of free-flowing sewage is never advised, but there I was, in my element, eating as fast as I could because I wanted more of the same. It's not that I wasn't aware of the health risks posed by my proximity to waste of all kinds. Put simply, I didn't have a choice. The situation was purely circumstantial: good food had been found in one of the dirtiest necks of an Agra-vated back alley. Two bowls later, I inched further down the alley, craving further delights. When I stumbled upon a shop serving hot milk in disposable clay vessels, I realised that I was on a roll in terms of discovering and sampling food and drink of the tastiest, cheapest and most authentic variety.

As much as I was tempted to delve even deeper beyond the invisible 'limits' imposed by the Taj Mahal, I spun on my heels whilst sipping the dregs of my milk. Having arranged to hook up with Si and Sheetha for tea, I had to return to our guesthouse. In spite of initially not having the heart to tell them I'd already eaten, I wound up confessing everything. Disturbingly, I was still hungry, devouring a 'thali' for dessert.

It wasn't until the early hours of the following morning that my greed returned to haunt me. I shan't do myself the indignity of relating too many details. Truth be told, the way I felt surpassed description. But did I learn from such gross overconsumption? Ensconced in 'Treat Restaurant' in the sun's firing line, I had a continental breakfast placed under my nose. That's why I'll leave you to decide.

~

TEMPORARILY DISTANCING MYSELF FROM THE TAJ MAHAL, I'd ventured over to the train station beside Agra Fort to book an onward ticket for the following evening with my friends. Eager to head east to the holiest of holy cities in Varanasi, we strode into the reservation hall brimming with cynical hope and dud cheer. Scanning an information board detailing train arrival and departure times, we were shocked to discover that only one train per day embarked for Varanasi. Furthermore, a sleeper berth on the service came at a high price. Indeed, the three-hundred and seventy rupees it cost for a ticket meant we'd have to instigate cutbacks on other things during the proceeding day, our budgets dependant on self-discipline. As we left the hall, a fellow foreigner asked where he could procure a reservation form. 'I can't see them anywhere,' he shrugged, crestfallen. Simon was ruthlessly direct with his response. 'There are some on the floor over there,' he advised, pointing to the darkest corner of the lightless hall. Eschewing all sense of logic, essential items are commonly found in the most obscure places in India. Should you routinely expect the unexpected, you shouldn't go far wrong. Take nothing for granted, and remind yourself that realistic patience is virtuous.

The rickshaw driver that had conveyed us from Taj Ganj to the station was awaiting our return on the road. We no longer needed his services and informed him as much. It was imperative that we curbed our collective spending on cross-city travel via taxis and rickshaws. In any case, our next stop was set to be Agra Fort. The main entrance was a mile distant. Our honesty upset him, but there was no way he was going to strong-arm us into taking a ride we didn't need. 'But the entrance is four miles away,' he lied, eager to convince us, desperate to take us for a ride in every respect.

Sick and tired of being lied to, we strode off, stalking the railway line towards the river before swinging in front of the fort's heavily embellished façade. A procession of middle-aged women bruised past. They were carrying bundles of thin wood. Even though they were working, they were dressed to the nines in exceedingly delicate, blindingly colourful saris.

The entrance to Agra Fort teemed with touts. Once we'd made it through the main gate, hassle of a wholly different nature attacked, a grassy knoll of monkeys getting the better of our attention. Elsewhere, cute chipmunks foraged for food as the oldest and slowest monkeys looked on in bemusement. Many of the Indian children in the vicinity were enraptured by the interactive antics of the animals. It was encouraging to see the kids look upon the monkeys and chipmunks with such awe. The way they stood back and admired the creatures from a respectable distance was a far-cry from what we'd witnessed in and around Taj Ganj. There, we'd spotted a litter of achingly cute puppies shuffling around at the side of the road, a hairsbreadth away from speeding rickshaws and a sensationally disgusting conduit. In an unbelievably cruel twist of fate, a couple of kids had dropped one of the puppies into a cylindrical concrete bunker from which it would never be able to escape unaided. The offending child had probably done it to generate a cheap laugh without paying heed to the possible consequences. Fortunately, Sheetha saw the puppy and instructed the child to lift it out of what resembled a dreadfully confined oubliette. Such puppies weren't pets, yet they certainly hadn't done anything to inspire such gross mistreatment. All they did was playfully tumble about with one another whilst looking utterly adorable. On the far side of the road, in a similarly heartbreaking episode of outright neglect, a gentle-souled goat stood tethered to a pipe. Stuck between a wall and the road's secondary but no less deadly ditch for waste disposal, the animal literally had nowhere to walk to exercise. Nor did it have any food or drink at its disposal. It had simply been abandoned to bake in the midday sun. The shocking scene further re-iterated the fact that most animals in India get a raw deal. Coming from Europe, where love is showered upon pets, it was upsetting to see the extreme extent to which many animals are routinely exploited and blatantly ignored in Asia.

Agra Fort is India's most important fort. Thankfully, it has been wonderfully preserved. Once the home of Emperor Shah Jahan, its grounds were laid in such a manner that their spacious and tranquil nature has a profound impact on the hearts and minds of visitors as standard. As beautiful as the Red Fort in Delhi is, Agra Fort seems all the more exquisite for myriad reasons. Its epic views over to the Taj prove a major bonus. Just two miles separate both edifices, yet they couldn't be further apart in terms of style and substance. The fort in Agra bears much in common with Delhi's Red Fort, though. Both are constructed from red sandstone, both preside over the same river, and both possess a history so thrilling that neither fort's story should be overlooked or undervalued. Perhaps the most compelling story within Agra Fort's history harks back to how Shah Jahan's son, Aurangzeb, wound up imprisoning Shah Jahan, awarding him the tiniest glimpse imaginable of his masterpiece, the Taj. It's often said that some things are worse than death, and it's safe to say that being allowed to look at but not touch something you conceived is a type of intolerable torture. Given that Shah Jahan built the marble mausoleum for his most beloved wife, Mumtaz Mahal, his final years at the mercy of his son must have been excruciatingly lonely. However, upon his death in 1666, Shah Jahan was ultimately laid to rest beside Mumtaz, at the heart of what still stands as one of the world's most awe-inspiring testaments to true love.

Skulking around the fort's airiest courtyard, an armed guard shuffled towards me. 'You smoke?' he asked. Ignoring the question's irrelevance, I told him the truth. 'No,' I said, staring him down, wondering why I'd been singled out. 'You have a laptop?' he continued, his moustache aquiver. 'Yes,' I responded, in no mood to lie. 'You are not allowed computers in here,' he sourly stated, glancing at my metrosexualised bag of tricks. 'Sorry, but I did not realise,' I said, suspecting my 'Netbook' was two seconds shy of being confiscated. 'Give me your laptop. It is a security issue to have them in here,' the man went on. 'Otherwise you will have to pay a fine.' A shiver of unease hit the base of my spine, detecting deception on the guard's part. Nowhere had we encountered a whiff of forewarning about not being at liberty to carry laptops. Fortunately, Si and Sheetha noticed I was being harangued. Edging over, they asked the official, decked in brown fatigues, why laptops were seen to compromise security. Three against one, the man's nerve faltered. 'It is not allowed. I do not make the rules. I simply enforce them.' Si pressed him further. 'My friend here has kept his computer in his bag. He needs it because he's a writer. Do you understand?' The man gaily shook his head in the affirmative before pacing away. Thanking my friends for intervening, I still wondered why the guard had picked on me. 'It's probably due to your bad posture,' offered Si. 'When a person's hunched over, like you are, some folk detect weakness. Such a posture suggests you're feeling too sorry for yourself to keep a straight back. In a more literal sense, a stance like yours implies you have no backbone, rendering you infinitely more vulnerable. As a result, people might think you'll be less likely to stick up for yourself if affronted. Think about it; act upon it. I guarantee you'll garner more respect, not to mention attention, if you focus on maintaining a strong, upright approach.' Absorbing his advice, I marched out of the fort, my realigned head held higher than ever.

Striking the streets running, a tout tailed me as soon as I emerged between two strategically parked drinks stands. 'You want rickshaw?' he uttered. 'No. We walk,' I responded, scissoring the forefingers of my right hand to clarify our intention to see Agra from the comfort of our own feet instead of the crippling confines of a rickshaw. 'You want helicopter?' he subsequently asked, throwing me completely off-guard. Intrigued by his offer, I asked him if he really had a chopper. 'Sure,' he grinned. 'It's over there, in the park.' Half-sceptical, half-convinced, I strained my eyes to popping point. Not a single rotor-blade was in sight. 'Are you being serious?' I shot back, smirking at the apparent absurdity of the conversation's unexpected development. 'You come with me and I show you. Please. Follow and I show.' Even if he did own and operate a helicopter, I still wanted to walk, to embrace the shadows of Agra that most folk stepped out of their way to avoid. Glancing at my feet, I nodded to myself. Walking: there's nothing more rewarding.

~

'DON'T LEAN TO YOUR LEFT WHATEVER YOU DO!' Si advised. Surveying the road conditions whilst observing the uninspiring driving 'skills' of the evidently agitated man sat to my right, I did as instructed, fighting gravity with utmost urgency as we sped towards a roundabout, a hurdle in our journey that was bound to necessitate physical anguish for all embroiled.

Desperate to reach Agra Fort Station as quickly and as cheaply as possible, our group of four had persuaded a rickshaw driver to take us for sixty rupees: a round figure that could be sliced into digestible quarters upon arrival. Simon, Sheetha and I had caught up with an independent female traveller from Zurich. She, too, was determined to catch the train to Varanasi. Without further ado, we'd piled into the same rickshaw - much to the driver's surprise. He'd initially hoped that Fabienne would be his sole passenger. More bodies meant more work for him and his trusted mode of transportation. Even more weight was added to the equation when we revealed our backpacks. With Si, Sheetha and Fabienne cosily jammed onto the back seat, I sat up front beside the nonplussed driver. Our gear had been rammed into any acceptable space available. Exiting the guesthouse-littered Taj Ganj area at a speed faster than strictly necessary, we rocketed onto the main road - and that's where the fun really began. Weaving in and out of vehicles making haste in both directions, we literally hung on for dear life. Fond of his horn, the driver wouldn't take his fist off it until all traffic in our path had ceremoniously shifted to one side. To all intents and purposes, he believed he was King of the Road, an Emperor of Instinct. Affairs became progressively more tangled and stressful as we neared the station. The number of roadside food stalls failed to aid the flow of wheeled death-traps. Leaning inwards due to the dangerous weight imbalance on the backseat, I wound up getting too close to the driver for comfort. We were as relieved as each other when the time came for us to hop out and drag our packs into the station.

Fabienne was a self-confessed 'hardened traveller'. Negotiating the roads and rails of India alone, she didn't seem fazed about a single trial. A fan of escaping to hot countries during European winters, she was in the midst of a sixth-month journey that would see her touch base with Melbourne in December for a three-month break. Physically drained in the wake of a busy day spent in Agra (I'd baulked at the grandeur of the Taj while Si and Sheetha visited Akbar's Tomb beyond the city limits), we shuffled onto the platform and waited patiently for a train that threatened to never come. It arrived thirty minutes later than expected, thankfully spawning no hardship at all.

Having been allocated sleeper berths in different carriages, we said our goodbyes to Fabienne as she readied herself to trudge along to 'S10': sleeper carriage number ten. Off we paced in the opposite direction. A couple of fellow Brit travellers had been awarded two berths adjacent to ours. Naturally, we quickly fell into conversation about our respective travel plans. It seemed that Andron and Joy had been at the mercy of bad luck for much of their journey. We thought we'd had it hard through being ripped-off and psychologically exploited, but even our most cringe-worthy stories failed to rival their rousing wake-up calls. We dared not believe our ears as they related details about how they'd been duped into visiting war-torn Kashmir by a scheming travel agent in Delhi. Such an agent was evidently at the top of his evil little game; he'd gone so far as to 'borrow' the couple's guidebook in which a certain paragraph had clearly stated that under no circumstances whatsoever should travellers consider booking a trip to Kashmir from Delhi. Given that the agent had essentially sabotaged their guidebook so they couldn't read such a paragraph and subsequently decide to cancel their flight to Srinagar, Andron and Joy gamely trusted the con-man for all he was potentially worth. So they flew to Kashmir, hoping for the best, only to emerge into arguably the most dangerous area of India, the only two Westerners for miles around. 'You should have seen the might of the military up there. So many personnel; so many military vehicles. It was as if they were waiting for something to go off,' Andron grimaced, still struggling to laugh about the unsettling situation into which they'd unwittingly flung themselves two weeks earlier.

I was coming down with something, I knew it. I felt my body slumping into sleep mode before shutting down completely. I didn't want to be rude by not involving myself in the conversation, but I needed a modicum of shut-eye. Wrapping my near-threadbare blanket around a homesick torso that wouldn't quit shaking, I tried to splay my bones holistically. On a speeding train, in a claustrophobic's worst nightmare, it's easier slurred than done. However, I somehow managed to score a sliver of rest before being rudely awoken by a volley of raised voices at the foot of my berth.

I cracked my eyelids open wide enough to read my watch. It had just gone three. I awarded my self-pity an additional five minutes before mustering the energy to roll over, gagging to hear what the fuss was about. The intensity of the commotion had heightened. Worryingly, Sheetha sounded to be at the heart of the melee. It soon transpired that Joy's backpack had been stolen as we'd slept. Aghast at what had happened, Sheetha had started asking questions, attempting to ascertain details surrounding the theft. Within minutes she posed a theory. A few hours earlier, an Indian man had butted into the animated conversation she'd been enjoying with Joy. He'd fired standard 'getting to know you' questions at speed in Joy's flustered direction. Thinking nothing about the possible consequences of the spontaneous exchange, Joy had obliged the man, going so far as to surrender precise details about who she was travelling with and where she was due to alight. It was wrong of us to peg such a man 'prime suspect' without hard evidence to consult, but it was possible that he'd been in some way involved. Thieves, like touts, work in gangs.

Joy was inconsolable. In her favour, she was also level-headed, summoning the motivation to detail what she'd lost to a rifle-carrying policeman, summoned from his post elsewhere on the train. She still had her passport, camera and money. Clothes had constituted the bulk of her backpack's contents. It was the loss of her diary that appeared to upset her more than anything. Genuinely irreplaceable, its sentimental nature reminded us about the real value of those things we hold closest to our hearts, compared to material possessions which can be replaced on a whim.

I couldn't have sympathised with Joy any more. If she could have, I'm sure she'd have changed her name to better reflect the dramatic lull in her mood. An opportunist theft had got the better of me in Bangkok just over a year beforehand, and I'd found the principle of the matter to be the hardest aspect to reconcile. For the remainder of my Asian odyssey in 2009, my defences had railed at an all-time high. If anybody so much as swayed within five metres of what remained of my satchel-swathed gear, I instinctively informed them that they'd better back down. I was unwilling to take any more chances with strangers. I had too much to lose.

We attempted to coerce Joy back into a trusting mindset, in spite of the betrayal that had occurred. Sheetha, to her eternal credit, did more for Joy than anyone. She was the first on the scene, so-to-speak. Even when the policeman casually bumbled his way into the fray, it was Sheetha who proceeded to ask the most pertinent questions. Perhaps a degree of misunderstanding soured the ensuing Q&A session, but the uniformed officer seemed distinctly disinterested in the prospect of obtaining information about the crime. Instead, he whispered and chuckled in the ear of a casually-dressed cohort who hung about simply to suggest he was concerned.

Eight hours down the line, the train finally rolled into Varanasi... over three hours late. Simon, Sheetha and I were expecting to be met by a rickshaw driver who'd been asked to pick us up by the owners of 'The Taj Guesthouse' in Agra. Some of their friends ran 'The Yogi Lodge' in Varanasi, so they'd done their duty in making a sound recommendation. Exhausted and upset for Joy, we were essentially putty in the driver's hands. As for Andron and Joy, they sadly shuffled off along a different platform. Bound for the nearest police station, it was time for them to make one of the boldest statements of their lives.

~

SITTING PRETTY ON MUNSHI GHAT, admiring the broad sweep of the River Ganges, I felt at total peace. Then I glanced to my right and saw a dead bird in a basket. Such is life - and death - in the holiest of holy cities.

One of the oldest settlements in the world, modern-day Varanasi isn't all that different from ancient Varanasi. Sure, chain stories have moved into premises clogging the main thoroughfares, but tough labour goes on as normal beside the river. Such work is of a non-retail nature. Indeed, one of the main 'in situ' businesses has been borne out of death, as ironic as such a concept might be to digest. The most sacred city to Hindus, Varanasi is the most popular place for people to be cremated if family or friends of the deceased have the ability to transport the body before it decomposes of its own accord. As I sauntered upriver towards the most prominent Burning Ghat, I reflected on how one of my friends had remarked upon an oddly-shaped bundle wrapped in a blanket at Agra Station. The way it had distinctively flopped in the middle suggested that a fresh corpse lay within, having been rushed to the station before the stiffening signs of rigor mortis developed. Time is of the element in the interface zone between worlds.

Determined to further my research into what possibly lay beyond, I warmed to the idea of rebirth, inspired by the way Paulo Coelho had simulated death in the name of living a fuller life as he acquainted his soul with El Camino, *The Pilgrimage*. I might have been a near-penniless drifter who related to Knut Hamsun's *Hunger* more by the hour, but I wanted for nothing. The sound of a man caning a dog into paralysis encouraged instinct to desert inhibition. Stepping forward to voice a plea bargain on behalf of the mongrel, I reflected on the importance of telling loved ones how you feel. Repeatedly.

En-route to the hottest 'ghat' in the city, I soaked up the riot of sights and sounds presented in sense-attacking succession. Hindi classes, English academies, yoga centres, silk houses, funky cafes, dirt-cheap guesthouses: they all had advertisements crudely painted upon walls overlooking the continuous run of concrete steps. One crumbling boundary granted philosophic perspective: 'Poverty is not lack of money, but lack of hope.' With each pace marked, a new tout seemed to approach with an offer of some sort. 'Hi. How are you?' was the most popular opening gambit flung into the stale air by people who wanted something, be it for me to purchase a postcard from them, take a boat ride with them, or sample a crumb of their hash. Indeed, hashish is plastered all over the city. I couldn't help but laugh when a supposedly lame Holy Man sidled up to me, panning for 'spare' rupees I didn't possess. As soon as I passed him, he sped up, whispering in my ear, 'Hash, you want some hash, my friend?' It's amazing how some con-men conveniently 'forget' about physical limitations when they believe they can nail a sale of some kind. Pay more attention, and you'll notice it happen all the time: right in front of your eyes, and under your nose.

Attuned to the comical chorus-line of dodgy drug-dealers and guesthouse-affiliated reps, I shuffled on, careful to watch my step as I zigzagged between five cows that had parked their rumps beside a fruit-seller. Unimpressed by their holiness, the man behind the table of bananas and apples refused to serve them. I'm not sure if his attitude could be aligned with racism; at the very least, I thought he might have forsaken a used skin or two if only for the trace element of goodness they might have provided such noble beasts.

Beneath the mackerel sky, cute kite-runners shrieked with carefree delight as they aspired to out-do friends with turns of kite-twirling derring-do. I was astonished by the extent to which some of the boys could remain in total control of their respective kites from considerable distances. Noticing my interest in the art of kite-flying, a bedraggled and shoeless boy of about five or six scurried forth, proffering the rein of his kite. Fearful that I might get his kite tangled with a rival, I politely declined, eager for him to do the honours.

Perched on a pedestal below one of the many riverside temples, a thirty-something man rocked his body, clapping his hands in time with an internalised melody. Chanting 'Hare Krishna' as he swayed, his eyes appeared to be on the verge of bidding adieu to his skull. He was still engrossed in his devotion two hours later. I looked at him more closely, only to notice his eyes were severely bloodshot. Concerned about his welfare, I asked a boatman if the body-rocker was all right. 'Do not worry about him,' the diminutive Indian huffed. 'He is, as you say, off his rocker.'

In the wake of a late-afternoon siesta, I began to edge ever closer to the most fascinating 'ghat' of all. It wasn't hard to find. The smoke and stench gave it away. Acknowledging the brown sludge-filled face of Mother Ganges as I continued walking, I doffed my metaphorical hat to the man who'd made it his life's work to clean up the river at Varanasi. Believe it or not, for forty years an Indian man has been campaigning for change on the stomach-churning section of river that evidently curses the city as much as it blesses it. The extremely high level of pollution is enough to spread disease even from arm's reach, hence why the sight of people washing and bathing downriver from cremations is enough to give any fan of health and sanitation a sleepless night.

What can be said about Burning Ghat that hasn't already been imagined? Night and day, it speaks for itself, bridging the gap between states of being. Consisting of a number of steps reaching down to the river, the 'ghat' hosts cremations en-masse every single day of the year. For Hindus, this is the 'in' place to be released and remembered. To surrender one's earthly remains to the Ganga lifeblood represents the pinnacle of life itself, hence why devout Hindus from across the subcontinent make the journey to Varanasi on behalf of loved ones, respecting their wishes and aspirations to essentially return to where they came from, completing the circle of life as their ashes flit, to be carried out to the river's delta, or to be feasted upon by birds harbouring a taste for death. At night, Burning Ghat assumes the guise of a truly timeless sight. Up to twenty separate cremations can rage simultaneously while 'untouchables' wade through the water in search of jewellery. Backing Burning Ghat, a preposterous tangle of haunted alleyways adds to the eeriness. Groups of men are to be seen and heard stomping around blind corners at full-tilt, carrying makeshift splints upon which new arrivals are wrapped. For those who wish to gain a closer view, it's possible to pay boatmen to cautiously row alongside the inferno. But be warned: renegade photographers aren't tolerated. A newfound American friend of ours had attempted to shoot a reel of images, only for a group of men to approach him once he regained dry land. They duly extorted a bundle of US dollars from his wallet to help absolve him of the disrespect he'd shown. The heat generated by each individual pyre is surprisingly intense, even from twenty yards away. As the flames whip in the wind, it's natural to reflect upon one's own mortality. Is death the end, or is it merely the beginning? At the end of the day, who really decides?

~

IT SOUNDED LIKE CHILDBIRTH. Anywhere else, the agonising scream expelled by Sheetha would have been enough to stop traffic. In the throes of hassling a shopkeeper for directions, I wrenched my neck around. Rubbing the back of her right leg, Sheetha howled her disgust at a man lurching past. Wielding a meaty hunk of wood, he'd walloped her behind the knees. Si responded in an instant, tripping into a sprint, leaping upon the man's back. Both of them smacked the road with a dull thud. Keen to reprimand the man for the unprovoked attack, Si administered a choke hold: the most effective form of restraint. Glancing around with a bloody cheek pierced by gravel, Si motioned for us to alert somebody about the incident. The shopkeeper stepped up, suddenly mute. Never before had he seen a Westerner bring a local to his knees. 'He's crazy,' the sideliner grimaced, keeping his distance in case the attacker miraculously bust loose from Si's unremitting grasp. His 'craziness' aside, the man also reeked of booze. Sheetha shook in shock, confused by the inexplicable whys and wherefores of the situation. A couple of policemen sauntered over in due course. Instructing Si to let go of the wild-haired man, the police kicked Sheetha's attacker out of the gutter, into deeper misery. Ironically, we felt guilty, worried that The Wooden Warrior might have the sense beaten out of him upon being dragged to the nearest jail. None of us supported the 'eye for an eye' excuse to inflict unnecessary violence on a wastrel prone to random outbursts. Had his abuse been verbal, we'd have felt more inclined to let things slide. The truth was, he needed help, yet mental health issues appeared to be ignored across the board. Instead of integrating their psyches as a result of receiving counselling, many schizophrenics wound up in cells, subject to beatings. Better education about mental health was essential. The last thing we wanted was for the man to slip into a mire of self-pity at the hands of a station stuffed with close-minded staff who potentially didn't understand the tender intricacies of a beautiful yet flawed mind out of time. Opting against making a statement, we gathered our gear and turned tail, praying the law would display common courtesy.

~

'THERE'S NO CHANCE.' Rolling with fate on the station platform, we took one look at the stinking 'GC' and winced. Out of desperation, we'd bought three tickets in the General Compartment. Vying to reach Bodh Gaya for a religious festival to celebrate Buddha's Enlightenment, we were willing to forgo comfort if it meant bagging a cheap ride. Tagged right at the back of the sorry snake of carriages, the compartment burst with passengers, the majority of whom were men. They all looked exhausted. From where we were hunched, not a single seat could be glimpsed, indicating a 'Standing Room Only' nightmare. I dropped my backpack and squeezed between four guys hanging out of the door. For them, it would have been unusual to spot a Westerner joining their ranks, but we had no choice: every single seat in second-class was otherwise engaged. Refusing to breathe in, the men made it difficult, amused by my determination to forge inroads on behalf of my friends. Sharing their distrust by glaring, they looked me up and down, suspicious about our motives. Overcome by nausea, I elbowed my way past the shoddy excuse for an on-board toilet: a murky hole in the floor. Turning around, I was horrified to see the gap through which I'd passed sew itself up, The Starers crushed chest-to-chest. Had I been claustrophobic, I'd have ceremoniously freaked out. There must have been five-hundred people metaphorically locked in a compartment designed for less than half that amount. Regurgitating dead air, I elbowed my way back to the door, raised eyebrows communicating vital information. It seemed we were due to stay in Varanasi for another night.

Further along the platform, five leashed dogs could be seen sniffing around a group of men humping what could only be construed as excess baggage. Within two minutes, transparent bags of cocaine came to be laid in plain sight of wannabe train users. Revelling in rumbling a haul of mind-bending proportions, the police personnel on the scene could do nothing to arrest their close-knit circle of crooked smiles.

~

CHEERED BY A CHAT WITH TASMANIAN MUSICIAN EMILY JOHNSTON, we emerged from Howrah Station to face a passion-fuelled fracas. Disappointed by the distinct lack of auto-rickshaws in front of the station, we had no choice but to wait in line for a yellow Ambassador taxi with hundreds of other new arrivals into the city. As we organised ourselves, I processed my first impressions of what I hoped to be a Bengali-influenced city with a glaring difference. The temptation to head over to Dhaka, the capital of Bangladesh, was almost too much to suppress. Also known as Kolkata, Calcutta is India's second largest city. At one time, it was considered to be the most poverty-stricken urban area in the entire country, but large-scale clean-up operations have done much to improve its image in recent years.

Confused as to how the queuing system for taxis worked, we stood our ground on a kerb behind approximately fifty people. Below us, on the level, a secondary line edged forward. We asked a lady beside us why there was a need for two separate lines. Hers served family groups, apparently. Overhearing her claim, a man behind us shouted that there was no such thing as a dedicated 'family line' to his knowledge. Believing her own lies, the woman fairy-stepped a couple of feet closer to a vacant car. It was enough to catapult the man into a rage. Pointing his finger and spitting abuse as though his life was on the line, he worked himself into such a fit that a policeman hurried over to try and defuse the tension. Ironically, it provided us with the best opportunity to grab the next taxi, leaving those geared for arguing in a cloud of exhaust. 'Sudder Street,' Si said to the driver. Evidently sleep-starved, he looked as vacant as his backseat had been a few seconds beforehand. 'You know Sudder Street?' The driver tilted his head to the right. It was a fifty-fifty chance. Travelling in hope, we instructed him to engage the meter.

So, there we were: rattling away from the iconic shadow of Howrah Bridge, crammed on a relatively plush leather backseat of an Ambassador that was confidently nosing its way through late-night traffic at the behest of our non-English speaking driver who could feasibly have been taking us anywhere. Shocked at how wide and clean the roads appeared to be, we couldn't believe we'd just arrived in Calcutta, a short distance away from the border with Bangladesh. Given that we were travelling by meter, the driver took his time, maximising profits. He even had the cheek to pull over, casually step out, spit residual 'paan' into the gutter, and urinate in bushes at the roadside. We looked away in disgust, conscious that the meter was ticking on all the while. The man returned precisely ninety-seven seconds later: a little lighter, yet marginally richer.

The road was deserted. I was reminded of the night I arrived in Mumbai when I resorted to commandeering a cab through what resembled apocalypse-blitzed neighbourhoods north of Colaba. Signs of life were beyond recognition. We eventually rolled up to a toll booth. 'Ten rupees,' our driver mouthed, eyeing his rear view mirror as though it was too much effort to twist around to talk face-to-face. I proffered a ten-rupee note in a flash, desperate for us to reach Sudder Street. Plagued by fatigue and stomach pains, all I desired was a bed for the night. If the bed was located beside a toilet, so much the better. Pining for a gulp of fresh air, I thrust my head through the window. There was nothing even remotely fresh about the air quality, so I retracted my head, mentally pushing the car's rusty bulk over the Hooghly River, a tributary of the Ganges, via a seemingly never-ending road bridge. Slowly but surely the meter ticked on: marking time, making money.

The Victoria Memorial was located in the vicinity, as was a simple but effective memorial to lives lost in the so-called

Black Hole of Calcutta. Shame it was too dark to appropriate our bearings from the back seat. Amazed at how orderly the traffic seemed, we were even more amazed when we flashed by a 'McDonald's', juddering to a halt at the end of a narrow yet insufferably busy street. Stabbing a finger towards the action, the driver grumbled, 'Sudder Street.' Having scant idea about what to expect, we were cautious, refusing to slide out until we'd hailed a passer-by to confirm our location. Satisfied with the man's answer, Simon and Sheetha stepped out to retrieve our backpacks from the boot. I stayed inside the car just in case the driver floored it before we'd had chance to grab our gear.

I clocked the figure on the meter, hopping out once Si had hoisted my backpack onto the kerb. Handing over the sixty rupees we evidently owed, we collectively reeled when the driver demanded double. 'One-hundred and twenty-two rupees!' the man squirmed. 'No,' Sheetha countered, pointing at the meter beaming through the darkness with a clean figure of sixty. Detesting dishonesty, we were about to trail off in search of a guesthouse when the driver began shouting, kicking the kerbside dust into a crowd-attracting storm. At the other side of the railing, five Indian men gathered, not wanting to miss the latest and potentially greatest altercation they'd seen between a bunch of foreigners and a driver. Hoping they might be willing to tell us why the driver was demanding far more than expected, we asked one of the youths to speak to our man. It turned out that the figure on the meter wasn't the amount we were supposed to pay after all. It was a code... and 'Code Sixty' equated to one-hundred and twenty-two rupees. Desiring the sacred formula for calculating future fares in the city, we asked the man to explain the system. 'Okay, so you double the figure then add two. If you get a Code Thirty-Two for a relatively short journey from here to Motherhouse, you'll owe sixty-six rupees.' As much as we disagreed with the overly confusing way in which the code system worked, we understood. Going thirds on the fare, we sloped away from the taxi with something of a defeatist attitude, anxious that 'hidden' costs might be added to other things we required in Calcutta.

On the upside, we'd made it to Sudder Street in one piece. It was just a pity that it had gone nine and we still faced the arduous task of securing two rooms for the night. Nursing the energy-sapping consequences of heatstroke, I was happy to crash into bed anywhere so long as it wasn't going to cost more than four-hundred rupees for the privilege. As soon as we began walking along the traveller-rutted street, a tout chased us, diligently directing us down a side alley to a guesthouse from which he'd score a handsome commission were he to successfully persuade us to stay. Savvy enough to realise that any room would cost more if we rolled up to a guesthouse with any kind of tout on our backs, we shook him off, telling him straight that we'd find a place on our own terms. On the downside, securing lodgings proved difficult so late at night.

Nearing the middle of the street where the guesthouses and shops gave way to a lifeless junction of iniquity, 'Times Guesthouse' tempted us up its creaking stairs. Silently screaming with joy upon being told that rooms were available at very competitive rates, we told the female proprietor that we'd sign in and pay up for three nights.

The noise on the street below didn't faze me. The fact that the en-suite toilet had no light and didn't flush failed to rouse my common sense. Far from provoking me to decline the room and to continue searching, I locked the door, fell onto the mattress, and snoozed like a foetus. I awoke twenty-four hours later, not knowing where I was, when it was, or who I was. I only fully came around after forking my way through a plate of vegetable fried rice served by a sneering side-street vendor. It was a Thursday night, I was still in Calcutta, and the passport in my pocket suggested that I was a British man bearing the name of Steve Rudd. Having caught up to speed with myself and my whereabouts, there was just one thing lacking in my new-fangled life: my friends.

~

WE WERE THERE TO HELP, yet we were made to feel like a hindrance.

Having learnt of the volunteering programmes organised through Motherhouse on AJC Bose Road, my friends and I had opted to work with the sick and dying for what we'd hoped might be a day that would genuinely make the people we were caring for glad to have us around. We'd purposefully visited Motherhouse to learn more about Mother Teresa's work. The 'house' is where she lived and worked for much of her time in Calcutta. It's also where she's laid to rest. Visitors can see and pray at her marble tomb if they so wish. Prior to learning more about the remarkable lady's truly compelling life, we edged into the spacious chapel of rest, to reflect, and to pay our respects. Atop her tomb, a quote had been sprinkled in stunning orange petals: 'A clean heart can see God.' As we shuffled around the tomb in an anticlockwise fashion, a flurry of people came and went, all pausing for thought, the sisters among them dropping to their knees, clutching rosary beads, praying.

Born in Skopje in Eastern Europe in 1910, Mother Teresa spent the bulk of her life in India, witnessing the worst aspects of poverty in the process. The Bengal Famine of 1943 claimed in the region of two million lives, and it forced untold millions of people into extreme hardship. Food was scarce; living conditions were dreadful. Just three years later, violence afflicted the streets of Calcutta in the run-up to Independence.

In 1948, Mother Teresa went into the slums. Shocked by what she saw, she vowed to do all she could to help.

Missionaries of Charity continue to help the poor and needy of Calcutta three-hundred and sixty-five days a year. What's more, the nerve centre for all cross-city projects run by the charity is Motherhouse itself. The best base conceivable, its relatively central location - a short walk from the vibrant ghetto of travellers populating Sudder Street - means that it's the easiest place for volunteers to converge on a morning. We'd been told we could attend Mass if we liked, but that would have meant getting up at five for the 5.45 a.m. start. What we did instead was roll up for breakfast at seven.

We were immediately directed to the main meeting room in which volunteers can freely roam and mingle whilst consuming their breakfast of two slices of bread, a banana, and a heavily-sugared 'chai' to savour. There were a few one-day-only volunteers, but most people had been toiling on a long-term basis, many of them cogs in groups that had stuck together for the duration. It was the final day of work for one group in particular. Ushered to the heart of the room, they were duly thanked and awarded gifts for their time and devotion. A prayer was also said before a sing-a-long overwhelmed such seriousness with camp jollity. 'Leaders' subsequently brandished cards upon which the names of the various hospices were colourfully scrawled in felt-tip pen. Sheetha, Simon and I jovially accosted the man with the 'Kali Ghat' card over his head, chatting with him as the rest of our group relayed dirty cups and plates to the sullen washing-up crew. Although he'd only been working at the Kali Ghat hospice for a short while, Korean traveller Sup hadn't been backward in rushing forward with his capacity to lead. Coincidentally, he was three years into an around-the-world cycling adventure. In conversation, he reminded me of a friend from Hull: Karl Bushby, an adventurer who'd set himself the challenge of walking in the region of thirty-six thousand miles back home to the UK, via the Bering Strait, from the tip of South America. Like Sup, Karl had once described how hours could pass without him being conscious of time's unforgiving passage. Not only that, he also admitted feeling like 'a prisoner of the white lines' when the going got tough, psychologically trapped in an inescapable 'world' of his own making. Adamant that hope had to be nurtured on a daily basis, Sup cited the sight of mountains as 'the ultimate inspiration' to him. Relating to his connection with nature at its loftiest, I told him that I regarded mountains to be spiritual touchstones of the highest order. Charged with divine wisdom, they've witnessed the best and worst of what nature has to offer. Reflecting upon Crystal Therapy, I wondered if there might ever be a strain of therapy known as Summit Therapy. As unquestioning as they are uncompromising, sky-scraping peaks speak to those with an allegiance to the unseen and mystical, harnessing the purity of light beyond the darkest of realms. Above all else, they foster strength.

Kali Ghat was within walking distance, sparing us the hassle of finding our way via the pitfalls of public transport. Other groups, meanwhile, hopped onto public buses to locations elsewhere in the city.

It was exhilarating to see the Calcutta backstreets thrum to life as we walked to work. Industrious to the hilt, all manner of enterprises appeared to be revving to their own respective tunes. There were greasy motorcycle repair shops; tiny sweat-shops rammed with young sewing machinists; open-fronted butcheries frequented by flies. Further on, general grocery stores - awash with bread, drinks, sweets and cigarettes - groaned through persistent power outages. Then there were lavish hotels interspersed with budget-preserving dumps. The forty-five minute stroll couldn't have been any more eye-opening if metre-long matchsticks had been jammed between lashed lids. Ducking through a heartbreakingly impoverished slum flanking a run of railway lines, we entered the Park Circus area, striding parallel to one of the lines in order to reach Park Circus Station. It was abuzz with a mixture of commuting businessmen, sari-clad women clutching babies, hip teenagers on their mobiles, and dirt-caked toddlers with their hands out. Beyond the station we sliced through another section of the slum before being directed through a door into the airy hospice grounds, children hurling sarcastic sound bites as they slid down a concrete embankment behind. Taking deep breaths in light of what we'd seen, and in anticipation of what we were about to experience, we followed Sup to a cage in which we could stow our belongings. Donning an apron each, we wondered what might be in store.

In a sheltered area of the hospice, ten men were sat in a row, in the shade, out of the heat, chatting amongst themselves. Just beyond them lay the women's quarter where a couple of sisters tended to the needs of two wheelchair-bound ladies. Sheetha rushed straight over, eager to assist. Attempting to suss out what was expected of us, Simon and I entered a slightly elevated area set aside from the men and women. Having received no clear instructions about what to do, we asked a sister if we should ingratiate ourselves with laundry duty. A laughably ambiguous headshake was all the impetus we required. Rolling up my sleeves, I warned my hands they were about to get dirty.

~

GIVEN THE CHANCE, INDIANS LOVE TO MAKE A RACKET. Unfortunately for us, a deafening festival coincided with our stay on Sudder Street. Just around the corner, a gazebo had been erected. Beneath its rain-deflecting roof, three men took it in turns to play music, sing and chant as though their religion depended on it. Heavily amplified, their voices must have echoed clean across The Hooghly. As tired as we were, sleep was not an option. It was like being on the front row at a Slipknot show. My ears bled. But what could I do? I had no ear plugs, and I'd neglected to pick up sleeping tablets for such occasions. All I could do was stare at the ceiling until I cracked, hopped out of bed, and paced over to the window. In the shadows of what smelt like death, I could make out a trio of entwined condoms just below the shutters, lying forlorn and forgotten about on the adjacent roof. The sight hastened to remind me that the 'Times Guesthouse' was alleged to be one of the main places for prostitutes to bring their clients. That would at least explain why I got chatted up every time I descended the front staircase. The previous day, a twenty-something man had tried pimping out his own mother by placing her in front of me, saying she'd wash, cook, do anything I asked. Prostitution: it's a filthy business.

If you can't beat them, join them. That old adage hangs truer than ever when faced with a sleepless night. I certainly didn't want to dumbly stare through my window until dawn. Entranced by the music, I fled the guesthouse, shrugging off two middle-aged women who appeared to be loitering for no valid reason. I wheeled around the corner, bought a 'Sprite', and sat down near the edge of what represented a stage, but what in reality was a glorified fruit stall large enough for the performers to perch upon. A sitar, tabla and flute all participated in the musical proceedings at select points. A veteran of 'open mic nights' in the UK, I had to constantly restrain myself from hopping on stage. After a while, I accepted my fate and shrunk back to a safe distance from which the sitar had no chance of getting hurt. The music washed over me. The monotonal drone of the alpha guru somehow hypnotised me. However, a gurgle of bad-mouthed words soon thrust me back into reality. A couple of men clearly disapproved of such festivities, as though the words spilling through the loudspeakers went against what they believed. The differences in opinion forced me to relive a day that had been spent trying to help people in an environment that discouraged compassion as much as it did patience.

Having volunteered to work in Kali Ghat Hospice, we'd been expecting to deal with the men and women there on a one-to-one basis, assessing their individual needs and making them feel as comfortable and cared for as possible. We began work at nine, and the first job of the day involved doing the laundry, followed by washing and drying the cups and plates used for breakfast. Supervised by a fellow volunteer in the form of a matronly Japanese woman, we'd been instructed to hunch over a series of bowls filled to their brims with soapy water. For the first ninety minutes, we scrubbed and rinsed clothes and bedding, disappointed by the fact we had so little contact with the Indian men and woman glumly sat on the sidelines. After a short break for 'chai' and biscuits, we returned to the same workstation to thoroughly clean metallic cup after cup after curry-smeared plate after plate. Amongst our crew of six stooped a non-communicative Frenchwoman, a down-to-earth Malaysian girl, and a free-spirited lady from Hong Kong. Some of the volunteers shared our disgust at the way some of the people staying in the hospice were treated. After dinner, the military-style routine asserted itself with surplus 'shock value'.

The second shift began with a few of us doing more laundry, much to our chagrin. We wanted to help residents in a more direct manner. Nevertheless, we were mature enough to realise that whatever we did would indirectly help them in some way or other, hence why I didn't mind when the Japanese lady began shrieking because I'd hung washing to dry in the wrong area on the roof. From where I stood, it seemed the garments would dry quickly regardless of where they were arranged on the lines. Impolite and pedantic, she was a control freak of the most intimidating and spirit-crushing kind. Craving an easy life, I complied with her demands, shifting all of the washing from one side of the roof to the other so the legion of standard-issue trousers neatly filtered into two lines of flapping bed sheets. She evidently took as much pride in arranging washing as some folk take in tending to their gardens or washing their prized cars. The integrity of her routine could not be compromised in any way, shape or form.

Descending the stairs beside her in order to return to the main section of the hospice, she stabbed a finger through a divide, pointing to a blanket that had fallen off the roof onto a ledge. Maybe it had had enough of her, too. 'Reason why no washing put near edge of roof,' she huffed, as though I was to blame for the runaway hunk of wool. She then flung her attention to the opposite side of the stairwell, in the corner of which a number of bamboo poles were stacked. 'You get pole and catch blanket,' she said, providing me with little in the way of choice. Having made her sensational demand, she scurried down the stairs, out into the courtyard, and back across to where dinner was being served, chomping at the bit to cause further uproar amidst fellow volunteers and sisters. In the wake of adopting a pole with a view to spearing the blanket and hoisting it into arm's reach, an Indian labourer ran up the stairs, instructing me to forget about the washing and to help him instead. Apparently he was in the throes of helping to erect a stage in the courtyard for a Nativity play that was to be premiered later in the afternoon. The bamboo poles would make ideal posts upon which lights and speakers could be hung. Knowing full well I'd intercept an ear-bashing of the most deafening nature for abandoning the blanket to the elements, I accepted the man's plea bargain, realising that there was more urgency attached to setting the stage than to fishing for a mangy old cover. With my heart set on helping the man, I followed him downstairs, being careful not to cause structural damage to the building as I rounded corners in the stairwell. I would have felt guilty had I accidentally scraped the harsh concrete walls with the pole's tip. Outside, it was baking. The temperature had suddenly blasted off the scale of what could be deemed reasonable. Before me, chaos reigned, a trio of carpenters hastily smashing nails into the poor excuse for an elevated platform. I placed the pole in a hole that had been excavated earlier. As I exited stage left, a near-limbless Christmas tree was placed at the centre of the stage around which the labourers continued to toil, sweat streaming from every pore.

I returned to the ward empty-handed, explaining to the Japanese lady that duty had called me elsewhere. She said not a word in response. Her demonic stare was enough. Fortunately, it was the busiest time of day in terms of work needing to be done. Various concoctions of medicine were relayed to patients prior to their main meal. I joined the queue of volunteers to help dole out white plastic beakers filled with a tablet or two, along with a nut chaser. It was obviously imperative that the right person was given the correct medication, but the system in place meant there was huge potential for human error. New volunteers who had no knowledge about which patients were owed which tablets were liable to make mistakes through no fault of their own. A stressed sister relayed the beakers whilst stood at a desk, flicking through a ledger that detailed each patient's personal requirements. The mixture was then made up and passed to a volunteer. The sister subsequently shouted a number and a name, then it was down to the volunteer to weed out the relevant person by walking down the corridor, calling out each number and name in turn, hoping the correct person responded. I was told to relay medicine to the men. Each time I approached them, one man in particular lunged forward, unfurled both hands, and yelped something in Hindi. No two ways about it, he wanted all the medication for himself. Terrified that I might award the wrong combination of medicine to the wrong person, I checked, cross-referenced, and then double-checked each name and patient number. Nobody was going to die on my shift.

Once the medicine had been distributed, it was time to eat. A Frenchman and I were summoned to fetch the food. Two cauldrons awaited us in a back room: one brimmed with plain rice, the other steamed with 'dal' to delight. Careful not to spill a drop, I lugged the latter cauldron to the serving area. One plate at a time, a couple of sisters ladled the 'dal' onto the rice before asking us to once again distribute the bounty. As expected, the man who'd wanted all the medicine desired all the food as well. I'd never encountered an appetite so raging - or so potentially destructive. A self-appointed leader, he radiated power. It seemed the other men were too afraid to say anything that might knock him from his lofty perch of self-importance. Offering him nothing more than a wide berth once served, I ducked into the dormitory to check on four bedbound men. Lowering a food-loaded plate onto an adjacent bed so one of them would be better positioned to eat, I received a shock when the man shouted at me, grabbing the plate. If looks could have killed, I would have been pushed facedown onto the floor and deprived of my ability to breathe within a second. Fortunately, he flung the plate down instead of me. Sensing that he wanted to eat in peace, I forged a slow retreat, asking him if I could do anything else to help. Shooting me a follow-up look of disgust, I took the hint and readied myself to serve somebody else, hoping they might be more appreciative of my helpful demeanour. Upon returning to the serving area, I was told to take what remained of the 'dal' and follow the Frenchman. For what reason I knew not. All became clearer as he squatted to offer second helpings. Pursuing his lead, I ladled extra 'dal' onto each plate until a sister stormed up and told me to surrender the cauldron at once. Apparently I was giving the men too much. To add insult to injury, I was told I was too slow. In that respect, I couldn't win. Above all else, I wanted to converse with the men as I carefully laid more 'dal' atop their rice. I begged for the time to be able to look in their eyes, to understand what kind of a life had ultimately brought them to the hospice. Had I been proffered supplementary time, I would have dared to ask questions, not out of nosiness, but out of genuine curiosity. I didn't want their stories to go unwritten, unvoiced. Alas, the chance was rudely snatched away as the sister beckoned me over. It was time to wash the crockery; time to live a lie.

~

MOSQUITOES CAN SEEMINGLY SENSE SWEET BLOOD FROM A THOUSAND PACES. I'd just slumped onto an already-lopsided bed in 'Harshini Guesthouse' on Poonamallee High Road, a short walk from Chennai's Egmore Station. When I'd checked on the quality of the room two minutes earlier, not a single bug had corkscrewed kamikaze-style through the cracked shutters. They waited until I'd paid my dues of three-hundred rupees. To be honest, the guesthouse was a dump. Or, to be more precise, it was a dump beside a dump. I had hoped to find a cheap room closer to the station, near where my friends were staying, but all the single rooms on Kennet Street cost at least five-hundred rupees. A handful of men-only guesthouses offered reasonable rates out front, but the grave look fired by each receptionist suggested that I wasn't going to be welcome on their premises. The sex-segregated guesthouse regulation was explained by the fact it was a Muslim-dominated area, hence why we were given a cold reception at certain guesthouses if we strolled in together as a trio of travellers. Wisening up, we subsequently took it in turns to make enquiries.

Tucked down a back alley of Chennai (more commonly known as Madras), 'The Harshini' was the cheapest place in the vicinity. Si and Sheetha took an auto-rickshaw back to their hotel as I sadly surveyed my hopelessly humble pad. For my hard-earned cash, I was rewarded with a bed (off which the bulk of my torso hung), a randomly placed plastic chair, and a squat toilet circled by green grime. Spying a mosquito climbing up the wall nearest the shuttered window, I leapt for my can of insect repellent and let loose. I'd been wondering why so many guesthouse walls were covered in downward-tapering stains. Now I knew.

Feeling peckish, I marched back to the run of shops facing Egmore Station. Sheetha spotted me from a restaurant and called me inside so I could join them to eat. Si had ordered a chicken-based curry. Feeling hungry but lacking money, I ordered a bowl of hot and spicy vegetable soup. It was served in record time. As we ate, we debated. Having taken a twenty-eight hour train ride all the way to Chennai from Kolkata, we deliberated about what to do next. Our initial plan had been to head a little further south in order to lap up the vibes at Pondicherry. However, we were running out of time. We couldn't afford to potentially squander a day or two there when Kerala and Goa were simultaneously demanding our attention on the west coast. All things considered and then reconsidered, I was half-tempted to buddy-up with a Canadian guy we'd befriended on the train. The following morning, he was poised to board a boat to Port Blair on the Andaman Islands. The journey was due to take him three days.

Never a fan of talking whilst eating, I coolly gestured my way through the ensuing conversation. In the time it took me to slurp a small bowl of soup, we decided to return to the station bright and early so we could reserve tickets for the next ride over to Kochi. Si had already collated quotes for bus rides to Kerala. On average, they spun in at almost one-thousand rupees: scandalously expensive for a bus ticket. Trusting trains, we conspired to stick with them, especially since they'd served us so well since our last bus ride from Ajmer to Jaisalmer. Indeed, trains tend to be the best and most fun way to travel around India, unless you're brave enough to straddle a Royal Enfield and ride around the subcontinent to both accelerate and ameliorate the freedom in your grasp. Having extolled the virtues of train travel, a few issues had nevertheless been niggling, not least the way in which a number of Indian men on train journeys routinely made Sheetha feel uncomfortable by constantly staring at her, making her feel as though she'd done something wrong. Such perverted behaviour on behalf of the men wasn't just confined to when we were chatting during daylight hours; affairs invariably worsened upon attempting to sleep if Sheetha was 'up top' and a man lay in the adjacent bunk. Their prying eyes, it seemed, knew no bounds.

Sleep proved hard to come by in Chennai. Conscious that mosquitoes were abuzz about my guesthouse, I tucked my mosquito net under the bed's mattress cover. I proceeded to climb between such sheaths. With a chink of light filtering in from outside, the second I fell out of a dozing fit, I was horrified to register the stark silhouette of a cockroach a few centimetres above me. Stifling a shriek of shock, I impulsively curled my right index finger, flicking it with the express intention of propelling it off the net and onto the floor so I no longer had to stare at or worry about it. I realised they were harmless, but that didn't make them any less intimidating in stature. Ironically, what happened next almost killed me: instead of witnessing the outward-bound flight of the roach, the big black bug of burden slammed down upon my forehead. There it rested for a couple of long seconds before I lurched to my senses, flicking it into the net. Mystified and terrified in equal measure, I yelled. I couldn't help it. The guesthouse reception was next door to my room, so the guys working the desk must surely have succumbed to fits of hysterics. I concluded that the roach had climbed up the inside of my net from the point at which I'd tucked it beneath the mattress where the shelled monster had been hiding all along. In that respect, a lesson had been learnt the hard way: always check the state of play beneath your mattress before doing anything else. Ignorance might be bliss on a short-term basis, but if you don't wish to wake up in the middle of the night with a roach on your back (or, even worse, exploring the cavities of your mouth), then it's wise to check on what's lurking in the darkest recess of your bed. I could have complained to the proprietor, but what would he do? He'd laugh in my face for being foolish enough not to have carried out a more thorough check of every nook and cranny of the room. My cursory glance into the corners and at the toilet had failed to highlight the ugly bedbug infestation. Thenceforth, I vowed to peer under mattresses as a matter of priority.

It was late. Alternative lodgings would be hard to find. That in mind, I traced a line of dead bugs back to the source of my problem: an airy crack in the bed's base. I dared to take a closer look, mindful that the cockroach had vanished. Or had it? No... it was still there, crouched just below the crack's opening. I slammed my mattress down, hoping to provoke the roach to retreat. Craving sleep, I reconsidered my options. I needed to be up for seven in the morning in order to rush to Egmore Station's reservation centre. I surmised that the only way I'd be safe from further roach attacks would be if I wrapped myself in the net as tightly as possible, leaving no room for the roach or any of his bug-eyed friends to come between me and a beat of much-deserved rest.

Five hours later, I woke. The first thing I saw was the roach: spread-eagled atop my net, mere millimetres from my mouth. Somehow suppressing my shock, I flicked the critter off. It clattered to the floor on its back, immediately righting itself. I possessed neither the heart nor the speed to stamp it out of existence. My ears would take too much offence at the severity of the consequential crunch. Instead, I let it be. After all, it wielded just as much of a right to live as me. I was becoming more of a Buddhist by the day, it seemed.

~

THE PAIN WAS TANGIBLE. I'd been run over, a car having rocked over my right foot without the driver realising. To be fair, I shouldn't have been stood in the middle of the road. Shaking away the shock, I thought back to the time I'd trapped my fingers in the hinge of a door whilst struggling to remove a foot from an ice skate. With nowhere suitable to balance, I had no choice but to curl my fingers into the dead space, neglecting to see a man through the crack, aching to swap sides.

Shuffling across the road with a limp in my step, I steered my body around a bus heading to Bangalore. A stray arm patted my head, its possessor hyperventilating with laughter. 'You come to the city of technology?' he sang. I shook my head, forgetting that such a gesture meant 'yes'. I'd heard much about India's version of Silicon Valley in which outsourced call centres incessantly fielded misinterpreted enquiries. At my heady command, the bus screeched to a halt. 'You join us, friend?' the driver harrumphed. 'No! I didn't mean to shake my head; it was a mistake,' I apologised. I had no intention of lurching anywhere near Bangalore, my ambition being to sever my soul from technology, conscious that people were literally losing their minds as mobile phones and social networking sites fought to suppress people's sense of self, sedating their best interests. My worst fear dreaded a point in the future when people could no longer communicate by talking, meaningless abbreviations truncating the longevity of words. On countless occasions, I'd chatted to old friends on 'Facebook', only for them to blank me when I'd dared initiate a live conversation in real time as I passed them in the street, as though words created by sounds, amplified by one's larynx, no longer carried half as much gravity as garbled sentences punched into portable devices. The sad truth is, a lot of people don't listen anymore. Simple as that. Unless massaging their own egos, they don't want to know. Needy products of 'Generation XXX', they scoff at the old-school importance of individuation, convinced that the world exists not beyond arm's reach, but in their unread palms, or at the end of their dearly manicured fingertips. In a world where most talk is rooted in slanderous gossip, there's not much room left for folk courageous enough to think and act differently.

As India pandered to globalisation's demands, I strove to smash happiness into component parts, fortifying the outdated integrity of the concept as I carefully reassembled it, one piece at a time. Chennai street-life appeared despondent, its lust for life tarnished. 'When did life get so tiring?' I wondered as I wandered, reminding my inner demons that happiness is a state of mind. Subject to internal adjustments in approach, I thanked Jesse Malin for secreting his P.M.A. (Positive Mental Attitude) through music. Societal expectations break people in a way that primitive lifestyles never could. Shouldering such a realisation, I wondered how an Ethiopian friend living in Los Angeles had coped whilst working in The Primal Institute. Helping broken individuals to regress to the precise point at which their innocence, awe and motivation whisked their confidence and, in some cases, sanity away, he'd risked losing sight of what was real in the emotionally draining process. I was also reminded of an actor friend who regarded my prowess at networking to be inspirational as a result of being unconventional. Amassing friends with selfless zeal, I told Vince that confidence is key when it comes to selling oneself. Breezing through Asia, I'd learnt that the less you take, the more you get to give. In an era preoccupied with acquisitions and consumerism, I reasoned that ownership of any kind made less sense than killing in the name of progress. Possess the strength to effect a positive change. Foster forgiveness and let go of grudges. If spiritual development inhaled the capacity to keep pace with industrial development, then progress would to some extent abolish hierarchical inequality. If only truth wasn't plundered by oppressive buzzwords reeking of violence. Regardless of what we imbibe, all of us are infrequently guilty of consuming without properly digesting, living our lives on mobile phones as though hearing voices is all we've ever known: as deaf as we are dumb. It's an empowering moment when somebody recognises your potential. A person shouldn't have to pimp their soul. Life should take care of itself. Tragedy lies in the gross sexualisation of children: a precursor to the premature disintegration of family units, served with a collective loss of identity. Sapped of self-respect, and duped into believing that the lives of celebrities are more important than theirs when they're not, the weak-willed become content to exist instead of being ecstatic to live. And that's when alarm bells become too deafening to tolerate.

~

CONTRARY TO POPULAR OPINION, Chennai has much to recommend it as one of India's largest and most populous urban centres. Its position, low on the east coast of India, means that its prosperity has always been determined by the value affiliated with international shipping. For sure, there is only a minimal amount of money trickling into the city's coffers from tourism. On its streets, Westerners are a very rare sight. During a four-hour walkabout, I didn't see one fellow foreigner as I peeled away from the bright lights of Kennet Street towards the waterfront. Encouragingly, Chennai could and should appeal to more visitors given its laid-back nature, not to mention its architecturally astounding buildings which owe much to the distinctive Tamil influence. The Madras High Court dominates the skyline from the Fort area with its high domes and colourful exterior. If only the city carried more parks. On the upside, a plethora of monuments and statues are worth seeing.

After scurrying along what I hoped might be a road to South Beach, I swung over a bridge beside a slum into the shadow of a statue immortalising a man on horseback. As I swiped a reel of photos from the roadside, a horn blasted from behind, demanding my undivided attention. I neglected to turn, instead striding further along the road. To my left, an ecological park, a golf course, and a military zone kept each other company. All three compounds shared the same entrance, either side of which stood heavyweight examples of vintage artillery. There didn't appear to be a single person on the golf course. Little wonder really. Perhaps all potential golfers in the area had read the day's dire weather report. The leaden skies looked a sight for all the wrong reasons. Turning around before the impending downpour soaked me to the bone, I scurried beyond the statue, only for an arm to shoot through the window of a smart white car parked on a roundabout. 'Excuse me, but did you just take a photo of the statue?' the cigarette-twirling man asked with a condescending air of superiority. Fearing the worst, I hesitated, sensitive to how photograph-shooting is often prohibited near military compounds. 'No,' I fibbed, betraying The Truth, sensing the man already had me nailed. He'd been right behind me when I'd stopped to engage my camera. Naturally, he would have seen everything from the air-conditioned comfort of his vehicle. 'Do you know why I tried to get your attention by blowing my horn?' he went on to ask. 'No,' I said, keen to get moving since the relatively refreshing drizzle had morphed into a raw downpour. 'Well, I wanted to direct your attention to the statue's history.' I launched a look of bemusement across the divide. 'Yes, you see the man who built it forgot two details which completely undermined the statue's integrity. Can you spot what the horse-rider is lacking?' The statue stood roughly thirty feet distant. As much as I squinted, I couldn't see what he was getting at. Turning away from the high and mighty example of artistic imperfection, I looked to the skies, hoping to subliminally confide my desire to return to Egmore before my 'Netbook' short-circuited. 'The man is without a saddle and a stirrup. The sculptor was branded a disgrace because of his inattention to detail. There was only one way the man could appease his detractors. Suicide!' the man belatedly elaborated, sagely nodding his head as he hammered hard facts down my ear canals. Shame I didn't know what to do with them. Regardless, I thanked him for his time, still paranoid that he might have me arrested for taking photos so close to a military enclosure.

Retracing my muddy steps, I trailed the nearest railway line in a northerly direction, somehow missing the fort altogether. Opposite Fort Station, a banner proclaimed Chennai to be 'India's first smoke-free megacity'. Given that smokers en-masse continued to strut their cigarettes in public, it would probably be a good decade or more before the city could legitimately take pride in its dubious status.

On the hunt for further examples of Tamil architecture, I paced back towards Egmore beside a train line upon which services shuttled between the Central and Fort stations with acute regularity. Opposite the extravagant Ripon Buildings complex, I literally stumbled upon a building site where women were doing the bulk of the hard work as male labourers looked on. A couple of middle-aged women piled five bricks on their heads at a time before relaying them to the bricklayers approximately thirty yards away. Decked in eye-spearingly beautiful saris, they were hardly dressed in appropriate attire, but they certainly went to work with the best kind of attitude, keeping their heads in line with earning an honest crust, as opposed to taking to the streets to beg. I nurtured utmost respect for them, returning their smiles as I plunged through the dust.

Between there and Egmore, a series of technicoloured murals detracted attention from the wall of traffic. Daubed on the side of a building, such murals depicted a multitude of scenes: from Shiva-dominated arrangements with religious connotations, to epic vistas of waterfalls and boat-strewn beaches. Around the corner, as if bookending the art, an advertisement had been hand-painted on a wall leading to a railway overpass. Rallying for people to attend The World Atheist Conference, it brazenly divulged details of where and when the event for non-believers was slated to take place.

I'd been impressed with what Chennai had to offer. For those visitors with patience, it proves to be a city teeming with modest surprises. Though it lacks the cosmopolitan buzz of Mumbai, the jaw-dropping history of Delhi, and the wide open spaces of Calcutta, Chennai wields subtle charm in abundance. What's more, one of its barbershops opposite Egmore Station had an extra special treat for customers. On a plaque outside, an advert for a shampoo used on the premises promised to reduce dandruff and improve a person's sight in one fell swoop. Having had my head shaved a few days previously, I strode straight by the offer of a lifetime without batting an eyelid. Next time, I thought. Should laser eye treatment fail me, I'll know where to turn. If only the shampoo had promised a relaxing ride to Kochi in addition.

~

A SCOOT AROUND THE ROYAL ENFIELD motorbike factory would have to wait for another trip. The premises resided on the outskirts, but we had neither the time (tours are only undertaken on Saturdays) nor enough money (the six-hundred rupee entrance fee was far too expensive) at our disposal. Nonetheless, the story of the Enfield motorbike is a fascinating one, especially when you bear in mind that the original factory in England closed down years ago. The base in Chennai now exports bikes back to the UK for sale. It's ironic, but it works, and a lot of money is made in the process.

On the train ride to Ernakulam, I had a dream. It involved taking to the road on a bike. I'll be straight up: I'd never been at the helm of a motorbike in my life, and I'd only ridden pillion on a few hair-raising occasions. However, inspired by stories from friends, I suddenly fancied the idea of renting or buying a motorbike and rumbling off towards the farthest horizon where routine-based responsibilities would struggle to find me. A friend called Frode from Denmark had zipped around India on a trusted Enfield in 2009. If he could do it, then so could I. Si was something of a seasoned pro on bikes. We'd planned to hire a Yamaha in Jaisalmer in order to explore nearby villages amidst the Thar Desert, but a spare bike proved hard to attain at short notice. A dealer outside the fort had offered us a bike for two-hundred rupees, but it was late in the day, so we'd foolishly declined his genuinely unbeatable offer. Simon had gained experience of riding motorbikes as a child in Thailand, having grown up in a village environment. In spite of the dangerous nature of Asian roads, he seemed unperturbed, simply thrilled about the idea of being able to explore lesser-visited regions in greater depth.

We were poised to travel by train all the way to the west coast. Booked onto an overnight sleeper, we scrambled to find our berths, anxious that one of our party might be refused the right to travel since we'd only been able to book two berths for three people. Indeed, we'd scored the last available berths. This meant Sheetha had to be put on the dreaded waiting-list. The man selling the ticket assured us she'd be fine because she was travelling with us. Even though we boasted bona fide reservations, we remained worried. Our middle bunk was down, enabling us to perch on the lower bunk until the conductor checked our tickets and decided our fate. I offered to alight if the absolute worst came to pass. I could always catch up with Si and Sheetha in Kerala. As things were, the conductor didn't say a word about our supposed predicament, inconsiderately squiggling his initials over the most important details on the ticket. He might have obliterated the name of the station at which we needed to disembark, along with our estimated time of arrival, but we forgave him, relieved we were still together, making glacial tracks from one coast to another.

Democratically sharing responsibility and potential blame, we took it in turns to look after any tickets we purchased. I was on ticket-duty for the duration of our ten and a half-hour ride. Prior to safely stowing it in my shirt pocket, I studied it intently for future reference, memorising its layout so I'd be able to find the number and name of our train at a glance. A bright yellow banner ran across the bottom of the print-out.

Keen to make a point, it screamed: 'Stop Discrimination against People Living with HIV & AIDS!' The socially-conscious message was loud and clear, but surely a better statement would have boldly streamed along the lines of: 'Stop the spread of HIV & AIDS by practicing safe sex!' The truth is, sexually transmitted infections and diseases are rife across India, partly due to poor education, religion, tradition, and the inability to procure reliable contraceptives. All factors play a part in the country's shocking statistics. India hasn't come to boast a population of over a billion for no reason. Similarly, half of the men who scratch their crotches in public aren't doing so for the good of their health. More often than not, they're scratching because they are in pain due to having contracted something in the wake of unsafe sex. If talking about sex, bringing the subject into the public domain with more panache, helps to reduce the spread of infection and disease, then it can only ever do the nation a favour. It can't be denied that sex is used 'to sell' on the subcontinent like never before. Everywhere 'chai'-wallahs, petrol pump attendants, and sharp-suited businessmen look, they're violated by photo-shopped images of beautiful women provocatively sitting on cars, slurping ice-creams, or giggling on mobile phones. Traditional, conservative values are becoming more and more compromised on a daily basis as India feels increasingly obliged to imitate Western ideals, fearing that if it doesn't, it might struggle to retain a competitive foothold on the world's fast-moving economic ladder. India can't risk losing ground; there's too much money at stake. Glancing north, the nation is following China's lead. However, India must be careful not to get ahead of itself. In some parts of the country, women are frowned upon if they wear tight jeans in public. There's nothing wrong with aspiring to be modern and trendy, but if some men think that a woman's choice of dress can act as an invitation to exploit her, then something has clearly gone amiss. In its favour, India is a relatively liberal country at large, and more and more women appear to be enjoying the benefits of equal rights both at work and at home. And that's the best kind of start.

As we approached Ernakulam Town, we were roused by fevered chanting emanating from the adjacent recess of sleeper berths. Peering around the corner, we were faced with fifteen men, the majority of whom were topless and sporting streaks of white and yellow paint across their faces and midriffs. Incense was wafted around as the men clapped in time to entrancing mantras. Outside, flower garlands, attached to the windows, flapped wildly in the breeze as the train whipped west. Paying homage to a bovine deity, the men didn't let the fact they were ensconced on a busy train stop them from indulging in standardised rituals. Fifteen minutes later, the group disbanded, the men returning to their respective berths as if nothing had happened, eyeing us - the token foreigners - as they passed. As wake-up calls went, it was unique and compelling in equal measure. It sure beat the insistent bleat of my watch alarm that alerted me it was six-fifteen in the morning a second later. And not a second later.

Paying closer attention to our ticket, we noticed that the train's name was 'The Trivandrum Mail' which suggested the service pushed on to the city of the same name after pausing at Ernakulam. Since buying the ticket, we'd decided that if we were to see the best of Kerala, we should head all the way down to Trivandrum. Our original idea to stop at Kochi had been flung straight out of the window upon learning that the beaches at Kovalam constituted some of the finest in all of southern India. Daring ourselves to stay on the service to see if it did indeed stalk the coast south from Kochi, we ultimately opted to ditch the train as originally planned at Ernakulam, not wishing to be crippled by a fine for free-riding.

Ernakulam Town Station was a dream: near-spotless and chilled-out. There was no pushing or shoving, and not a single rickshaw driver drove contemptuous hassle in our direction as we emerged into the early morning light of yet another beautiful neck of Mother India. There was a very good reason why no drivers were forthcoming, though. The truth was, they were on strike, protesting against the pay they received and the way they were treated. Instead of hustling up to ask where we wanted to go, the drivers - all five of them - huddled in a circle a few metres from their rickshaws, conversing amongst themselves in hushed tones. However, a deserter lurked in their midst. 'Hey, where you go?' he whispered conspiratorially as we loped towards the busiest restaurant in sight, keen to score a 'masala dosa' for breakfast. 'The bus stand,' Si and Sheetha chirped in unison. 'Okay. One hundred rupees,' the man shot back as quietly as he could so none of the other drivers realised he alone was still touting for trade, looting the strike's significance. 'We weren't born yesterday, and we certainly didn't arrive in India yesterday,' Sheetha confirmed. Shaking him off, we formed a united front whilst crossing the road, pining for a hunger-appeasing potato-filled snack like no tomorrow.

~

THE BEACH LIFE ISN'T ALWAYS AS EASY AS IT LOOKS. It's often buoyed by non-stop hassle, with confrontational boatmen rallying to take you for rides, and seasoned shawl-sellers vying to convince you that the 'genuine silk' in their wares really was sourced in Kashmir. At least it's non-stop hassle if you choose to base yourself on the busiest beaches in India. It's all about location.

The beaches at Kovalam on India's west coast are renowned for their relaxing vibes and surprisingly clean blankets of sand. Made all the more romantic by its lighthouse, sited upon a rocky promontory, Kovalam has become something of a Mecca for trendy travellers and ageing hippies alike. All budgets are catered for in the form of cheap backstreet guesthouses and expensive beachfront residences. For those fond of food, almost all restaurants serve a selection of Indian, Chinese and European dishes. Local restaurants place as much emphasis on their seafood as possible, delighting in sharing their taste for good food in breathtaking surroundings. Lobster, tuna, barracuda and prawns feature heavily on the majority of menus. Should you be entertaining a tight budget, it's advisable to overlook the fish-based options entirely. Settle for a rice-riddled option instead.

South of the photogenic might of the striped lighthouse, a smaller and infinitely more secluded beach gives way to a rocky headland upon which a beige-coloured mosque imposes its history with reverential pride. I paused for a few moments of reflection, awed by the distance I'd covered since arriving in Mumbai two months beforehand. At my feet, a couple of emaciated black goats casually gnawed on the ropes tethering them to a wall, preventing them from falling to their deaths. Directly below the ramshackle structure, a ghastly waterfall of litter crudely cascaded towards an apparently inaccessible beach. Upon it, nothing stirred. Only an unseaworthy boat basked in the middle of the lip of sand, a rotten shadow of its former self.

I'd heard that a vibrant fishing community lay within walking distance of Kovalam. Sensing it was a little further south, I eased around the back of the mosque, covering my ever-sensitive ears as a call to prayer blared through a pair of speakers hung atop the nearest minaret. It was obvious that few Westerners ventured so far south, a smattering of invasive stares making me feel far more uncomfortable than anticipated. I walked on regardless, spurred on by the promise of another mosque around the corner. It appeared to be more lavish and well-attended than the one on the hill. Perhaps it was the slight issue of gradient that resulted in the lower-level mosque being favoured if push came to shove. A couple of hundred yards away, a riot of boats bobbed in the bay. Many of them were being treated to licks of paint and wood preservative before they were dragged back into action. Waltzing along one of the piers, I could taste the salt in the air. It unwittingly acted as an agreeable chaser for the copious amount of sugar I'd feverishly stirred into my breakfast 'chai' at the 'Swiss Restaurant'. The timeless scene of toil literally looked a picture. Ancient, bare-chested men with heads of thick hair and thicker beards were involved in all manner of back-snapping jobs. At their ages, they should have known better than to labour in the unforgiving heat of the midday sun, but if a job has to be done, it might as well be completed to the highest possible standard sooner rather than later.

I'd seen very few beaches on my journey around India. Chowpatty Beach in Mumbai aside, Kovalam Beach was the first I'd really had the opportunity to explore and enjoy, hence why I was in my element. Aching to ascend the steps of the lighthouse to its lookout point, I was disappointed to learn that it was only open to visitors between three and five in the afternoon. Instead of waiting for the required four hours, I strode north, around to Samudra Beach via a slip-road flanked by a thick canopy of palm trees. The crowds contaminating the main beach suddenly seemed a million miles away as I introduced my feet to Samudra's welcoming sands. The net effect was delightful. Splashing into the sea, I excitedly scanned the water for the types of fish which teased taste buds in the area three hundred and sixty-five days a year. Either I didn't look hard enough, or such fish populated deeper water further from the coastline. The only entities I clocked on the beach came in the form of smashed oyster shells, an intriguing trail of blackened bananas, and a coven of fiendishly observant seagulls that evidently wanted a part of me. Why, I will never know. I was in no fit state to be eaten, that's for sure.

The further north I trekked, the quieter the series of beaches became. A run of extravagant hotel complexes shouldered the main stretch of beach for a few hundred yards. As a result, strategically positioned sun loungers catered to the comfort of residents. A mixture of middle-aged couples on holiday flaunted their relative wealth beside sun-baked retirees who weren't ashamed to expose more flesh in their sixties than they had in their twenties. I kept my train of thought on the straight and narrow, wondering how the beaches at Goa might differ from Kerala's heavily salted selection. I speculated that those further north would be just as stunning, if not more so, though I feared guesthouse prices would reflect the prestige attached to the world-famous parade. The fact that Christmas was just around the corner would mean prices would be even higher than normal. Swallowing a dry gulp of dread, I allowed such seasonal concerns to slip out of my head, into the ether, evaporating completely. A flush of surfers sprinted into the swell, addressing my kind of board meeting. On the sand, a helmeted teenager slogged a cricket ball towards the road, worshipping Sachin Tendulkar, whooping with delight between invisible wickets.

Goa could wait. I aspired to live in the present like never before, so I marched onwards, astonished by the ferocious will of the land-bound waves. I looked out to sea and cleared my mind. I'd made it to the southernmost tip of Mother India. I was living the dream.

~

AWAY WITH THE FAIRIES, I'd stumbled upon a small patch of paradise. After an hour's worth of walking, I'd found the main drag of Alleppey Beach. At one point, I thought I'd wind up perishing of dehydration. In spite of picking up cold drinks every twenty minutes, it was approaching midday, and the heat had made me delirious. Bored of water, I bought a bottle of 'Sprint' in a poky store. A poor man's 'Sprite' for want of a better comparison, it would have to do, quenching my thirst if not contributing to my health in any positive way. In less than sixty seconds, I found myself to be essentially supping boiling water. Given that 'Sprint' consists of little more than carbonated water, along with more sugar than is strictly necessary, the contents - once exposed to direct sunlight - begin to taste altogether more off-putting. If only a shred of fruit pulp blessed the fizzy elixir. Uninspired by the drink, I hopped off the main road to duck into the delightful 'Dreamers' restaurant. Although the joint shouldered the road, its shaded and tastefully landscaped courtyard provided a tranquil sanctuary for those seeking good food and drink in friendly surroundings. Cowering in the shadow of arching palm trees, 'Dreamers' proved to be one of the finest places to dine near the beach. In the wake of ordering a 'chapatti'-accompanied bowl of corn-based soup, I couldn't resist honing in on the conversation freewheeling with glee on the adjacent table. Directed by a British couple, the bulk of it was inane to say the least. In the course of twenty minutes, the only conversational gambits the man and his partner thrust forth revolved solely around the words 'cool', 'right', and 'chill'. In that respect, they weren't really holding a conversation at all with the Indian man beside them. Voicing their laid-back intentions for the rest of the day, they planned to do nothing else other than sunbathe and swim. As they prepared to saunter along to the nearest beachfront café, the vacationing male asked the Indian if he used 'Facebook'. The

Indian confirmed that he did. The Brit seemed somewhat taken aback, spluttering 'God' in such a clipped and sensationally posh tone that he sounded like Bill Nighy. For some reason, he couldn't conceive that the Indian man possessed a profile of his own. 'Wow... well we'll look you up, and you'll be able to speak to us in England when we get home,' the woman butted in, keen to discuss the pros and cons of living in an increasingly well-connected world. Personally, I suspected that the Indian was glad to see the back of them: as soon as they left, he promptly burst into laughter, evidently ridiculing the happy-go-lucky naivety exhibited by the couple.

Between mouthfuls of soup, I wrote, noting how I felt. I wanted to be totally honest with myself. In doing so I realised that I was floundering beneath a tidal wave of loneliness. I was in one of the most stunning areas of India, if not the world, yet I'd have preferred to have been trudging through the snow-laden UK. As reluctant as I was to admit that depression had engulfed my soul, I knew that to be the case. I missed home, in spite of constantly professing to adore the flexibility, unpredictability and raw excitement awarded by a root-severing life on the road. I was only human at the end of each day, craving genuine intimacy as much as the next man. The love of my life had just returned to England after a two-week jaunt through Nepal. I couldn't deny I missed her dearly.

My head soon began to hurt as a result of such procrastination. I should have meditated instead. The mood of the drifting music proved to be the perfect foil. Acoustic-based tunes put me at ease, a reggae-styled version of 'Cecilia' serenading me as I left to stroll further north.

Fingering its way into the Arabian Sea, Alleppey Pier looked more than a little worse for wear, having succumbed to a battering from the elements over the years. It was over one-hundred and forty years old - and you could tell. Given that a couple of mangled tracks could still be seen leading up to the pier, it must have been employed as some kind of docking point in its time. I'd just met a lone traveller from Cornwall called Charlie. He'd jokingly recommended trying to walk to the end of the pier, unaware that we'd need to be acrobats to accomplish such a feat. Indeed, no wooden walkway exists: all that remains are the rusted metallic struts which once supported the rest of the structure. Nevertheless, it looked imposing in its state of blackened disrepair in the same way the burnt-out pier at Brighton seethes with malicious serenity. It no longer served a purpose, but it remained somehow iconic, posing as a history-flecked landmark. It can be seen for miles along the straight patch of coastline. Unlike at Kovalam, Alleppey's lighthouse stands back a couple of hundred metres. Squat in nature, it took some finding beyond a seductive uprising of rustling palm trees.

While Charlie scouted for a suitable eating-place for breakfast, I asked him how he was finding the act of blitzing his way around India alone. 'It's easier than I thought it would be,' he smirked. 'I've encountered fewer problems than I feared I might.' He'd started out in Rajasthan and was now heading south... next stop: Kollam. 'Then I'm flying to the Andamans,' he boasted, niggling my jealous bone. 'Do you plan to do any diving off the islands?' I wondered. 'Maybe,' he hesitated, 'but saltwater crocs are quite common. Somebody recently got eaten whilst diving in open water there. I might just stick to snorkelling, depending on the safety aspect.' I'd never been diving before, but friends had suggested that I get qualified in Indonesia. Only time would tell if I ever got around to surrendering myself hook, line and sinker. I asked Charlie about other places he'd visited on the subcontinent. He confided that he'd just come down the coast from Goa. I told him it was my next destination. He shrunk back in horror. 'Do you realise how much some guesthouse owners are charging for even the dingiest of rooms at this time of year? The cost of some rooms is multiplied by as much as ten from mid-December to mid-January owing to the fact that Goa becomes one of the most popular places in the world to escape to.' So, a room that would normally cost three-hundred rupees per night could wind up costing three-thousand. Mentally, I began to make premature allowances, praying that Charlie was exaggerating about such festive price hikes. Irrespective of the accuracy of his claims, I thanked him for the warning.

He ducked into 'Dreamers' in due course. Just before he slunk away, he confided that he'd been hoping a revelation would hit. Having quit his job in IT, he didn't know in which direction to usher his life. 'Epiphanies can be hard to come by,' I reassured him. 'A degree of enlightenment might descend, but I think you're more likely to decide what you want to do in terms of pushing life forward in a more fulfilling capacity once you return home. Only then will you be able to process all you've seen and apply what you've learnt. Perspective will shift, I guarantee it.' With those words we parted, Charlie loping off to further nourish his mind, body and soul. I, meanwhile, lurched onto the beach, observing how legions of sand-flies subtly made tracks around a group of sand crabs. The behaviour of the crabs proved fascinating to watch as they shuffled sideways in short but sharp bursts before plunging into deep holes. Temporarily lost in their world, I almost failed to notice an Indian man on my heels. Had I not heard him cough and then spit in my general direction of ignorance, I wouldn't have known he was there. I spun around to see him crouch above a pronounced cleft in the sand. Armed with a plastic bottle filled with water, he scanned the sand for shells, plopping any he found into the bottle for safekeeping so he could subsequently carry his cache inland to fashion delicate jewellery. Amassing an impressive collection in no time, he grinned as he passed me by, suggesting that he was cultivating a rupee-spinning winner with the trinkets he produced. Inspired by his actions, I realised that I needed to nurture an original venture of some description: something that would generate assets which could be relied upon to provide long-term financial security.

The beach had definitely got me thinking. All I had to do now was act. Downtime on the overnight train to Goa was destined to be my salvation.

~

HOW OFTEN DO YOU SEE two grown men being taught the intricacies of kick-starting a motorbike? To be honest, it's a relatively common sight in India when inexperienced travellers rent bikes in the hope they'll be able to gad about at their leisure without breaking down. Should the worst possible scenario become a pulse-quickening reality, almost any Indian man, woman or child will be willing to lend a hand... or foot.

Renting a motorbike had seemed like a good idea at the time. It's undeniably the best way to make the most of a stay in the Goa area, especially if you're not fond of getting crushed on suspension-lacking local buses bouncing between the main resorts. Having had Anjuna Beach recommended to us by an Ecuadorian friend in Alleppey, we'd travelled to the northern area of Goa in good faith. An early morning train from Madgaon had delivered us at Thivim for seven. Still some distance from the coast, we had no choice but to travel forth and prosper by bus or rickshaw. Worryingly, not a single rickshaw driver was willing to drive us for less than one-hundred and fifty rupees. We wandered along a quiet country lane to the main road. 'Bus to Mapusa?' I enquired of a man loitering outside a beaten-up shack of an exceedingly well-stocked grocery store. Doubtful that he'd understand my English accent, let alone my broad Yorkshire dialect, I was stunned when he flung his attention to the far side of the road by flicking up his head. There was a strong possibility he was simply being polite, happy to tell us anything so long as we left him alone. But he was right. Buses to Mapusa halted directly opposite the store. Furthermore, they stopped with staggering regularity. In the wake of getting on and then immediately back off two services bound for the town (both were unhealthily rammed to capacity and beyond), we wound up being ushered onto a school bus. Standing tall over approximately twenty children under the age of ten, just one thought jolted through my mind: only in India. It seemed the kids had never before seen anything like our entourage, a noticeable hush pervading as we stood to attention in the gangway until seats became available. Nobody got off until we rolled up outside the school. Then, amidst a noisy flurry of excitement, the children dived for the door, clearing adequate space for us.

I knew I should have sat closer to the front. A few stops later, every spare seat had been filled. The gangway groaned its annoyance at being abused by so many standing passengers, the floor threatening to collapse. If I'd needed to alight before Mapusa's bus station, the only way out would have been via the window through which my left arm gaily dangled.

Brusquely bus-hopping our way to the beach, a frantic run around the station concluded with us scrambling onto an altogether quieter service bound for Anjuna. We could finally relax, allowing our eyes to savour the scenery, our ears to catch the entrancing quality of birdsong, and our noses to be stimulated and repulsed in equal measure by incidental scents which happened to engulf the vehicle as we peeled due west. Thick vegetation flanked the twisting ribbon of cement, sky-skimming palm trees looking down upon a plethora of fruit trees more diminutive in stature. Ever the fruit aficionado, Si pointed out the wealth of papaya and banana trees within grabbing distance, vying to thrust his arm through the window to pick and eat as we went, boldly pioneering the eminently consumable concept of 'Fast Fruit' in real time.

The landscapes out of which India is composed are so diverse that it's sometimes impossible to believe mountains, deserts and lazy backwaters can all exist in the same country. The refined quality of light in Goa helps to focus a person's senses on the area's exquisite beauty, its verdant hills harbouring tumbledown houses, whitewashed churches, and luxurious guesthouses. Primary colours enrapture the soul, the essence of vitality frolicking in green as the earth's folds surrender to the serrated coastline where dirt roads trickle onto ghost-polluted beaches with modest gusto.

We were deposited near a shop-crowded road junction at the so-called heart of Anjuna. On first inspection, the village appeared to be the sleepiest place we'd encountered in all of India. Once we'd settled into our respective guesthouses, we marched towards Anjuna Beach, halting at 'Yash Restaurant' for breakfast. It was eleven. The last explosion of sustenance we'd awarded ourselves had been a tray of 'chicken biryani' on the train north from Ernakulam Junction over fourteen hours beforehand. Languishing a few hundred yards from the sand, the small but amicable joint was evidently a popular place with food-craving foreigners. In light of Goa being the be all and end all for a lot of Westerners visiting India, the majority of menus highlight dirty fry-ups as standard. As much as I fancied eggs and beans on toast, I'd become addicted to 'paratha' over the preceding two months. It required considerable willpower to stop myself ordering at least one from every café and restaurant I patronaged. 'Aloo paratha' swung in as my favourite variety of all, its potato filling complementing the texture of the wheat-based wrap. If no varieties of 'paratha' were available, I opted for a 'masala dosa' without fail, yet I was still sorely tempted to try 'appam', 'pathiri', and 'ladu' at some point. 'Idly' also appealed: a rice-based snack not too dissimilar to the 'upma' first sampled in Aurangabad.

At first sight, Anjuna Beach suggested it was all rock and no sand. It wasn't until later in the day that we discovered the 'real' beach beyond an inconspicuous track bound by stalls selling shawls, shades and sandals. Having hired a couple of Honda motorbikes, we bounced our way over the ruts and weaved our way through the crowds, circling to a stop where the track bluffed its way to a drop over which a quiet but perfectly located restaurant presided. The sand looked sumptuous, so we parked up and ambled down. Even though it was exposed and unadorned by waves, it would make an ideal sunbathing spot later in the week.

If we were totally honest, we'd been somewhat disappointed by Anjuna, having hoped there'd be a more raucous buzz in the guise of better nightlife. Steering our mangled thoughts to a couple of beaches a few miles south of Anjuna, we re-straddled our bikes and struck the road to Baga. In spite of speeding perilously close to a ditch on the outskirts of Anjuna, I savoured every second on the bike, opening the throttle whenever a straight section of tarmac hove into view. When you're familiar with a road and its quirks, riding becomes formidable fun. However, if you lack the basic knowledge about where the most treacherous corners are located, or how best to swerve around the profusion of rumble strips running across certain roads, it can be a rough ride. As if to lampoon my caution, sandy corners perpetually taunted my bike, joking with their tyre treads as we skidded at gravity-abusing angles. Umpteen times, I told myself: 'Slow. You must go slow.' But would my desire for exhilaration listen?

~

I'D FINALLY DISCOVERED A ROUTINE WHICH NOURISHED MY SOUL: writing at dawn, philosophising with friends over breakfast, motorbike-aided beach-hopping in the afternoon, then another intense burst of writing, with prose wrestling poetry. I was slowly beginning to fast. In doing so I felt significantly stronger, mentally and physically. I'd also begun to meditate twice a day, working a succession of push-ups and sit-ups into a regime that would enable me to more effectively stimulate then calm my mind and body in equal measure.

Having indulged in the beach-life south of Anjuna, my friends and I decided to strike north - via the petrol station - to Mandrem Beach. We had a map to hand, but we still didn't count on the considerable distance between Anjuna and Mandrem. As fish-chewing seagulls flew, it didn't look far on paper. Once we'd factored in the mileage covered on the gently meandering coastal road that ushered us through the tiny but incredibly vibrant settlement of Chapora, we calculated that we'd trundled about fifteen miles. En-route, tree fronds brushed our shoulders as we cautiously steered a course past a shelter for women and girls in distress, not to dismiss a patch of roadworks that required workers to labour in the middle of the road as traffic dangerously streamed around them. Why bother shutting a road to undertake essential repairs when there's enough room for everybody to swerve and toil in situ? Trying in vain not to become too distracted, I slowed to survey the scene, surprised to see a group of women heaving baskets full of gravel on their heads. They carried such gravel further down the road to lay it in the holes needing filling. Once the gravel had been levelled, a guy ambled over with a steel can crudely spouting tar, spreading the steaming gush of blackness clean across the relevant area. A steamroller was subsequently employed to pound the sticky mixture of gravel and tar into a form of submission so extreme it can only be termed 'unquantifiable' in nature.

Though the beach took some locating in the wake of a few misdirected turns, we soon pulled up behind some attractively landscaped gardens, beside three rickety wooden walkways which ran parallel to one another over a stream leading to the sea. Guesthouses in the area came in every colour under the sun, while the profusion of beach shacks fronting the sand proffered the bare essentials in terms of providing mattresses and air-circulating fans. Leaving Si and Sheetha to their own lounger-based devices, I joyously shook off my non-designer sandals. Having bought a pair the previous evening, their cheapness haunted my every step, the plastic footholds literally shredding wedges of skin between my toes.

Stamping north, the width of the beach gradually expanded. In spite of moving fast, I was stalked by default. If it wasn't an Indian man on my tail, trying to offload an armful of bracelets, it was an impossibly skinny man on a bicycle, attempting to flog me an ice-cream for the frankly ridiculous amount of fifty rupees. Bear in mind I'd hired my motorbike for a mere two-hundred rupees and you should wisen up to such injustice. Such is life: for an ice-cream on the beach, it seemed to be the going rate whether folk desiring such refreshment liked it or not.

Coincidentally, the day before, on Candolim Beach (south of the party epicentre of Baga), Si had fallen foul of a mean ice-cream vendor. He'd simply pointed to one of the 'Walls' products advertised on the board atop the man's ice-box. Without being polite or patient enough to inform Si how much the ice-cream cost, the man extracted one from the box and whipped off its wrapper in one fell swoop, thereby pitting Si in an awkward position had he deemed the price to be in excess of what it was worth. 'Fifty rupees,' the man said as he relayed the ice-cream with deft sleight of hand. Si took hold without intent. 'No way!' he half-laughed in bemusement, half-groaned in fury. Refusing to pay what had been demanded of him, Si engaged in a bartering battle. Thirty rupees was the vendor's final offer, but it was still too high a price for what was little more than a tiny stick of artificially coloured and flavoured ice. Who'd have thought that people could lose their temper over the price of ice-cream? However, in the cruel light of day, anything's possible in India if you feel you're being swindled as an unfairly exploited victim of daylight robbery. 'I'll pay twenty rupees. No more,' Si reasoned. 'If not, I'll put the ice-cream on your board and walk away.' It sounded like a threat... and it was. A second later, sensing that any vestige of a positive response wasn't going to be forthcoming in the foreseeable future, Si placed the ice-cream on the board as promised: an action which motivated the man to curse Si's admirable decisiveness. Hitting the beach in due course, we wondered if the man would dare to damage our bikes as a result of the way in which he'd been put in his place, having been publicly earmarked as a cheat: a so-called businessman who evidently didn't realise that the best way to build business is by being honest in order to generate trust, respect and customer loyalty.

Ever the beach connoisseur, I was becoming increasingly addicted to life beside the sea. In my eyes, Baga Beach had been too busy, its modest beauty overshadowed by the level of hassle from touts. Calangute Beach wielded serious potential, but a filthy stretch of sand in its realm meant the quieter and cleaner beach at Candolim had almost effortlessly triumphed in being hailed the most enticing beach I'd so far seen in Goa during the four days I'd lolled in the area.

Arambol Beach promptly changed my mind. A natural successor to Mandrem's delights if you happen to be kicking sand in a northerly direction, Arambol couldn't be any more chilled, its clientele of dreadlocked foreigners keen to be seen committing lazy beats to bongos as friends strum lightweight tunes on acoustic guitars emblazoned with hip quotes. As I approached the rocky headland which literally stops the beach in its tracks, a man twirled a baton around his hand before rolling it down his arm. He looked at me as though he expected a wave of applause to emanate from my hands. Meanwhile, his stone-faced girlfriend threw random shapes, hula-hooping herself into a profound state of dizziness. Curiously, she wasn't the only person I'd seen who gave the impression that she was unhappy or in some way disappointed with the reality of Goa. On every beach I'd visited, I'd noticed glum men and women sprawled on loungers, nonchalantly texting or reading trashy paperback novels, looking for all the world like they'd be just as appreciative of a package holiday to Bognor Regis. What did I see that they didn't? A child of nature, I lapped up every incoming wave, recognised faces in every cloud, and ached to be able to count every grain of sand that I could sieve through the fingers of entwined hands.

Later, I found myself back in 'Yash' to indulge in a bowl of soy sauce-soaked fried rice. Dining on a budget to a wealth of UB40 tunes, I couldn't stir enough sugar into my 'masala tea' for the life of me. It now took at least four tablespoons of the sweet stuff for its quality to register, my tolerance levels having been severely affected by the staggering amount of sugar lacing a huge proportion of drinks in India. Highlights of what I assumed to be the day's play of cricket colourfully rippled across the big screen. England were slogging their hearts out against Pakistan. In spite of having never been much of a fan of the sport, I soon became entranced. It's so much better when the boring bits are edited out, leaving the most exciting taking of wickets to grasp one's attention. I readily accepted the fact we were losing. What I struggled to come to terms with was the make-up of the team we were fielding. Undiluted shock caught me out the second Alec Stewart began his shameful trudge back to the pavilion. Graeme Hick and Allan Lamb followed in his wake. But wait a second, I thought. As much as I was willing to suspend my disbelief, there was no way it was possible for Allan to still be slogging sixes like no aging batsman's business. He'd been playing way back when I used to attend matches with my dad in the early nineties. I distinctly remember asking Allan for his autograph in Scarborough. All became clear as the highlights segued into a batch of enlightening adverts: the match was from 1992. Such highlights were followed by a retro football match from the eighties, suggesting there was very little in the way of current international sporting events that could be deemed of interest.

Darkness fell with as much delicacy as a stairwell-negotiating drunk. Coming down from my sugar-induced high, I requested the bill. It came in at the one-hundred rupee mark, itemised as follows: eighty rupees for the fried rice, and two cups of tea at ten rupees each. No stranger to the restaurant, I'd eaten there four days in a row. I knew for a fact the fried rice cost seventy rupees, not eighty as stated. Disappointed that my unwavering loyalty to the place seemed unvalued, I made an issue out of the glaring mark-up as a matter of principle. 'Ah… New Year, new price,' the owner coyly remarked, a mischievous grin smothering his face. For the record, I can deal with the fall-out of inflation, but I couldn't help but be flabbergasted for two reasons. First and foremost, a restaurant can't start charging specific prices for certain dishes without adjusting its menu accordingly. Secondly, the excuse that it was a new year couldn't be used in any capacity to get him off the hook. It was only the twenty-first of December for Santa's sake. What were the wheelers and dealers of Goa thinking? More intriguingly, what on earth were they smoking to fortify the collective belief that it was all right for them to rip people off whenever they felt like it? Left alone to wonder as the man went to fetch the paltry cache of change I was owed, I stared at a stone relief of Hanuman peeping through the window of an artisan's store opposite the restaurant. If the cheeky monkey knew the answers to my questions, he clearly wasn't prepared to tell me. At least not for free.

~

'IS ANYBODY IN THERE?' Through the dark, I peered at my watch. It was 4:48 a.m., and long before time to rise. I couldn't understand what the commotion might be about, but a man was outside my room, pounding the paint off my door. More sleep-deprived than ever, I was understandably reluctant to get out of bed. However, if I failed to open the door, it sounded like the innocent hunk of wood was slated to be elementally deconstructed. 'Yes. There is somebody in here. What do you want?' I called back. 'Open up and get out. This room is taken,' the ill-mannered stranger seethed. Praying there'd been some kind of misunderstanding, I slid my backpack from behind the door, unbolting it with trepidation. I cracked it an inch to score sight of the man who was seemingly accusing me of stealing a room that had allegedly been assigned to him. I was greeted by a middle-aged Indian man with a moustache tickling his upper lip and an old Nokia phone resting in his palm. Eager to resolve the situation and slump back into bed, I told him how I'd rocked up to 'St. Anthony's Guesthouse' eighteen hours beforehand, where and when I'd been told I could take a room for five nights. In a fit of booking confusion, I'd initially homed up and hosed down in a room set behind the proprietor's house. I'd subsequently been shifted to a room up a flight of steel steps, directly above the lady's living quarters. She'd promised me that I'd be able to stay until Christmas Day morning, at which point I'd have to check out by ten before trudging over to a different guesthouse.

The fact that Christmas and New Year loomed on the horizon meant that prices for rooms across the Goa region had skyrocketed beyond what could be deemed acceptable. As soon as my friends and I had been dropped off by bus in sleepy Anjuna, we'd split in search of cheap accommodation. The first ten guesthouses we visited were either booked up or presenting us rates so astronomical they became laughable. An hour after arriving, Simon and Sheetha found a room at 'Henmil's Guesthouse' near the main crossroads. It just so happened that 'St. Anthony's Guesthouse' was next door.

Although I'd not paid for the room upfront, I still regarded the bare cell as mine. I'd already become attached to the brown writing desk and the light-catching bed beneath the window. I even admired the grey refrigerator from afar; in spite of being out of action, it somehow made the room feel more homely and aesthetically pleasing.

On the shrine-encrusted balcony, the man refused to budge. He looked to be as fatigued as I felt. 'It is my room,' he said without a hint of sympathy to my fast-developing plight. I honestly feared that he alone had the power to barge past me, sweep my belongings off the table, and kick them outside. His straight-backed posture and pockmarked face were great allies when the need arose for him to intimidate the meek likes of yours truly. Woefully bemused by proceedings, I

asked if he'd spoke to the lady-owner to see if his room might
be located around the back of the house instead. I detested the
level of tension developing between us. With eyes locked on
one another's, it was an impasse, a mutiny, a stand-off.
Disgruntled, he glanced down the stairs. Another middle-
aged man was strolling along the driveway. Beyond him,
only the open gate to the guesthouse could be seen. There
was no auto-rickshaw to suggest they'd been brought from
the nearest bus or train station with luggage in tow. My
suspicions were bolstered as a result. I looked at the man
before me, trying to place him. I thought to myself: I know
this man, but how? Had I seen him selling sunglasses,
massacring coconuts for consumption, or walking on one of
the rocky spits extending into the Arabian Sea? Perhaps he'd
been sat beside me at '5th Avenue Smoothies' earlier in the
evening when I'd kicked back with a cup of herbal tea whilst
using the free Wi-Fi on offer. Maybe I'd not seen him at all,
but what if he'd clocked me somewhere? Yes. It was entirely
plausible. He could have seen me using my 'Netbook' and
then followed me to see where I was staying. As it was, my
guesthouse was literally a few doors down from the smoothie
joint. Suddenly consumed by overactive paranoia, I
wondered if the man was a prospective guest, or simply
someone who was poised to manipulate me and potentially
steal my belongings. I couldn't have been cornered in a more
vulnerable position, hence why I suggested he go downstairs
at once to speak with the lady who'd booked me in. She'd
seemed decent and honest... certainly not the type of person
to double-book a room at such a busy time of year.

By this point I'd stepped forward, foolishly allowing him
the chance to see what I had in my room. My 'Netbook'
modernised the table, silently charging. He saw it and wanted
it, I knew it. 'This is my room,' I affirmed, sick of the charade.
'Speak to the lady and you will see.' He glanced down at his

friend. They conversed in Hindi. He wasn't going to allow his impressive grasp of the English language betray his intentions. He then solemnly nodded his head, apologised for the early morning wake-up call, and hopped down the stairs. Shaken and stirred by adrenaline, I locked the door, duly returning my backpack to its original resting place for added security and peace of mind. Outside, I could hear the men mumbling. On the inside, all I could hear was my pounding heart, readying my senses for further unsolicited confrontation. Sleep might have been a necessity, but it was no longer an option.

~

I FELT THE BIKE LOSE POWER long before it unceremoniously rolled to a stop. Having just traded in my previous Honda Activa for a 'new' one, I'd been hoping that I'd experience fewer problems with my latest scooter. Given that it was only three days before Christmas, bike-lenders had begun to raise the bar with prices. The man we'd been hiring bikes from suddenly demanded three-hundred rupees for each scooter when we skidded up to offer the usual two-hundred that we'd been forking out on a daily basis. Unimpressed by his unwillingness to offer discount to loyal customers such as ourselves, we were blunt: 'We'll shop around for a better deal,' we chirped. 'We'll return these bikes within the hour.' Confident the man would buckle upon learning we were bound to defect and favour a rival, we were surprised when he nodded his consent, allowing us the luxury of sixty minutes to find somebody still willing to loan us a pair of bikes for just two-hundred rupees in the heated run-up to the twenty-fifth.

Time was running out, and we had to scoot elsewhere before attempting to strike deals with the money-grabbing bike owners near the beach. Our first stop was 'Philip Olinda Guesthouse' where Simon and Sheetha needed to leave photocopies of their passport and visa details so they'd be able to check in on the morning of the twenty-fourth. The lady proprietor clearly had a lot on her mind. It was understandable since she had so many guests arriving. Introducing us to a beautifully designed and pulse-calming alcove in which classical statues stood before enlightening mirrors, she reassured them they'd be able to move from their current lodgings to her guesthouse without any hassle on Christmas Eve so long as she could submit their details to the authorities in advance. Everywhere we'd lodged in India, guesthouse owners had been vigilant: heavy fines can be imposed on establishments housing unrecorded guests. Back in Delhi, we'd had to pose for a mug-shot upon checking into a couple of guesthouses, their owners having trained grimy webcams on our heads so the grainy images captured could be compared to our respective passport photos. Had our passports been fake, they'd be traced and destroyed. Once Si and Sheetha had scrawled their signatures at the foot of the necessary paperwork, the lady offered to contact a friend of hers who loaned bikes, promising us we'd be able to hire two bikes for four-hundred rupees in total. 'He's on his way now,' she confirmed, making an abrupt end to the call. Her so-called 'friend' was less a person to confide in on personal matters, but more a business associate who helped her accrue custom so long as she helped him in return.

As we waited for our new bikes to arrive, the lady matter-of-factly stated that we must remain constantly on our guard whilst riding around Goa. She then related a shocking story which thrust everything into perspective. 'Yes, yes,' she stuttered in preamble, 'so these young guys come from Dubai. They hire bikes and head to the petrol station near Vagator. They're all from very wealthy families and are wearing much bling. Seeing this, the pump attendants begin to make fun of the men. This results in the bikers, my guests, assaulting the attendants who are ridiculing them. A brawl results, the police get involved, and the men are fined four lakh.' Our jaws dropped, but not to the extent that we couldn't muster a response. 'How much does four lakh equate to?' Si wondered. 'Oh,' the lady hesitated, executing an approximate conversion in her head. 'Let's see... I think three lakh is about seven-thousand US dollars, so that should give you an idea.' The moral of the story boiled down to how it's best not to metaphorically join 'Fight Club' whilst ebbing around India. The consequences could cost more than the actions might be worth.

The lady also warned us not to pay upfront for bikes. 'Pay by the day, even if the guys renting the bikes try and convince you that the only way for them to broker a deal is for you to pay there and then. Another one of my guests, a young lady, decided to hire a bike for four days and paid for all four days at once. However, she got bored two days in, saying she'd seen all she'd wanted. She took the bike back to the man she got it from and asked for a refund for the two days she wouldn't need it, but the man said that no refunds were given. Upset by his reaction, she got so angry that she hit him. He slugged her back in shocked retaliation. I saw this from the other side of the road, at the main junction where the buses stop. I ran over, prised them apart, and brought the girl back to my house. She was in a rage, you know, feeling like she'd been cheated. She had, in a way, but it's difficult to argue with these guys. It's sometimes better not to bother.'

She wound up her pep-talks in the nick of time, the lady's friend announcing his arrival by way of the squeaky oil-deprived gate out front. He shook our hands prior to launching into the hard sell. 'So how many days would you like my bikes for?' Unsure of our plans, I glanced at Si. He was looking at Sheetha. 'Two or three days,' Si said, 'so long as they cost two-hundred rupees per day.' The man softly chuckled to himself. 'It's nearly Christmas, so I give them to you for two-hundred and fifty per day,' he grinned, subtly strong-arming us into believing he was an honest man who wouldn't even dream of ripping-off foreigners. 'But we were told the bikes would cost us two-hundred,' Si retorted, launching a frown of miscomprehension in the lady's direction. Feeling cornered into coming clean, the lady confessed that she had indeed said we'd be able to take the bikes for such a price. Steeling ourselves through a momentary stand-off, the man eventually - and reluctantly - offered us the bikes for two-hundred, ordering us to return them on Christmas Eve without fail.

Beaming with delight at how things had worked in our favour for a change, we rumbled down the perilously bumpy track from the guesthouse to the main road. From there we set out for the petrol station, reflecting on the bike-related stories we'd absorbed. Accelerating out of sleepy Anjuna with liberated glee, all was well until I eased off the throttle to negotiate a set of speed bumps, only for my bike to cut out completely. Fortunately, we'd been enjoying a straight section of downhill action, the momentum I'd gained from bouncing over the bumps serving to propel me a further twenty yards closer to the station. Shame it was still half a mile away. When I eventually rolled to a halt beside an isolated house, I instinctively lifted the seat and unscrewed the fuel tank's lid. As suspected, the tank was far from high, but unquestionably dry. Cursing my luck with bikes, I stared at the throbbing sun, conscious of its indifference, yet thankful that it hadn't as yet attained the burning pinnacle of its diurnal journey. Midday had no choice but to keep its distance for another half-hour, yet the sun was already blazing, branding cancerous tattoos onto my exposed neck, forearms and shins.

Burning by default, I had to kick my Doxycycline tablets into touch. Since beginning to use them for malaria prophylaxis, my skin had become pathetically photosensitive. Guiltily flagging Si to a sudden stop, I laughably begged for a push. Fortunately, he obliged, ecstatic to be of service. He knew I'd return the favour if and when the need arose.

~

IT WAS CHRISTMAS EVE, and I had no intention of staying in to stew on thoughts swishing around my mind. Having bought tickets for the 'Hilltop' party, I'd made the effort to get glammed up, excitedly anticipating the sight of raving Goan folk.

The original plan was to travel by motorbike, but I'd handed my Honda back to its owner an hour beforehand amidst a fit of confusion. No sooner had I relayed him the key, he told me to sit. This was on a narrow lane leading to South Anjuna, directly outside his house. In no mood for engaging in an impromptu game of 'Simon Says', I eyed him suspiciously. 'Why do you want me to sit?' I asked. Never one to waste words, he refused to explain, simply instructing me to once again sit. Then, just as I feared that some kind of distasteful joke might be hovering in my presence, the ignition switch in my mind gave a fraction of an inch. He didn't expect me to warm the gravel-soaked lay-by after all. He was trying to persuade me to sit behind him so he could speed me to my guesthouse out of sheer kindness. Laughing my way through the fog of embarrassment, I assured him there was no need to go out of his way. Shaking hands, we wished one another a Happy Christmas. Slaying fanfare, he gunned the sorely dented Activa towards the crossroads, leaving me to choke on a festive mix of dust, fumes, and mozzies.

The fabled 'Hilltop' venue was further away than I thought. I'd ridden there in the morning to scope out the setting for what was expected to be the biggest and best party in the Greater Anjuna area. Although I'd heard whispers that the 'Bamboo Forest' event was bound to be a serious contender in terms of being a DJ-decked party to dance for, the fact that advance tickets for Hilltop's impending extravaganza cost just one-hundred rupees inevitably impacted on my loyalties. I just wondered how many people would make the effort to show up given that the venue was set back from the beach. Furthermore, it awarded not a single glimpse of the remarkably beautiful coastline.

Stepping forth at a brisk pace, I nosed my body out of Anjuna's streetlight-infused glow of warmth. Unused to encountering lone pedestrians so late at night, stray dogs roaming the scrubland on either side of the road to Vagator whined their envy. Up ahead, an Indian man walking in the same direction heard the clip-clop of my shoes. Turning around, he shot me a malicious stare as if to suggest I should give him more space if I aspired to survive the night. Had I truly known what was good for me, I would have dowsed my neck and arms in mosquito repellent. If not by ravenous dogs, I was doomed to be savaged by malaria-enriched insects which routinely bite without serving barks of warning. I hooked a left beyond the police station, hitting a steep side road that curved around to the party without so much as a single mast-plastered poster to point the way.

I heard the music long before I caught sight of the venue. Out front, a patch of land had been cleared to act as a car park, even though the majority of partygoers were arriving by scooter. Somehow clearing security without a cursory pat-down, I squeezed through a turnstile, rounded a blind corner, and edged into the fray. The scene that greeted me resembled *The Magic Faraway Tree*. A retina-scarring assortment of fluorescent 3-D stars made from cotton tenderly collided on the branches. Neon lights had been strung up to enhance the effect. A regimental line of trees saturating the main arena reflected the strobe lighting, their glow-in-the-dark paint having been artistically applied in psychedelic patterns designed to hypnotise the mind's eye. Two bars served ridiculously priced drinks as standard. Large bottles of 'Kingfisher' cost one-hundred and twenty rupees, which wasn't so bad, but a bank loan would have been necessary had I desired a cheeky cocktail or two.

The only thing worse than missing a party is getting there too early. It had just gone nine, and less than fifty people were dancing. The stage inspired awe through being so visually impressive. The sound system, meanwhile, threatened to put the integrity of amplifiers used by the likes of U2 and Metallica to shame. Behind the stage, a white screen deflected a miasma of random images projected from above. Planting myself beside a yellow tree, I allowed the frantic series of images to override my sense, smothering my sensibility. Ancient symbols were juxtaposed with still images of Buddha and Hanuman, fuelling my imagination as much as my paranoia. Fearful that subliminal messages might sully my intellect, I focused on the DJ who was in the throes of leaving the stage. He sprinted to the nearest bar, leaving the most devoted ravers to worry about what might become of the music since the nerve centre of sound had been so unexpectedly abandoned. But there was no need to stress: he returned within seconds, a bottle of water in hand. In spite of craftily splicing trance samples together, I'd expected the DJ to embrace more of a rock 'n' roll attitude by staggering back with a half-necked bottle of JD in his grip and a syringe sticking out of his arm. But he was clean - which was reassuring.

I took a walk to shake off boredom. Shouldering the perimeter of the venue, approximately thirty stalls had been erected. The majority of them stood ready to whip up omelettes for the energy-starved attendees. Small candles atmospherically flickered at the centre of each stall, faintly illuminating the faces of the Indian women silently crouched behind. Moseying around the back of the stage, I sauntered full circle, eventually halting beside a grounded blanket upon which a dazzling collection of bracelets and amulets had been arranged for sale. Returning my attention to the dance pit, I was astonished to see a man literally bouncing off the speakers. Surprisingly, around ninety per cent of the ravers were Indian. Since the event had been poorly publicised, it was understandable that many of the foreigners staying in Anjuna wouldn't have been made aware of the Hilltop's bounty until it was too late.

I prayed for a couple of Counting Crows numbers to smash the monotonous drone, but the mish-mash of noise continued unabated. My sensitive temperament was more suited to the emotionally rich variety of sounds expelled by the likes of Alastair Artingstall, Edwina Hayes, Miles Cain, and Glen Strachan. For the most part, the hopping DJ's set was as tuneful as a spluttering chainsaw, a daft cacophony of sound effects indifferently clashing with a billion beats a minute. The net effect might have been deemed 'phat' by some, but I remained distinctly unentranced until an extraordinary combo of beats syringed my ear canals. Perhaps I would have appreciated the 'music' to a greater degree if a drink had been wedged in my palm. Realising that I wasn't in the correct frame of mind to enjoy the party, I pinpointed what might have been contributing to my psychological downfall. My hands were jammed in my pockets for a start. I wasn't properly attired. I hadn't smoked any weed. I was stone cold sober. Oh… and I was lacking company. I spun on my heels, observing what everybody else was doing, and how they were acting in the face of the overwhelming light and sound beaming down. Crass SFX bounced out of the speakers with even more urgency, the distorted sound of a thousand elastic bands being twanged simultaneously preceding a five minute sample of a plumber spilling the contents of his toolbox upon a steel girder. It was too much to take standing still, so I urged my right foot to tap, vying to ease into an appropriate groove. Aspiring to blend in, I began to nod my head in time to the reverberating waterfall of screwdrivers. Meanwhile, the man directly to my right sought to assume the guise of Billy the Kid, drawing imaginary guns from invisible holsters. He was sporting a cowboy hat, sure, but his actions constituted a leap of the imagination so great that it could only have been aided by drugs. He subsequently started running on the spot, slapping his knees, hypothetically dodging rifle-to-feet bullets. Closer to the stage, a Japanese woman went one better by taking liberty with John Cleese's Ministry of Silly Walks, striding and stretching as though she wanted nothing more than to be the centre of attention for all the wrong reasons.

Partied out for half-past ten, I ditched the Hilltop and braced myself for the unsettling walk home along a couple of deserted roads, around a slew of blind corners. I only began to relax upon reacquainting my dancing feet with the tarmac strung between Vagator and Anjuna. That was until a motorbike on the far side of the road slowed down, suggesting its riders wanted to challenge me about something. Chewing back my apprehension, I strode forth, recognising two familiar faces with empowering relief. Simon and Sheetha had decided to come out! But where could we go together? I still had their unused tickets in my pocket for the Hilltop party, but I'd neglected to ask for a stamp so I could get back in. At my time of disgruntled departure, I'd nurtured no intention of returning.

It was eleven. Our options were limited. 'How about a late-night ride to Baga to see what's going on there?' queried Si.

Given that he was driving, it was really up to him. Sheetha and I agreed that there would probably be a lot more going on in the resort. Thus, I saddled up. En-route, 'Cocktails & Dreams' - a funky bar teetering on the edge of the middle of nowhere - urged the bike to rest-up before chugging further. A cluster of all-smiling, all-giggling twenty-somethings awarded the joint an energetic atmosphere. Even better, cocktails were on offer. Ever conscious of the fact we couldn't stray too far if we all craved alcohol, we wound up staying put, and although the bar's 'Manhattan' mix of spirits failed to impress, Si's 'Mojito' won me over instantly. Even so, at the end of the night, I lusted-after another 'Pina Colada' more than anything. Christmas had come to Goa, and there I was, shamelessly supping what was purported to be the ultimate girly drink.

~

WE WONDERED WHY HE WAS POINTING THE FINGER. All became clear as we were instructed to pull over at the side of the road. My friends and I had just eaten out in Baga. We were returning to Anjuna by motorbike. Simon was driving and Sheetha was precariously perched right at the back of the seat, sandwiching me in the middle. A bored traffic cop clocked us a mile off. Naïve foreigners make easy pickings. He knew he could demand whatever he liked. Si dutifully slowed down and parked up. The cop in white beckoned us behind his vehicle where he could talk to us in a discreet a manner as possible. Scared of the potential consequences of our innocent misdemeanour, we waited with baited breath for what he was about to tell us in terms of our crime and our rights, along with our inevitable fine. 'Show me your license,' he wheezed. Confidently taking the lead, Si remarked that his license was cowering in 'Philip Olinda Guesthouse' where they were staying. 'You leave bike, take taxi, fetch license. Otherwise you pay fine here and now,' the official nonchalantly replied, bobbing his head over Si's shoulder, evidently eager to bust more people.

Because we were a party of three, we'd been sitting targets. We'd been warned in Baga that it was illegal to have three people on a scooter. Annoyingly, traffic police swarmed over the main roads and junctions in Baga like wild-eyed ants, inspiring the need for Sheetha and I to constantly hop off then back on every time we saw an official lurking in the distance. 'Does a UK driving license cover us?' wondered Si. 'No. You need an International License. You should know this, you should have one, you should carry it at all times.' None of us wielded an International License. That left us with no choice but to meekly swallow our pride and cough up. 'How much is the fine?' asked Sheetha. It was one-thousand and fifty rupees: approximately fifteen pounds. Having just dined in an expensive Baga restaurant, we were riding fairly dry in financial terms, but a crisp five-hundred rupee note I'd stowed in my back pocket made a delicious dent in the fine. Simon and Sheetha contributed the rest before calculating how much they owed me. 'Can we have a receipt?' Sheetha chanced. If we attained some form of official documentation to indicate that we'd been caught and fined, that would hopefully lessen the chance of us being fined again further down the road. We were roughly four miles from Anjuna, and there was bound to be a heavy police presence surrounding the Saturday Night Bazaar. We couldn't afford to be fined again, but the official scoffed that there was no such thing as a receipt to show how much we'd paid. For all we knew, our hard-earned cash could have been destined for his back pocket. There was no record whatsoever of the unprofessional exchange.

Having been filthily extorted, we trudged back to the bike

feeling violated. We were wise enough to look on the bright side, though. As fines went, ours had been tiny. He could have demanded ten or twenty-thousand rupees from us if such a greedy desire had consumed him. We got the impression that some officials concocted rules and levied fines however they saw fit, often dependant on their moods, or how well-off they judged the guilty-until-proven-innocent perpetrator of any given 'crime' to be. Corruption of the highest order is rife across India, and we'd heard a profusion of tales concerned with innocent travellers being ripped-off to the hilt by touts, taxi drivers, guesthouse owners and police personnel. Relieved to have got off relatively lightly, we decided to play it safe. Knowing that traffic police would be around the next corner, I volunteered to start walking, vowing to deal with the dark and dogs on my own freshly liberated terms. The plan was for Si to rush Sheetha back to Anjuna before speeding back to retrieve yours truly. It was foolproof in theory, so we followed it through, even though Si only drove as far as the bazaar, confident there wouldn't be any more police checks as the road narrowed and surrendered to a series of bends prior to forking, the road more travelled curving inland to the town of Mapusa.

The Saturday Night Bazaar is legendary. It's also a tourist-trap of the most laudable variety. Aimed primarily at wealthy tourists, its open-air stalls sell traditional garments, delicate jewellery, hand-carved trinkets, and generic tat. It's laid out in such a way that visitors are liable to spend a couple of hours there, if not the entire night. Food and drink stalls make a killing by default. We'd stopped to have a look around before entering Baga, and we'd seen a modest plate of vegetable 'momos' handed over for one-hundred and twenty rupees: an extravagant price which literally said it all. In the bazaar's favour, an area adjacent to the mightiest cluster of food stalls was dedicated to showcasing live music. A reggae-flavoured band was playing when we passed, reminding me that Graeme from UB40 was due to perform in Anjuna later in the week. Indeed, reggae music is unavoidable in Goa. If Ali Campbell's voice isn't drifting over the sand towards the glistening Arabian Sea, the legacy of Bob Marley's music informally asserts itself.

Having had our fill of the bazaar before being busted, Sheetha and I trustingly resaddled, adamant that we hadn't passed traffic police whilst travelling in the opposite direction. Breezing past blindingly colourful temples and chapels, rumbling over spine-jolting sets of speed bumps, and leaning into the harshest corners with adrenaline-accelerated excitement, we conspired to laugh at our folly, coming to terms with the realisation that we could have been locked-up instead of making headway home. Had we made a scene with the official, anything could have happened. Our fine would have been significantly raised without a doubt. Thankfully, our genuinely apologetic nature had rewarded us with what had essentially been a casual warning. Though we were irked that the money contributed to the pesky official's benevolent fund could have been splurged on cocktails at 'Om', we still refused to bear a grudge. In truth, we'd made a mistake. We'd just be sure to thoroughly research license and insurance requirements before hiring motorbikes elsewhere in Asia.

Unsteadily swerving around a sandy bend on what could safely be deemed as the home-straight, we couldn't believe our eyes. A couple of rifle-clasping traffic cops were patrolling the junction ahead. It was too late to turn around or shed weight from the bike: both men were staring directly at us. The joy underlining our free-spirited bout of night-riding evaporated. We were about to be busted again, we could tell. Amidst a whirlwind of expletives, we decided to take the only sane course of action. Nodding in agreement, and holding on for dear life, we turned a blind eye as Si caned it.

~

THE KID WAS A LIFESAVER. He knew exactly what to do. Running over from the far side of the road, he placed his bananas beside the streak of gravel upon which Si and I were hunched, willing my Honda Activa back to life. 'You need to kick-start it,' the boy spat in a manner so curt it suggested we should have known precisely what to do should the engine not judder into action by pressing the back brake and ignition button together. Although Si had mounted his fair share of motorbikes in Thailand, he was impressed by the breadth of the boy's knowledge, and his confidence in instructing those who had only basic mechanical know-how. The boy duly motored: 'Pull the bike back, get it on its stand, then kick the pedal as fast as you can!'

To its credit, the bike was trying its utmost to start in order to please me. It whined and it groaned. It spluttered and it choked. The choke! Yes… perhaps that was why it refused to start. Maybe the choke had to be pulled out. Convinced that we'd stumbled upon the solution to my woe, Si reached for the choke, yanking it back with his left hand whilst attempting to initiate ignition with his right. 'Have you checked you've not run out of fuel?' the boy offered, half-prepared to shed tears of mirth were we to subsequently unscrew the lid to reveal a dry inner wall like last time. But we'd checked already, and there was more than enough juice swishing around. Si then began to rock the bike back and forth so the fuel would be more likely to get where it needed to go. 'Come on!' Si whispered, urging the bike to help us out with dignified confidentiality. Pushing the choke back in, we conspired to hit the ignition button one last time prior to conceding. As Lady Luck had it, the black beauty roared to life, telling me in her racket-laden language to hop on and hit the road before impatience consumed her and she once again assumed the strike position.

Si's bike was fine. It started first time. Unhappy with mine, we rode to the junction where the man who owned the bikes hung. We explained that my bike had refused to start, begging for a replacement as compensation for the inconvenience. Worried he might blame me for something I'd blatantly not done, I sucked on a sigh of relief the second he pointed to a different Activa, saying I could have it for the same price. As all India-stationed bike enthusiasts will know, it's simple to bag any kind of motorbike in the country, especially in beach areas such as Goa where visitors seek ultimate flexibility, yearning for absolute freedom from the constraints imposed by designated bus routes which very often leave beach-goers at random locations, miles from their desired destinations. Daily rental charges for bikes vary, depending on what kind of bike you want. Generally, scooters are the cheapest, owing to the fact that they're not as fast or stylish as bikes in the beautiful Enfield's league. What's more, if you're straight up and tell the owners you'll require a bike for more than one day, they often oblige loyal custom by proffering a money-saving deal mutually beneficial to both parties.

With a new bike beneath my legs, Si and I hastened to re-locate the nearest petrol station on the way to Vagator. Pulsing away from Anjuna in a northerly direction, we were careful not to bottom out on the succession of humps warning road users they were entering an area where pedestrians or turning vehicles were likely to hog or block the road. Giving the blink-and-you'll-miss-it settlement of Small Vagator the slip, we hooked a right, at which point I noticed that not a single gauge on my dashboard functioned. I had no idea how fast I was travelling. As for the meter keeping track of distance covered, it had jammed at the thirty-five thousand kilometre mark. Fair enough, I mused: the number of kilometres covered wasn't important. The amount of fuel remaining in the tank was, on the other hand, something I needed to note. Dispiritingly, the fuel gauge was locked on red, indicating I required fuel without delay. Nothing changed in the wake of procuring one-hundred rupees worth of juice. The needle, if anything, descended yet further, obliterating any shred of confidence I'd initially invested in the bike. Unprepared to waste fuel going back to have words with the owner, Si and I zoomed on, aiming for the beach with both eyes locked hard on the debris-strewn road ahead.

It was essential that I got to know my bike on intimate terms so I could come to trust how it handled on corners and steep gradients. With my left index finger touching base with the back brake, and my left thumb hovering above the horn, I kept pace with Si as we raced up and over to Vagator Beach. Breezing past the 'Doroga Club' as we went, we decided to give the biker's bar a miss, at least until we could call ourselves real bikers with time-served experience on Indian roads. By and large, the road network gracing the Goa region is ideal for experienced and inexperienced bikers alike. So long as you stay off the main inland highways upon which helmets are required, zero bother should affect your time behind the steering shaft. Although it took me a while to stop braking whilst accelerating, my confidence increased dramatically once we rode south in tandem. Sheetha had by this point hopped on the back of Si's Honda, so off we blew, taking it in turns to lead as though we were Charley Boorman and Ewan McGregor. Surprised at how speedy the small bikes could be, I gradually began to ride like the locals, jamming with the horn every time I overtook wayward pedestrians or slower-moving vehicles. Mindful not to cultivate ideas above my station, I eased off the gas whilst approaching 'rumbler strips', standing up as the bike shuddered its sleek body over each individual set of three humps. I soon learnt that objects in the rear view mirror really do appear closer than they are. Should you not be able to see any objects at all in your mirror, then you might want to adjust it before potentially veering into the path of an overtaking water tanker or hell-bound bus. It's best not to take too many risks, and it can't be re-iterated enough how you should avoid involvement with the police at all costs unless you enjoy being extorted for more money than you might earn in a decade.

Basking in the sun-dappled scenery awarded by the road between Anjuna and Baga, we whooshed past architecturally astounding guesthouses galore, sensationally photogenic churches left behind by the Portuguese, an extensive temple complex out front of which a dolled-up elephant ingratiated itself with snap-happy tourists, and more restaurants serving fresh seafood than you could flap a shark's fin at.

Baga Beach shoved Anjuna's strip of sand firmly into the shade with its dizzying range of water sports to the tune of parasailing, jet-skiing and speed-boating. As we stepped onto the northernmost section of the beach, an Indian man accosted us. 'You want to do water sports?' he enquired. 'Sure,' I shot back, 'but only in the form of good old-fashioned swimming.' Visibly crestfallen, he dropped behind us in order to ask the next unsuspecting beach-goer precisely the same question, expectantly touting for any number of sea-based ventures with which he had ties.

Instead of paying exorbitant fees to be trailed in the air whilst harnessed to a parachute, we trained our hearts and minds on the rush of the swell, the blue forever. We dunked ourselves in the water, already plotting our subsequent escape to what were purported to be even more stunning and secluded beaches further down the coast beyond Candolim. Spying a hulk of rusting steel in the form of the eerily abandoned 'River Princess' tanker on the horizon, I soon traded swimming for walking, sand-pounding my way south, harbouring no intention of turning back.

~

IT APPEARED TO BE A SAD STATE OF AFFAIRS ON THE SURFACE. There I was, sat in bed, munching on a pack of 'Tiger' biscuits for breakfast. Theoretically, I should have been down the road, kicking back in 'Yash' and spooning up a bowl of fresh fruit. Was I feeling sorry for myself? If I'm honest - and I am - I couldn't tell. Reeling from dark dreams about LA, I woke with a start to stare at the corrugated roof of my room. Looking back, it was a wonder I'd scored any sleep at all. For some reason, a fellow guest had taken it upon himself to hose down his motorbike at midnight. It was parked below my window, and the mad swoosh of water had whipped the proprietor's dog into a frenzy, hopping around and barking for Goa. At the time, I'd swung my woefully sunburnt legs off the mattress with a view to sinking down onto the tiled floor, freshly awash with sand since I'd returned from Arambol. Five days remained before 2011 marked its territory, but I'd already resolved to get fit and bulk-up. That in mind, and with the dog still partying, I lay on my back, focusing on my toes, elevating my head, curving my spine. Ten sit-ups later, I was done. Pity the riled canine didn't join me in enjoying the hit of euphoria awarded by physical exertion, however protracted in scope. Feeling guilty for having given up so easily, I timed-out for thirty seconds, observing the re-emergence of an old friend in the corner of the room. Sprinting through a crack between the roof and the wall, Gandalf the Gecko froze as soon as he saw me. In a game of 'Statues' he'd win without trying. I wondered what he thought, if indeed he thought anything at all. I wonder if he even registered my presence, or if he always hauled his tiny body to a halt whenever he felt inclined to thoroughly scope out his surroundings. He was so small that he couldn't have been anything but a baby, out on his own in the world. I'd named him Gandalf because he acted in such a wise manner. Indeed, he was a sage gecko if ever there was one, intelligent enough to scout for potential predators before dashing forth with the kind of blind ambition that can get you killed. I scratched my arm as he blinked his distrust. Mosquitoes were definitely in the air, but ants were equally as keen to bite, cruelly plunging my short stay into scratching jeopardy. Rather than patrolling in packs, the ants attacked individually, stealthily nicking my skin as I lay prostrate in bed... or on the floor.

It was unfair to pin all my despair on the dog and the way it restrained me from sleeping; there was more to my restful evening than met the eye. I'd been looking forward to receiving a festive flurry of e-mails from loved ones. A smattering of messages had penetrated my Yahoo account, but the sentiments within had been garbled, rushed, altogether lacking in thought and feeling. It was a good thing I had Simon and Sheetha to rely on. Forever transforming negatives into positives, they'd helped me through so much since we'd first hatched our ambitious dream to encompass India. Now that we'd essentially flung ourselves onto the final leg of a trip which had swallowed tens of thousands of miles, we'd begun to reflect on what had been the eye-spearing, heart-attacking, horizon-broadening pilgrimage of a lifetime.

In truth, I'd loathed every second of my first night in Mumbai. It had taken a week for me to lower my guard, at which point Si and Sheetha swooped into the city, enabling us to experience Elephanta Island, Malabar Hill and Chowpatty Beach together during the firework-dominated Festival of Light. A few days later, we ambled onto an Aurangabad-aimed train, arriving in the city at four in the morning. Conned into staying at a guesthouse that clearly didn't warrant its high rates, we squandered no time in taking buses to Ellora and Ajanta, desperate to admire immaculately preserved caves once used by Buddhists and Hindus. Awed by the lush scenery at Ajanta, we decided to ditch our original plan, somewhat inconsiderately laying it to rest at the side of one of the country's busiest roads, where it was destined to be denied peace for time immemorial. Willing to forsake the beach-life until the very end of our trip, and in mutual agreement to visit Udaipur (undoubtedly one of India's most romantic cities), we caught a bus from Aurangabad to Indore, before scoring tickets on a train to take us further north. A dilapidated bus subsequently escorted us from Udaipur to Ajmer. We duly squashed ourselves onto a late-night service over Snake Mountain to Pushkar. Having timed things exquisitely, we downed our backpacks just as the annual Camel Fair climaxed. A sucker for savouring the widest variety of landscapes on offer, I adored the mountains which encircle Pushkar with such photogenic magnificence. Eager to witness more of India's visual diversity, we crawled upon an overnight bus service to the frontier town of Jaisalmer. It proved to be a night to remember for all the wrong reasons, the 'warp speed' nature of the suspension-destroying driving implying that the man behind the wheel was suicidal, homicidal, or both. Once we'd coupled the dreadful driving with the way the windows kept sliding open, allowing indescribably cold gusts of air to assault our bodies, we vowed to travel by train as much as we could from then on.

It can't be denied that we were travelling on extremely tight budgets, but we were a long way from becoming sadomasochists who enjoyed doing things the hard way for the sake of it. A couple of magical days out in the dune-flecked Thar Desert helped us to overcome the nightmares associated with the bus ride to Jaisalmer. As close to the border with Pakistan as we were going to get, we eschewed the idea of heading further north or west, erasing from our minds images of Amritsar's Golden Temple and the fourteenth Dalai Lama's 'home' in Dharamsala. We rolled in an easterly direction instead, vying to reach Jodhpur, followed by Jaipur. Both cities boast breathtaking forts. Only a fool nurturing no interest whatsoever in the mighty history of India would pass up the opportunity to walk in the footsteps of Emperors and warriors. It was only a short journey by train from Jaipur to Delhi, the wretchedly sprawling capital. Holding our metaphorical horses there for a weekend, we indulged in an early morning train ride to Agra once we'd had our fill of the Red Fort, along with what is surely the best museum in the world dedicated to the inspirational life of Mahatma Gandhi, the violence-abhorring, yarn-spinning gent who selflessly dedicated his life to helping India and its people. Leaving Agra's bounty in the form of its stunning fort and the Taj Mahal, we pushed on to Varanasi where we encountered the River Ganges for the first time. December had already descended, and I pulled out all the stops to bus myself north, vying to vault the border into Nepal at Sunauli to catch up with my girlfriend in the lakeside retreat of Pokhara. Due to a painfully restrictive multi-entry Indian visa which prevented me from entering Nepal for the two weeks required, I conspired to pursue the Ganges in the direction of Kolkata. Si, Sheetha and I stayed there for four days, during which time we worked on behalf of Motherhouse for a hospice in the deprived Kali Ghat area of the city. A Swiss friend recommended Puri, but we were running desperately short on time. Bypassing the coastal settlement altogether, we braced ourselves for the epic train ride down to Chennai. Gluttons for harvesting an abundance of miles in very short periods of time, it wasn't long before we clambered aboard a train bound for Kerala. There, we holed up for two nights in Kovalam, followed by a couple in Alleppey. It was then a race against time and money to reach Goa before 'Christmas prices' kicked in and guesthouses began charging room rental rates above and beyond our meagre budgets. Shouldering our backpacks whilst embracing persistence, we successfully walked into a barrage of semi-decent deals at Anjuna, enabling us to rest our bodies and calm our minds for an entire week before completing the circle by chugging back up to Mumbai.

Considering the pros and cons of being on the last leg of our trip, I surmised that there wasn't a single advantage of returning to Mumbai in anticipation of shaking the colossal country from our backs. As the subcontinent stood, it had become a part of us. Embedded in our disconnected yet collective consciousness, it would stoically refuse to defuse its electrifying hold on our impressionable imaginations. But that didn't matter; it was by the 'bai. What really mattered was the realisation that we would never really leave India. It would always be there: flaunting its wealth, haunting with its poverty, taunting with its intensity, inspiring with its majesty. Long before I left, I was already looking forward to going back.

~

TAPPING THE MAN'S FOREHEAD, THE CONDUCTOR ACCIDENTALLY DEFACED THE SLEEPING PASSENGER'S THIRD EYE. The man sat beside me had only boarded the bus five minutes beforehand, but the heat of the day had conspired to make him drowsy. 'Ten rupees,' the conductor wailed, desperate to fight his way along the rest of the rammed gangway to collect fares before the next stop. We were in Madgaon, more commonly known as Old Goa, aspiring to reach the train station before six. Our train north to Mumbai was unlikely to stall for stragglers. If we missed it, we'd be stranded in every respect given that all of the other services to the city were booked-up. Willing the bus to weave through the traffic with stealthier grace, we sighed in frustration upon halting at a random corner where we waited for fifteen minutes until the bus refilled. We'd been warned that some buses don't move until every last seat becomes occupied. At least the hiatus allowed us to gaze admiringly at the grand cathedral over the road, a whitewashed wonder of a structure constructed and used by the Portuguese back when they exercised their hold over Goa. Outwardly adorned with detailed murals depicting biblical scenes, the cathedral was topped by a chunky cross of the highest order.

It was still hard to believe that Christmas had come and gone in the dilation of a pupil. The day had jingled by in a blur. As I reminisced, the bus juddered into action, swerving away from the kerb into traffic thicker than an unconscious imbecile. We were left at the end of the road. Sooner than expected, I wound up scouring the station platform for fodder in the form of literature and food. I had to focus on nourishing my mind, body and soul. I also had to focus on getting out of Goa so the next part of our journey could commence on the last day of the year. Unwilling to return to the UK until physically reinvented and psychologically sound, I was bound for Indonesia. Furthermore, I would be in the air as the wrath of 2011 swept across southeast Asia, unable to ground myself until air traffic control signalled that it was safe to do so.

I stumbled into a trackside restaurant at the southern end of Madgaon's station where I bought a 'samosa' for ten rupees. The vendor placed it in a dust-caked microwave, assuming that I preferred the steaming variety. Snatching my money, he wandered off, having set the microwave's turntable spinning for sixty seconds. With fifty seconds remaining, the ground-shaking drone of a locomotive's warning horn shocked the station to life. The train was on time, rocking into the station exactly five minutes before it was due to depart. The restaurant was approximately one-hundred yards away from the arbitrary spot I'd abandoned my friends. They had my tatty backpack; I had our tickets to ride. The train's drone became unbearable as the engine nosed its way past the restaurant window, delivering a dilemma. In reality, the course of action I should have taken was obvious. I should have ditched the spinning 'samosa' and apologised to my growling stomach for any further upset I caused. Racing back to my friends and getting on the train was of utmost importance, yet no sense of urgency initially registered in the tips of my toes. My feet refused to move as my eyes pierced all four corners of the room. Where had the vendor gone? I considered vaulting the countertop as the train wheezed to a stop, straining its brakes beyond aural comprehension. My fashionably scratched watch told me no lies. It was two minutes to six: high time to scoot. Then the man reappeared, carrying a 'thali': a circular tray of 'dal', various curries, pickled cabbage, thick yoghurt, and a healthy 'roti' stash. Detecting my desire to intercept my food and flee, he sauntered around to his side of the counter. 'Come on, come on,' I silently yelled. He knew I was due to travel on the Mumbai-bound train, so what possessed him to merely saunter when the rest of our travel plans wielded the potential to be spectacularly slammed into jeopardy if we didn't scramble aboard the service within the next minute? To be fair, it was my fault. But I blamed my hunger. It was unforgivably inconsiderate at times.

Alas, a swift cash-for-snack exchange preceded an exhausting sprint along the platform. Simon and Sheetha were waiting beside 'S3', the sleeper carriage upon which we hoped to slip into slumber. 'Where have you been?' Si grimaced. As guilty as I felt for thinking of my digestive tract in a time of crisis, I confessed that I'd got stuck in a restaurant. 'What do you mean you got stuck? Did the power go off, preventing you from locating the door due to bad light? Did a rupee-pinching princess take a shine to you and refuse to let you go? Or did a strategically coordinated rat-attack mean you had to take to the tables as they ravaged the kitchen?' I stood shame-faced, finishing my 'samosa' as I scrambled aboard. 'I got stuck at the till,' I replied, glancing over my shoulder, through the door of the train, blessing Goa for its traditional charms, thanking fate for its unbridled patience.

~

IT WAS OUR FINAL EVENING IN INDIA TOGETHER, so what did we do? We trailed up to the closest cinema, of course. Having considered revisiting Chowpatty Beach before deciding to sit back and relax in the comfort of the air-conditioned cinema, we sought to have fun wherever we wound up. In the mood to celebrate the fact we'd travelled all the way around India, we indulged in a late afternoon meal to pre-empt the six p.m. showing of *The Tourist*, the latest Johnny Depp movie. Dining with the ravenous locals in a cheap eatery directly opposite the historic Regal Cinema, my friends and I chose three different dishes. Dining to a budget, I spooned up a value-for-money tray of 'aloo mutter' served with rice and a cup of tea so sweet that I prayed a dentist was present in case of emergency. Sheetha sampled 'chicken handi' as Si sank his cutlery into a ravishing okra-based curry. To say we were going to miss authentic Indian cuisine was an understatement of ridiculous proportions. Just as much as we'd consumed it, it had consumed us, yet we were still foaming at the mouth with excitement about the kind of food we'd be presenting to our lucky taste buds later in the week when we touched down in Indonesia.

Indonesia constituted uncharted territory for us all, but everything we'd heard about it from other travellers had been uniformly inspirational. Only the previous day we'd chatted with a twenty-something Alaskan fisherman who had spent time in Indonesia prior to visiting India. Having reassured us that buses, boats and guesthouses were cheap, he advised us to head over to Komodo Island on our own terms to avoid the disturbingly high cost of tours to the home of the beastly dragon of the same name. We planned to purchase a thirty-day visa on arrival at Juanda Airport, Surabaya, unless a sixty-day visa could be obtained. A second month in the country would be ideal since it consists of thousands of islands, hundreds of which are purported to be ravishing. A large proportion of visitors make a beeline for Bali if partying hard is their vice. One of the greatest places in the world to drink and be merry, Kuta Beach is renowned for its bars and clubs for good reason. I was fortunate enough to have a friend who lived on the island, so I prayed he'd be home. We would first need to flee the island of Java. When booking our flight from Mumbai, we had the chance to fly into Jakarta instead of Surabaya, but we figured it made more sense to head as far east as possible from the get-go to make backtracking less of a necessity. Indeed, if getting a thirty-day visa was our only option, we'd have to be doubly focused on sketching out an itinerary which encompassed as many island gems as such a restrictive time frame would permit us to cherish. Mutually wishing to climb smoking volcanoes, swim with sharks, and snare glimpses of orangutans living and larking in their natural habitat, it was essential we put our heads together in order to figure out where we were going to go after Bali. Having pondered that, we were getting ahead of ourselves. After all, we were still in Mumbai. The city deserved our undivided attention until the dying seconds of our Colaba-based stay in league with The Gateway.

While the Regal failed to live up to its name, it remains a beautiful building in its own right. Sitting beside the 'SBX Sportsbar', one of only a few places to hang out after dark in South Mumbai, the Regal - designed by Charles Stevens in classic Art Deco style - mixes Hollywood with Bollywood showings on a daily basis. Unfortunately, I'd still not ventured along to catch an Indian film, but I was desperate to do so in light of what I'd heard about the intensity of the crowd reaction when famous Bollywood stars stride into any given scene. Indian crowds are notorious for getting passionately involved with movies, thereby making the showing of a film a truly interactive experience by cheering, clapping and jeering in accordance with the strains of action on screen. Given the limited entertainment options for foreigners in Colaba, the Regal tends to be extremely busy with movie buffs of all nationalities. It seemed ironic that we wanted to see a film called *The Tourist* whilst ensconced in a Traveller's Ghetto. However, there was no need to attach drama to the reality since it was sheer coincidence. Seated and satisfied with punnets of caramel-laced popcorn, we were fools to get comfortable. No sooner had we sat, it was imperative we stood... for the Indian National Anthem. Standing with our hands clasped behind our backs, we stared at the screen upon which the image of a billowing Indian flag was projected, the circular heart of the flag's design paying homage to the type of spinning wheel employed by Gandhi. In itself, *The Tourist* touched base with elements of intrigue, comedy and romance, but the overall highlight was the Muse anthem that blasted over the end credits. No disrespect to the film or its producers, but it couldn't have been more formulaic if Michael Bay had manhandled the story via his favourite scriptwriters into something so unoriginal that the time wasted watching it could be classed as a crime. In the movie's defence, the neat twist come its climax proved surprising.

Out on the causeway, street children ran the gauntlet of taxi-laden traffic, violating the central reservation wherever there was a gap in the railings. Scouting for a new backpack, it was amusing to witness the lengths to which stallholders were willing to go in order to offload their gear. As I inspected a backpack for signs of wear and tear, suspicious it might be second-hand, the stallholder told me I could have it for 'the good price' of twelve-hundred rupees. Unfortunately for him, it was obvious the product's quality of stitching was so dire that both straps would probably rip from the pack's misshaped body within a matter of days. 'How much you give me?' the man yelped as I walked. 'Where you from? You English? Australian? Come back, my friend! I give you bargain of the decade!' I might have been desperate – but I wasn't that desperate.

~

STAMPING UP THE STEPS, Si didn't look best pleased. 'We've got a serious problem,' he explained to Sheetha. 'The ATM only issued one-thousand and six-hundred rupees instead of five-thousand.' We were sat in a plush 'Thomas Cook' office on the periphery of South Mumbai's Financial District, vying to exchange a wad of rupees for a fistful of dollars. We collectively craved such hard currency for buying a thirty-day visa upon arrival in Indonesia. A few hundred rupees short of the one-thousand four-hundred and forty-three required to initiate an exchange of thirty dollars, Si had clomped out of the office in search of a bank.

Sheetha and I had been wondering why he'd taken so long. Now we knew the instantly forgivable reason why we'd been left to sit-pretty for twenty wholesome minutes. Brandishing a receipt which implied the full amount of five-thousand rupees had been deducted from their balance, Si realised they had to get in touch with their bank without delay. We explained as much to the patient 'Thomas Cook' employee. Fortunately, a gargantuan branch of 'HSBC' was located a couple of hundred yards away. On the downside, the 'May I help you?' lady could only direct us to a small room inside of which a wall of phones squared up to a row of redundant teller machines. Understandably irate, Sheetha lifted one of the receivers, praying they'd be able to resolve the issue hand-in-hand. Three-thousand and four-hundred rupees was a lot to lose. The sting of the loss couldn't have been more pronounced since it was beyond their control, owing to a technical glitch. 'The ATM flat-lined mid-transaction,' remarked Si. A power-cut might have upset it. Who knew? It didn't matter what had caused the error. So long as they were granted an instantaneous rebate, everything would be fine and we'd be able to go about the rest of our daily business as normal.

Time was short. Si and Sheetha had just three hours before they were due to leave Colaba in a miasma of fumes. Psychologically bracing themselves for what was bound to be a two-hour journey through South, Central, and then North Mumbai, they would rather have been relaxing in the shadow of The Gateway of India whilst admiring 'The Taj Mahal Palace' from afar, the internationally renowned hotel in which Barack Obama had recently stayed.

Growling her annoyance, it was obvious that Sheetha wasn't getting the kind of helpful answers deserving of her polite telephone manner. Calmly replacing the receiver, she sulked: 'They can't do anything from here in India. We need to ring London.' Beside the rack of phones, an Internet terminal allowed full-blown access to the web. It was neither the time nor place to tap into 'Facebook', even though Si joked that he was tempted to check his messages since Wi-Fi was so hard to find. Adopting a sensible stance, Sheetha signed into their online banking account to collate details of recent transactions. Armed with dated evidence, we sloped out of the bank in search of a phone booth. We found one at the side of a busy road stretching between Flora Fountain and Chowpatty Beach. In spite of having been short-changed, Si's mood somehow remained buoyant. He was evidently excited about the prospect of greeting the large Indonesian island of Java. 'Have you got any STDs?' Si said to the man behind the counter. He meant no harm by the joke. The expressionless phone guardian didn't understand what Si was getting at. Nevertheless, given that the Indian man casually caressed his crotch whilst pointing at the phone, subscriber trunk dialling potentially came with sexually transmitted diseases as standard. Finally connecting with their branch in England, Sheetha relayed detailed information about what had happened, procedurally reciting a comprehensive list of dates, addresses, and withdrawal amounts. Reassured that they'd be reimbursed, we left the bank and returned to 'Thomas Cook'. Ten minutes later, we had ninety dollars at our disposal. On the painful flipside, we had just two more hours left before Si and Sheetha needed to set in motion the second leg of our Asian odyssey.

Retracing our steps through the Fort District, I paused beside Flora Fountain, just like I did every time I struck the heart of Hutatma Chowk. A beautiful structure carved from stone, it was constructed in 1864 and pays tribute to the Roman goddess of the same name. Momentarily succumbing to an Italianised flight of my easily influenced imagination, I was shoulder-barged back into reality by a hawker selling watches. Strolling further south towards Colaba, I allowed the rawest strain of awe to remodel my wildest dreams as a parade of architecturally astounding buildings secreted their history from every brick. The Army & Navy Building, The

David Sassoon Library, Jehangir Art Gallery: each structure
was a sight to behold. Having snooped around the art gallery
upon first arriving in Mumbai, we were familiar with the
types of paintings exhibited. The majority of canvases within
its circular sanctuary presented rural scenes of a traditional
nature, showing children at play and families at work. For
those searching for work of a more contemporary and racier
variety, The National Gallery of Modern Art is guaranteed to
satisfy specific tastes. If those two galleries aren't enough,
then the guarded doors of The Prince of Wales Museum
should be breached. One of the most beautiful buildings in
the entire city, The P.O.W. Museum is named after King
George V who laid its foundation stone in 1905. Its dome can
only be described as a masterful work of breathtaking
majesty. The mere sight of its graceful curvature is bound to
remind visitors of the Taj Mahal in the swift blink of an eye.

Having walked off their bank-related frustration, Si and
Sheetha asked if I'd like to join them for what would be our
very last meal together in the country. We once again loped
into the working man's restaurant beneath 'Hotel Majestic',
acknowledging the fact that we'd discredited our self-styled
spontaneity by becoming apathetic creatures of habit. Careful
to order dishes which wouldn't serve to blow our dwindling
reserves of rupees, we were understandably distraught when
the bill rang in far higher than expected. We re-requested a
menu for an attention-snaring bout of fevered cross-
referencing, adamant we'd been charged for something we
hadn't ordered. And we were right, so we argued our point
until the correct balance was restored. I glanced at my watch
in the midst of such wrangling. It was almost five: time for Si
and Sheetha to grab their backpacks from my room prior to
hailing a cab. I just hoped their driver wouldn't be in the
mood for trying to rip them off. Spare rupees were hard to
come by, adding up as we counted down. 'It won't be long

now,' I told Si. 'You'll be toasting on a wealth of Balinese beaches come New Year without a money-orientated care in the world.' Si mock-grimaced before grinning in retaliation. 'Ah... but you'll miss India once you leave, Steve.' Truer words had never been voiced.

~

IT HAD ALREADY TURNED THREE IN THE AFTERNOON, and I'd achieved less than nothing. My priority had been to get the straps of my backpack re-sewn before trawling the pavement-packed stalls of Colaba Causeway for a pair of hardy hiking boots. Having lost focus, I'd been wasting time on the Internet, aimlessly wandering around the Fort District, eating my way towards an imminent heart attack. It was the penultimate day of 2010. Positivity had to be awakened in my soul before 2011 plundered an exceptional year which had been inspirational and agonising in equal measure.

It wasn't my fault I'd become hopelessly addicted to the Indian 'thali'. Resistance is futile; once you've had one, it's inevitable that you'll start ordering a 'thali' at most meal-times without thinking. Arguably the best place to savour a 'thali' in Colaba is 'Hotel Majestic'. Its 'special thali' for the modest sum of fifty-two rupees comprised a value-for-money meal deal like no other. It was a fattening feast, no less.

The restaurant had the capacity to seat about seventy people. Almost every bench was occupied by men lapping up a variety of different platters. My 'thali' was deemed special in the sense it had the largest quantity of curries. Delivered on a circular tray, it resembled a work of art, a riot of loud colours serving to help the 'thali' resemble an undisturbed painter's palette. At the centre of the main tray, a hotter-than-thou 'roti' sat atop a bowl of veg-flecked rice. Radiating from the steaming heart, six smaller trays jostled for attention, three expertly folded 'chapattis' nestling between tiny tubs containing plain yoghurt and spicy pickle. Frankly, I had no clue where to begin, so I panned around the room, discreetly rumbling culinary protocol. It seemed that different people ate different curries in different orders. It was each to their own. Some folk ladled spoonfuls of each curry over the rice to produce a super-curry the likes of which could kill. Others meekly ripped their 'chapattis' into dip-sized bits before plunging the wheat-based accompaniment into the hot stuff. Given that the 'thali' is on a tray, it can be spun around like a turntable, making it even easier to dip 'chapatti' shreds into a multitude of curries at the same time. Watching Indian men munch their way through a 'thali' makes for fascinating viewing as they randomly stir tiny amounts of pickle into their yoghurt before sinking their 'chapatti' into the resultant mixture. Anything goes with food, yet it's surprising to see so much wasted. It's the way of the world that not all diners are going to devote their taste buds wholeheartedly to every kind of curry, but it's tragic that such leftover food is thrown away. Only in shockingly rare circumstances can a box be attained so uneaten food can be removed from the premises and distributed amongst the homeless. I've said it once, and I'll say it again: India possesses an abundance of food. There is no reason why anybody on the subcontinent should starve or suffer from malnutrition.

I half-considered seeing a Bollywood film to settle my stomach, but the forty-rupee stall tickets for *Band Baaja Baaraat* had sold out. The entire balcony had been filled, convincing me once and for all that Bollywood is the biggest kind of business imaginable. Scanning the posters for star-names, my mind cast itself back to the afternoon Si, Sheetha and I had ventured up to Malabar Hill. One of the wealthiest areas of Mumbai, the park-graced hill acts as a safe haven for all manner of actors, actresses, musicians and socialites. A beggar's leap from Chowpatty Beach, Malabar Hill remains one of my favourite areas of the city, not least because it's such a tranquil and clean neck of Mumbai, ablaze with beastly dragonflies, courting couples, and energetic children on the rampage. Even though it's only about three miles north of the perilously overcrowded Colaba district, it genuinely does seem a world away.

Veering left out of the cinema, I stumbled into 'Shankar Bookstall', one of the best places on the causeway to buy or part-exchange books. I'd nearly finished *The Ground Beneath Her Feet* and sought to score another Salman Rushdie book. Having exchanged my dog-eared copies of *Visions of Cody* and *The Greatness Guide* earlier in the week, I had nothing else to offer other than a palmful of rupees.

Roads leading towards The Gateway of India were barricaded to ridiculously restrictive extremes, rendering it near-impossible to reach the eighty-five foot high structure. Juhu Police Station had installed barriers around the perimeter of 'The Taj Mahal Palace' in the run-up to the New Year celebrations, perhaps fearing that terror might once again descend on 'Maximum City'. Only the other day, Si and I had been told how a commission-driven tout had helped to collect bullet casings from the floor of 'Leopold's Café-Bar' in the wake of the attacks which had shocked Mumbai to its core in 2008. 'Let's fight terrorism together,' urged a police-authorised banner. South of The Gateway, the waterfront played host to sad men selling balloons so huge and oddly-shaped that it was impossible not to laugh when they approached with a view to selling them. An army of younger men, meanwhile, patrolled the path with cameras and photo-albums, encouraging day-trippers to pose for a price. As elderly men promenaded with poor posture, I cut a circle around to the main road. Halting to commit an idea I'd just entertained to paper, I could sense I was being watched by a pompous security guard outside an Internet café. Eager to book a flight from Kuala Lumpur to Melbourne, I decided to catapult myself out of my misery by setting a date and paying my dues, praying that I'd be able to head to Oz at the end of January after what was scheduled to be an intense month of writing my way over a selection of Indonesian islands. Thus, I strode past the guard and through the door, only to be vocally reprimanded. He called me back, pointing at the pen and piece of paper in my hand. 'Give it!' he coughed. My scrawl was near-illegible to me, so Shiva only knows what he made of the squiggles invading his field of vision. 'You cannot go in there with this,' he stated, an air of authority defying his lowly position. Rather than having my notes confiscated in a fit of misunderstanding, I raised my arms in mock surrender, asking for the paper back before heading to the Internet place next door. In his eyes, you couldn't be too careful. I could have been plotting anything. Behind me, Canadian traveller Otiena Ellwand confessed that she, too, was a scribe. Defending my wanderlust, I lambasted work, saying it was a bad habit. I also aired grievances in relation to how the masochistic makeup of Western society places undue pressure on highly sensitive souls. She agreed by degrees, tapping her keyboard towards an early grave, updating her online blog.

Away from the maddening hustle and bustle generated by Colaba Causeway, the bulk of the district consists of desperately quiet, tree-shaded roads which are a joy to explore. Dilapidated Methodist Churches lean within praying distance of lively Hindu temples, religion naturally ducking and weaving around different beliefs in good faith. The Kala Ghoda Art District straddles the imaginary line of demarcation between the Colaba and Fort districts. Boasting a staggering number of museums, it's easy to understand why visitors flock to this part of Mumbai. A little further east, the Naval Dockyard takes no prisoners, yet it's most definitely off-limits to folk who aren't appropriately suited and booted. Guarded by grand gates named after wild animals, Elephant Gate gives way to Lion Gate before Cheetah Gate gets the opportunity to turn away those who have no business in the yard. Opposite the dockyard, I clocked a Naval Tailors advertising new stock, promoting a smart selection of boiler suits, boots, and stripes. What's more, a placard in the vicinity applauded those in service. Celebrating India's sixty years of Naval history, its slogan sang: 'Our Whites Keep The Oceans Blue!'

Cutting inland from Cheetah Gate, the intimidating bulk of Mumbai's stock exchange didn't take much finding. Offset by military posts in which uniformed personnel rested itchy fingers on machine-guns, the main building attracted attention courtesy of its overhead LCD screen. Across it, stock and share figures zoomed, blatantly highlighting profit and loss to those capable of translating such financial ups and downs into a form of language which actually meant something to the average man, woman and child on the street. From where I stood, it looked as though India was getting richer by the minute. However, I naively fielded such a judgement whilst looking up, my head in the clouds above the bizarrely-designed building. Reverting my gaze to ground level, the gutter-dwelling purveyors of poverty pushed everything back in line, unknowingly saluting *The Moneyless Man* in Mark Boyle.

Did the country's GDP have something to hide? Or did the gulf between rich and poor go deeper than that?

~

WE WERE NOWHERE NEAR. Where was he taking me? I thought I'd bagged a sound deal for three-hundred and fifty rupees, but my driver seemed intent on going the long way round. I'm just thankful that I was sensible enough not to travel by meter. Glancing through the window at passing rickshaws, I noticed meters colourfully courting the warning: 'Don't touch me!' I wasn't due to fly until ten p.m., but I'd taken heed of the widespread warning to get out of Colaba as soon as feasible. It wasn't uncommon for the journey between there and the International Airport to consume three hours and then some. Having pre-arranged to meet a specific driver outside the 'YWCA' building an easel's throw from The National Museum of Modern Art, I was disappointed when he didn't show. Fair play to him, though: he was probably busy. Conscious that time was ticking, I trudged towards the vehicle crowning the queue. Blithely ignoring 'No Parking' signs, drivers were either reading 'The Times of India' or catching forty winks on their backseats. One driver was trusting enough to leave his keys in the ignition as he slept, tempting me to quietly slide in and buckle up, psyched to take us both for a cross-conurbation ride to remember.

I asked the driver how much he'd charge. Between slurps of 'chai' he spluttered 'four-hundred.' I protested that the guy I'd spoken with earlier had been prepared to take me for fifty rupees less. The man eventually relented, instructing me to drag my backpack onto the springy backseat. From the off, he reminded me of the pie-eyed tour bus driver from the movie *Big Trouble in Little China*. He had one eye bigger than the other. When he spoke, he did so out of the side of his moustache-shrouded mouth. Given that taxi drivers could potentially have a long drive back to Colaba from the airport terminals without fare-paying passengers for company, it's understandable that not all cabbies are willing to undertake the epic slog north.

Si had been right when he said I'd be sad to leave. Tears began to well as we taxied west, away from Colaba, over to

Marine Drive. I thought it would have been easier and quicker to strike directly north towards CST, but my driver cultivated alternative designs, aiming for Chowpatty Beach, only to plough into an inglorious tailback. We sat without talking for ten minutes as his Ambassador purred on the spot. 'See, this is what happens! It's no good to go to the airport at this time of day.' Shooting me a malicious glance via his amulet-laced rear-view mirror, he wound up making me feel personally responsible for the fact his car had begun to overheat. A short while later we began to wend our way south of Malabar Hill's base, plunging into yet heavier traffic.

Ironically, only an hour beforehand I'd been chewing the fat of a chicken wing over a conversation concerning the best way to reach the airport. By sheer coincidence, I'd sat opposite an Israeli traveller for the second time at the same restaurant in the same day. He, too, would be on his way out of India later in the evening in the wake of a five-month trip around the subcontinent. Having finished his compulsory stint in the military six months earlier, he'd withdrawn from The Middle East at the first opportunity. It's extremely common to encounter Israeli guys in their early twenties on the proverbial road. Three years of being told what to do is enough to provoke anybody to do something on their own terms in liberal lands far, far away. Before asking him his name, I asked where his favourite place had been within Mother India's realm. 'Ladakh,' he beamed. 'People keep asking if I went to Nepal, and I tell them "no." The mountains in India are enough.' I then asked him where he'd spent Christmas. 'I don't know what you mean,' he snorted. 'When is Christmas? I am Jewish.' His abrupt answer silenced me. 'Oh. Er. Right,' I stalled, aiming to keep politics and religion out of the food hall. 'I live near Jerusalem,' he confided, scooping yoghurt dregs from his 'thali' tray before summoning a server. I suspected that I'd accidentally scraped a nerve, for he upped and left after suggesting I take a train to Borivali, and then a rickshaw from there to the airport if I was still in the mood for saving money if not hassle. I thanked him by nodding. But he didn't notice. He was back on the street already.

'You give me fifty rupees and we take expressway,' gurgled my driver. Once again, we were up close and personal with a jam so bitter that he could tell my patience had perished. Unsure if he was conning me or not, I acquiesced, agreeing to pay the necessary toll if it meant we'd catch sight of the airport within half the time it would take to pursue the scenic route. It was in the best interests of us both to get there sooner rather than later. With that, he punched his car into a different lane. A couple of minutes later we were racing over a causeway which extended into the Arabian Sea. Aided and abetted by a series of exquisitely designed bridges, the near-deserted causeway looked out-of-place, not least because so few vehicles were rumbling over its asphalt. At least it awarded a succession of breathtaking views, re-iterating the fact that Mumbai boasts one of the most mesmerising skylines in the world. The toll charge needed to be paid once we'd swung off the last bridge, away from the waterfront. Although he failed to understand that I needed to reach Gate B for international departures, I eventually persuaded him to ignore the volley of signs directing traffic towards the domestic arena. Short of reaching over and grabbing the wheel, I relayed precise instructions. As the most pedantic backseat driver in recent history, I pointed… forward. Forward! FORWARD! Maybe it wasn't his fault. Perhaps his car naturally veered to the right, making it more difficult for him to cut a straight course.

As expected, he charged three-hundred and fifty rupees, plus fifty for the toll. Peeling out of sight before I even had the chance to offload my remaining notes into his palm, I was thankful he hadn't tried to extort me. The journey had taken almost two and a half hours, the evil entirety of which had been endured without a single drop of water to rehydrate my flagging body. I hastened to find the relevant 'Air Asia' check-in desk. I'd never flown with them before, but I'd been assured that 'AA' was the best airline to use in order to whizz around the continent on the cheap. A budget airline operating in a similar no-frills fashion to 'Easyjet' and 'Ryanair', it provides cost-effective opportunities for people to hit the skies on a whim to some of the most exotic places on earth. Falling in line, I thought how strange it would be to wing my way out of one year and into another from the timeless space of the night sky. Midnight was fast approaching, and 2010 was doomed. It wasn't the only thing that was doomed.

~

IT WAS NO JOKE. The situation had surpassed being a joke. I was sat in a tiny office, behind the scenes of Juanda International Airport, Surabaya. In no mood to be patronised into submission, I eyeballed the TV to my right as the young man sent to deal with me posed puerile questions. 'Are you sure you checked your backpack in at Mumbai International?' he asked, as though I might have mislaid it before approaching the counter. 'Yes, yes, yes! A thousand times, yes! I checked it in. I distinctly recall it weighed just over eleven kilograms.' For once, the weighing machine had worked in my favour in the sense I didn't have to pander to excess baggage charges.

The two-legged flight from Mumbai to Surabaya had been blissful: an energising chat with Gold Coaster Stephanie Kingsmill pre-empted a smooth transfer at KL where I slyly slipped through a barricaded door that led straight to a special transfer desk able to issue boarding passes within a

'Slumdogs' heading north out of Mumbai's Churchgate Station.

Mumbai's Taj Mahal Palace Hotel squares up to the Gate of India.

Koli fisherfolk ply the dirty bay for sustenance.

Dhobi Ghat, Mumbai: the best place to get laundry done.

Mumbai's most famous necklace of sand at dusk.

The timeless elegance of Elephanta Caves.

Seeing the light through the water at Ellora.

Landscape-gazing towards Udaipur's divine Floating Palace.

More than enough fresh fruit and veg for everyone.

The alluring lie of the land around Pushkar.

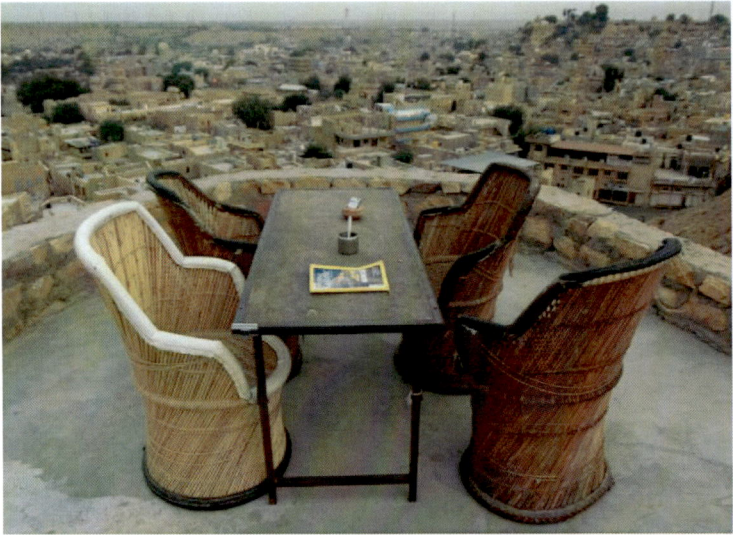

Catching breath & killing time atop Jaisalmer's formidable fort.

A heated bout of cooking and contemplation in the Thar Desert.

The 'Blue City' of Jodhpur on the greyest of days.

The dizzying approach to Amber Fort, Jaipur.

Waiting in vain for an opening at The Taj Mahal, Agra.

The Rowing Man on The Ganges, Varanasi.

Canal-based reflections in Alleppey, Kerala.

Religion hits the beach at Vagator, Goa.

Spying a 'Spider Boat' in the mid-distance.

Hitting the loneliest of roads on the northern tip of Nusa Lembongan.

One of the most timelessly mesmerising landscapes in the world.

Indonesia asserts its volcanic presence with Mount Batur.

A Rudd's eye view of the Indonesian capital, Jakarta.

The elegant facade of the legendary Raffles Hotel, Singapore.

The Singapore skyline in all its high-flying glory.

An uber-funky shopping arcade beside the Singapore River.

A Singaporean structure to behold: Marina Bay Sands.

The tropical bounty of Fort Canning Park.

A musical interlude in Singapore Botanic Gardens.

Tranquillity transcends Monkey Beach on the island of Penang.

At Muka Head Lighthouse; a fitting climax to a breathtaking journey.

Lost in thought: the author in Goa.

matter of seconds. From there, I was escorted to the departure lounge and awarded an hour to kill. I splurged it on writing and net-surfing. Things only began to go awry once I touched down in Indonesia. I appeared to be the only Westerner on the entire flight. I was certainly the only person who stopped at the unmanned 'Visa on Arrival' counter as everybody else charged towards Immigration. It was early in the day, for sure - but where was everybody? Okay... it was New Year's Day, but did that really constitute an excuse for such a conspicuous shortage of airport staff? Hoping the visa issuers were on their break, I hung around in front of the counter, pacing up and down the adjacent stretch of corridor. Before long, I was the only person on the corridor. When it came to making tracks towards Immigration, Indonesians moved fast. Sick of waiting, I hopped over to a foreign exchange booth. 'Yes, you can buy a voucher here for a visa.' I duly slipped twenty-five American dollars through the gap between the window and counter. The man then wished me a Happy New Year: a pleasant gesture. Since I'd squandered ten minutes upstairs, I wound up being the very last person from my flight to pass through Immigration. In light of what happened next, that was probably for the best; I would have felt guilty for holding people up.

'Can I see your return flight ticket?' the stern attendant asked. Well, he could have done if I had one. Sensing a rare strain of tension simmering in the air-conditioned space between us, I explained that I was verging on spending thirty days travelling across Indonesia by bus and ferry. 'Right,' he dryly remarked, tapping a pen against his desk, lazily issuing a glance of distrust. 'You need to guarantee that you'll leave the country once your visa expires in thirty days,' he bemoaned. Attempting to appease his concern, I withdrew papers highlighting the fact I was scheduled to fly from KL to Melbourne on the last day of January. I hoped such hard evidence might mould his mood into one of a more amenable breed. If anything, my subsequent flight plans agitated him even more. 'The purpose of your visit?' Dumbfounded by his paranoia-petting line of questioning, I confessed to being a tourist. I was tempted to go one better, to tell him I was a travel-writer, but I didn't think he'd understand. Instead, I said I worked in retail, not wishing to generate further questions about the nature of my writing in case he suspected I might write something negative about the country. Three of the man's colleagues edged over to see what the fuss was about. Clearly reluctant to stick a visa in my passport, he asked where I'd be staying. Having arrived the day before, Si and Sheetha had been kind enough to e-mail details of their whereabouts in Denpasar, Bali's capital city. I diverted the man's attention to the address at the foot of the page I'd printed for reference purposes. Without saying any more, he nodded, slamming a pre-stamped visa into the middle of my passport beside a year-old Cambodian bone of contention.

Steaming towards the luggage carousel, I reeled from a sinking feeling. Two carousels were within striking distance; neither were operational. They'd both been shut down. Not a single person loitered in the area between Immigration and the final set of security checks. It was an eerie state of affairs. Praying my backpack had been lifted off and stood to a side, I circled both carousels, feeling a sense of dread descend. This can't be happening, I mused. Distraught, I headlessly hurried across to the only person I could see: a disinterested cleaner. The second I launched into my tirade, he shrugged, thrusting out his chin to indicate that I needed to speak to someone with more authority. At this point, had I been in possession of my backpack, I would have negotiated another X-ray machine. Collaring the twenty-something guy manning the machine, I explained that there was no sign of my gear. Through with scanning my paltry hand luggage, he led me through a door, down a corridor, into a room flooded with paperwork. A desk sat in one corner, a TV in the other. A Saturday morning kids' show was playing; handsome pop star Anang crooned whilst softly strumming his acoustic guitar. A wave of pre-pubescent teenagers swayed and sang along behind him. It reminded me of 'Live & Kicking'. A trio of style-savvy presenters salivated with excitement about nothing in particular every time they were called upon to provide real-time links between performances. Disturbingly, I should have been paying more attention to the man attempting to converse with me. 'You come from KL, yes?' I nodded, clarifying that my journey had originated in Mumbai. I asked if somebody could double-check for my pack in the storage area out of which the carousels craned their ever-turning heads. Assuming the guise of a psychic, he assured me there was no chance my backpack could be anywhere in the airport. I wondered, could it have been stolen? The fact I'd been held up at Immigration for longer than necessary would have given any have-a-go thief the perfect chance to pretend my bundle of grime was theirs. A landslide of possible scenarios diverted my attention from a pop-punk quartet riffing across the screen; an Indonesian version of Busted, they had four guitarists, yet not a single guitar-plucked melody could be heard above the soulless vocals. It was obvious they weren't playing live, the overproduced nature of the song rendering the musicians surplus to requirements. Snapping my mind back to attention, the 'Air Asia' employee instructed me to fashion a list of what my backpack contained. He subsequently typed up an official report, stressing that he'd call me if it surfaced in Mumbai or KL. 'But I don't have my phone. It's in my backpack!' I balled. My e-mail address would have to suffice as a mundane means of contact.

I was in the office for over two hours. The 'AA' rep seemed

in no hurry to leave, perhaps using my predicament as an excuse for avoiding work in alternative capacities. Confiding that he usually worked on the check-in desks, it became apparent that he preferred doing as little as he could, hence why he'd sooner chat to me. 'Your name is Mr. Stephen, yes?' Paying less attention to detail than usual, I nodded, marginally impressed by the anthemic quality of Indonesian pop music. Noticing that I was more interested in the bands on TV, he attempted to engage me on matters concerning British fare. A colleague strolled in, equipped to begin his shift. A flash of banter erupted between them. If only it had been in English. Assuming they were laughing at me, I was disgusted by their apparent unprofessionalism. 'Can I have your autograph?' the shady shift-starter asked. 'Don't you mean my signature?' I responded, focusing on the desk, expecting to see the official report plonked beneath my chin. 'No... I mean your autograph. I think you are Mr. Chris Martin from Coldplay, yes?' In spite of feeling sick with anxiety, I couldn't help but smile. 'I do play sing and play guitar,' I gushed, 'but if I was Chris, I don't think I'd travel around the world as a backpacker - or via "Air Asia" for that matter. No disrespect.' Both guys chuckled prior to getting back to business. The Coldplay fan waltzed out of the room as the desk-bound gent asked after my plans for the evening. Fabulous, I thought... now I'm being chatted-up! 'Well, you know, I intend to, you know.' Nothing I said could buy the time required. 'I need to reach my friends on Bali,' I said, honesty betraying privacy. 'How?' he asked. Lacking the energy to explain, I refolded Si's e-mail and gave it wings. 'By bus, then ferry, then another bus,' I elaborated. 'That's why I need you to speed up this process so I can get on my way; if I miss the bus, I'll be stranded in Surabaya.' The man's brows furrowed. 'I think you better take a plane,' he remarked. The journey time between Surabaya and Denpasar is thirty minutes by air. If I made the journey by bus and ferry, it would take over fourteen hours. For the sake of spending what equated to ten pounds extra, I agreed to a flight: my third shot of fuselage action in twelve hours. Picking one up for thirty US dollars, I punctured the grey skies on a promise.

If my backpack showed, the rep would personally request that it be forwarded to Denpasar Airport in the first instance. I had his word: nothing more. The only other thing I received for free was a slice of cake on my Bali-bound flight. Wishing me a 'Happy 2011' in toxic icing, I didn't know whether to laugh or cry. I'd only been in Indonesia for six hours, yet I feared that I'd already spent more money in the country than I had during the course of two whole months in India. Food and drink in Surabaya was expensive enough, yet Bali prices grossly polluted a different league entirely. At least I arrived there safely. All I needed to do was convey my aching body to Poppies Lane. If only I had money for a taxi.

~

I WASN'T SURE IF I WAS IN INDONESIA OR AMERICA. Sluttish fast-food restaurants ogling the beach suggested I was stuck in the latter, yet I was most definitely on the island of Bali. Having swung around to the world-famous expanse of Kuta Beach from the shop-saturated Kuta Square, I'd been astonished by the high quantity of outlets catering to Western tastes. 'Starbucks', 'McDonald's', 'Burger King': they were all present and correct, their logos no different from anywhere else in the world. Aching to experience authentic Balinese cuisine, I sidled up to a roadside bench behind which a man tossed bundles of noodles into an oil-rich wok. 'Bakso' had been recommended, so I ordered a bowl with rice. Consisting of chunky chicken meatballs basking in a noodle-based broth, 'bakso ayam' is one of those meals which can be consumed at any time of day. Essentially a light snack, I didn't feel guilty for indulging, even though I'd only just eaten an egg and tomato toastie at my guesthouse on Poppies Lane. Careful not to fling too many notes around, I was still getting a handle on Indonesian currency, executing dual mental calculations. First and foremost, I was trying to work out how many Indonesian Rupiahs there were to one Indian Rupee. My life had been dictated by rupees for over eight weeks. It was difficult to let go of the Indian currency because it seemed so simple to convert. I now needed to work out how many rupiahs there were to a pound. It transpired that there were fourteen-thousand, so at least I had a rough idea of how much I was blowing on food, accommodation and transport costs around the island. Worryingly, I'd been overspending as though it was Groundhog Day.

It can't be denied that Kuta Beach is an expensive place to stay, especially if you're a backpacker. One of the world's most popular holiday resorts, this southern neck of Bali teems with luxury hotels. Seeking a draft of fresh air away from the women flogging shawls on the sand, I stamped south along the beach, treading grains onto the boardwalk. Although the beach is dirty, it constitutes a haven for surfers of all ages and abilities. I suddenly wished I'd taken lessons with a Mexican pal, Arturo, in the sleepy Pacific Coast town of Melaque when he'd offered to teach me the basics. As with everything else in Kuta's vicinity, surfing lessons didn't come cheap, so I bypassed each instructor with a spring in my step. The wide, meandering boardwalk plunged through a grove of palm trees. Between them, wooden boats lay redundant. Signs tacked to posts lectured visitors in no uncertain terms: 'Throw your rubbish at the dustbin!' Yes, you did read right. The sign really did instruct people to hurl their litter at, not in, the green and red receptacles. At least that went some way in explaining why an unruly heap of banana skins, crumpled crisp packets, and empty bottles of water could be seen beside one of the bins.

Immaculately maintained, the mile-long boardwalk effectively connects the jaw-dropping wealth of five-star resorts fronting the water. The majority of such resorts have prominent water features channelling fresh water into their centrepiece pools of distinction. Loungers, by and large, languish beneath funky gazebo-styled shelters, allowing sunbathers to drag them out into the sun when it's blazing, then undercover whenever rain rattles exposure levels. Bizarrely, there appeared to be invisible lines of demarcation separating the holidaying residents of some resorts and the Indonesian hawkers encamped on their peripheries. Outside each resort, groups of Indonesian men and women sat: waiting. If a resort resident dared to take a swim in the sea, the hawkers literally pounced on him or her as soon as they left the resort with a view to purposefully beaching themselves. It was possible to buy anything, from polished seashells and silver bracelets, to henna tattoos and fully-functional harpoons. Doubtful that I'd be able to tow even the smallest harpoon through C&I, I was reminded of the time I managed to bring a genuine Gurkha knife home from Nepal without officials in Kathmandu so much as raising their eyebrows when it crawled through the X-ray machine in my hand luggage. Suffice to say, it had been pre-9/11.

A spit of land on the near horizon embraced a succession of inbound flights, three planes slamming onto the runway with graceful brutality within the space of an hour. As it was, I needed to reach the airport to see if my lost-in-transit backpack had been traced. However, it was impossible to gain access from the waterfront, hence why I had to backtrack half a mile before slicing inland to the main road strung between Kuta Beach and Denpasar Airport. As I promenaded past a beautiful Hindu temple, outside of which square trays of offerings had been laid, a motorbike-straddling man swerved in front of me, pulling up outside a resort. Something seemed to be amiss with his neck. On the surface, it was badly sunburnt. Worse than that, there was something else making its presence felt on his skin. It couldn't fail to attract attention. 'Do you realise there's something on your neck?' I asked him as I readied myself to read the wave-battered beach its last rights. 'What? Like a spot?' Not knowing how to break the untamed truth of the matter, I chose my words carefully. 'It looks more like a monkey.' His broad grin looked at odds once squared up against my grimace of shock. 'Ha! This little fella's been hanging on for dear life for a few days now. I've kind of adopted him. He's too tame and too cute to leave on the wayside. I'm even letting him stay with me in my hotel.' Swallowing my surprise, I'd evidently heard it all. The man subsequently strode over to the pool bar. Taking its non-verbal cue, the monkey sprung off his neck to frolic beside the water, keen to show off in front of his newfound father. Lapping up the stunts being executed, the man smiled with pride. It was only then I realised how surreal the situation appeared to be. Cringing, I left them to it, stunned by the intense bonds humans have the capacity to forge with animals, and vice versa.

Facing an hour-long trek to the airport, I collected my thoughts and fortified my patience, praying that a miracle had lured my backpack out of the ether. If it still hadn't arrived from KL, I fancied staging a hunger-strike to prove a point. Shame I was ravenous... and pity I possessed no willpower.

~

'MAN! DON'T WORRY! BORROW MY BIKE AND TAKE A FERRY TO LOMBOK!'

Suan's maniacally-delivered proposal was tempting to be

sure. But did I trust myself with a faster bike than a bog-standard scooter? Suavely erring on the side of caution, I considered all options before declining his undeniably kind offer, deciding instead to take a shuttle bus to Sanur before hopping onto a public ferry as a foot passenger. I could always rent a motorbike once I got there. As things stood, I was stuck on Bali until 'Air Asia' reunited me with my backpack. According to them, it had been accidentally transferred to Solo City on Java. Inconveniently for me, there were no direct 'AA' flights between there and Denpasar, so my beloved backpack had to be sent back to Kuala Lumpur. Ironically, my luggage had suddenly become better-travelled than me, having been shunted from Malaysia to Indonesia, then back to Malaysia in anticipation of a second coming amidst the ultimate archipelago of adventure.

I'd first met Suan at Beverley Folk Festival in England. He ran a stall via which he sold an assortment of handicrafts lovingly produced in Indonesia. In the wake of purchasing a handful of bracelets, we got chatting, agreeing to keep in touch. Seven months later, there I was... on Bali, Suan's place of birth; his home. Although he was unable to show me around due to work commitments, he rushed to meet me for a round of beers, though we missed one another the first time around due to my guesthouse address being mis-communicated. It seemed there was more than one 'Taman Ayu' guesthouse in Kuta.

We eventually hooked up at a 'Mini Mart'. Craving an ice-cold 'Bintang', the shop seemed the most logical place to go in order to score bottled beer on the cheap. In hindsight, the atmosphere outside the 'MM' buzzed with just as much energy as the main bar scene did a mile back from the beachfront. That's the great thing about 'Circle K' and 'Mini Mart' outlets in Kuta: the majority of them have forecourt benches so you can eat and drink within easy reach of enough cut-price booze to bring a band of raging alcoholics to its ready-grazed knees. Furthermore, you're in luck if you've got a laptop, for free Wi-Fi is often available to customers.

The act of swigging beer outside a shop might lack a certain degree of sophistication, but the cost of beer in bars and clubs on Bali is scandalous. In any case, Suan was driving, and it was tough to find a decent parking place. He'd already encountered problems with his grey people-carrier, having got stuck within the narrow nightmare that is Poppies Lane. Indeed, there are only a few places along its length where vehicles can safely pass. Suan succeeded in staking a parking place in front of a hotel. Escaping the lane became our downfall upon crawling into the unforgiving beams of an oncoming car. A minute-long mutiny led to hand gestures from Suan. The man in the other car had no choice but to reverse the necessary two-hundred yards to the main road in order to let us through. To our right, a vehicle was attempting to leave 'Kuta Puri Bungalows'. It was a two-pronged attack; options were limited. Suppressing his frustration, Suan nudged forward far enough for our nearest neighbour to ease behind, out of the resort. Suan's graceless five-point turn at least enabled him to reverse into the resort's courtyard, thereby liberating the inconsiderate protagonist who refused to retreat a single inch. It was thirsty work. Suan was visibly relieved to make it back to the beachfront without his new vehicle sustaining any dents or scratches. He'd just bought it for his job as a tour guide. Its spacious interior could comfortably seat at least four passengers. He confided that he was busy with bookings as a result of his aunt who owned and ran a guesthouse. In time-honoured style, she recommended his services to her guests, ninety per cent of whom were holidaying Australians. Even though he would miss spending summers in the UK at festivals of Glastonbury's ilk, Suan confessed that he required a stable job which paid well. His hard-working attitude and personable nature would bear him in good stead as he built his reputation through word-of-mouth in tandem with a flashy website designed to further promote the tours on offer. His greatest asset boiled down to the fact he knew Bali as well as a bureaucrat knows paperwork. He vowed to escort tourists and travellers to off-the-beaten-track sites of wondrous beauty that very few visitors to the Indonesian island get to savour. In that respect, he was the best kind of guide, sagely fusing history and geography to a myth-shrouded range of legends.

We picked up a couple of beers for twenty-eight thousand rupiahs: approximately two British pounds per bottle. It was just after nine; the party was just getting started. Opposite us, a couple of guys mixed Coke with whiskey, only too happy to chat. Differences in linguistic capabilities initially inspired widespread confusion. Suan assumed the role of translator, passionately spouting off in both English and Balinese, the latter a Malayo-Polynesian language spoken by approximately four million people. I asked the guys if they spoke any other languages. In stunted English, the youngest of them nodded, mouthing what I mistakenly took to be 'Japanese'. Awed by their grasp of such an alien language, I asked him if he'd ever visited Tokyo. 'No, you misunderstand. I speak Javanese, not Japanese!' The hulk of an island anchored due west of Bali, Java plays host to the capital of Indonesia in the form of Jakarta, regularly voted as one of the world's ugliest conurbations for its sins.

Indulging in a four-way-conversation, we swapped stories with as much vitality as we passed around our mixed-up cache of beer and spirits. Glancing over the road to the sea wall that comprehensively shields even the slightest glimpse of Kuta Beach, I wondered if Suan was much of a surfer. 'I'm a mountain boy at heart. I'm scared of the water and not a strong swimmer. I prefer to have my head in the clouds instead of in the deep blue.' When it came to extolling the integrity of nature on terra firma, he was a thirty-something man after my own altitude-adoring heart. 'Surfing's fun, but its novelty dies if you don't cultivate patience,' Suan related. 'If I were you, I would head north to Ubud to see the temples and rice paddies. Beyond there, terrain becomes increasingly mountainous and wild. I only wish I had a day off to show you the most beautiful corners of my magical island.' He then admitted that he was feeling somewhat sluggish. It was the third of January: his body was still reeling from a heady New Year's Eve party that had cost a whopping eight-hundred thousand rupiahs to penetrate. 'I hit the beer hard, you know. It hit me back with twice as much force.' No wonder he aspired to take it steady. Two bottles later, it was time to seek authentic food.

Readying ourselves to leave, Suan listed other spiritually invigorating places in Indonesia. 'If you jump on an early morning shuttle bus to Sanur, you'll be able to catch the cheap "slow ferry" to Nusa Lembongan from the northern end of Sanur Beach. Once you reach the island, get yourself over to Jungutbatu. Check out Mushroom Bay and Dream Beach if you can. Kick back for a couple of days before moving on to Lombok and the Gili Islands. Your jaw will drop, Steve. The beaches, the forests, the locals, the vibes: they all help to produce heaven on earth.' Allowing me to neck the last half of his second bottle, Suan was fighting fit behind the wheel. Cruising parallel to the beach before swerving inland, we halted in front of a roadside stall vending food. Officially ravenous beyond respite, Suan ordered two plates heaped with plain rice, noodles and vegetables. The proverbial icing on the cake came in the form of two yellowed hunks of fried chicken. Desperate for a protein fix, I munched on the legs like an animal, yet the ferocity of Suan's appetite saw him clear his plate long before

I scooped the final grain of rice from mine. Chasing our food with iced tea, we reflected on what had been a humble but hilarious night outside the 'Mini Mart'. We'd been so engrossed in discussing Balinese culture that time had seemingly dissolved in the space between the past, present and future. That's why it came as a shock when Suan announced he had to hit the road speeding. It had gone midnight. He needed to be up at seven to start the day with his tour group by nine. Pointing me back towards Poppies Lane, he promised to meet me at my guesthouse the following evening for what I hoped would be an action-packed follow-up to what had joyously preceded.

He drove; I walked; we waved. As my gentle footfalls echoed along the deserted lane, I ruminated and concluded: any given place can only ever be as awe-inspiring as the people with which it's shared. Consumed by such a realisation, I slept long and deep through a new dawn of consciousness, dreaming about star-spangled pavements dating ghost-ridden beaches, and the beautiful but distant woman I loved above all else.

~

BALI IS CLOSER TO OZ than many people think. Little wonder then that the lush Indonesian island teems with Aussies on vacation. You can barely budge an inch in Kuta without hearing the Australian drawl. Worryingly, Indonesian men and women imitate Aussies by adding 'mate' to the tail-end of most sentences, whether they're making statements or posing questions. 'Yes, boss' is another phrase that's wiggled its way into casual street-talk. Fortunately, it has nothing to do with servitude; instead, it's projected in a comradely manner, trussing up trust.

So long as confrontations were avoided, I was content to

stalk the back lanes of Kuta, stunned at the plague of graffiti scarring walls. 'Love! Hate! Love!' screamed one particular burst spray-painted beside a ghoulish representation of Shiva. On Legian, the bars were hotting up, dancing girls strutting to rock anthems, trying to entice punters upstairs into soul-seizing darkness. 'Electric Avenue' promised live rock music every night. A rough-edged discotheque displayed placards advertising their best drinks deals, none of which were good value for money in any respect. Across the road, a lead guitar solo boomed through a stack of amps rooted to the pavement. The petite singer aimed to emulate Andrea Corr, her 'Breathless' version of The Corrs tune provoking a rumble of applause from the bar. Meanwhile, in a reggae gaffe a few steps away, a UB40 song smoothly surrendered itself to Pato Banton's nineties hit, 'Baby, I Love Your Way'.

Either side of the intense cluster of bars, shops sold a staggering range of genuine Indonesian articles offset by mass-produced tat fit only for the trash. The worst offender in the 'tat' department came in the form of a phallic can opener. Such novelty items might be regarded as good luck, supposedly having a positive impact on the owner's fertility, but they are hardly representative of the high-brow nature of the intricate crafts that most traditional Balinese artisans proudly uphold. As I marched towards the end of Poppies Lane, my eyes were accosted by 'Bintang' stubby holders, logo-laced vests, tour packages to Ubud, untrustworthy motorbikes for rent, and teen-aged girls offering 'special' massages.

On its high-octane surface, the road proved to be invigorating and exhausting in equal measure. A tang of seediness never failed to engulf it, many of the hustlers loitering at select points along its length as likely to slit your throat as shake your hand. Unable to afford a beer at Legian's bordering-on-extortionate prices, I swept a course past Kuta Square to the beach. Stamping onto the sand via a gap in the wall, I unconsciously clamped my eyes to an information board in reach of a giant replica turtle. The board highlighted the vein of action necessary in the event of an earthquake-triggering tsunami. A detailed map focused on evacuation routes extending from the beachfront. Cordoned into colour-coded zones, the red 'danger zone' consisted of the main road running parallel to the beach. Behind the red zone, the yellow zone constituted a safer haven, much further away from the waterfront. People were advised to seek shelter in high buildings if a tsunami warning sounded. On the downside, the board failed to divulge a single word about what to do should successive quakes plunge a balmy day at the beach to a juddering, no-nonsense halt.

A small temple complex sat camouflaged on the inside of a boardwalk curve. An ancient tree stretched its fantastically gnarled branches over the temple walls, presiding over the offerings placed at its entrance. Such 'offerings' are impossible to ignore around Kuta. It's not uncommon to see men and women lovingly preparing trays in kitchens, lounges, even in gutters. Primarily consisting of a selection of flower petals, smidgens of rice, a 'Ritz' cracker or two, and a jingle of loose change, the trays are left everywhere - not just in the immediate vicinity of temples. That in mind, watch your step: they can be placed on the beach, on steps, in the dizzying midst of busy road intersections, outside people's houses, and even on bottle-strewn ledges in sweaty bars. Given their widespread distribution, it's inevitable that some trays will be accidentally destroyed. Coincidentally, as I traipsed onto the sand, squeezing between a couple of stabiliser-clad boats, a motorbike sped over a tray of offerings, obliviously obliterating its prettily arranged contents. It's not that he didn't have any respect; he just didn't expect to see a tray in his path.

It was half-five in the afternoon: arguably the best time of day to hit the beach. Cool enough to tolerate, I whipped through the sand, skipping towards the surf. The tide was out, leaving a twenty-yard shelf of compacted sand which was a pleasure to walk upon. Although the sun embedded itself in a tongue of dirty clouds to irk those who worshipped the flaming star, it soon burst through the bottom of such clouds, bouncing rose-hued ripples of pure magic across the ever-darkening sky. Unperturbed by the loss of natural light, surfers continued to ride waves in sight of full-scale football matches. Heartened by the fact there was no sudden drop in temperature, I slowly backtracked, my peripheral vision overwhelmed by Sheraton's crane-tamed project every time I tore my eyes from the sea, the sky, the divide. Due west, planes lined up, gagging to be beckoned forth by Air Traffic Control at Denpasar Airport. Distant blinking lights drew attention to the bulk of their landing gears, the lowering of which amplified inbound passengers' hopes and fears.

The air smelt sweeter than usual. The sand looked cleaner than normal. My heart soared higher than ever. My friends had already flown east to Labuan Bajo. From there, they relayed 'Facebook' updates about their jealousy-arousing diving exploits. They planned to head back in the direction of Bali over the course of the coming week. I aspired to reach Lombok in the meantime. Our trajectories were bound to intersect.

~

'HE'S BEEN ON THE ROAD TWENTY YEARS. He travels until he's bankrupt, then he gets a job for a while before heading elsewhere.' I was talking to Myrthe from Groningen. Poised to undertake a three-legged journey back to Europe via Jakarta and Dubai, she'd waddled into the roadside eatery where I was munching on a bowl of rice and noodles. She looked shattered, having wrestled her huge backpack to the floor as though her bronzed legs were about to buckle. 'Yes, so this guy I met... he's from England,' she warbled on. Discussing the pros and cons of 'freebird' lifestyles, Myrthe admitted that she'd never be able to commit herself to long-term life on the move. 'I want to settle down and have kids. My boyfriend and I are studying right now, but we'll want to start a family in a few years.' She was taking a course in nutrition; he was living as part of a small community in Papua. 'I think if you spend a lot of time travelling, it gets harder for you to stop. You get used to making friends and then saying goodbye to them after a while. It becomes a mental challenge to adapt, to lay down roots.'

I wanted the best of both worlds and told her as much. I aspired to travel and yet remain grounded for as long as my heart allowed me to sustain such a dual lifestyle. I argued that it was possible to see the world whilst cultivating love and supporting a family on a tiny patch of its surface. In many respects, we saw eye to eye. She talked sense, and I found it difficult to believe that she was on the verge of finishing her very first trip outside Europe. She gave me the impression that she'd been travelling from a very young age.

We parted ways after an hour-long chat. She needed to reach the airport; I needed to tame a wild mutant of a manuscript set in America that I'd been diligently chipping away at, obsessed with sculpting something beautiful yet true. I empathised with what she'd said about the emotional upheaval associated with leaving friends, knowing there would be no chance of ever seeing them again unless by a minor miracle. A friend of mine appreciated the risks involved: facing the dilemma of a lifetime, he'd opted to pursue an expedition at risk of losing his Colombian girlfriend for good. I, too, had metaphorically fornicated with fate.

I stepped out into the mid-afternoon heat, conscious that a rainstorm was primed to unleash its refreshing fury within the hour. Out west, over the sea, gross banks of grey clouds steeled themselves for a furious downpour to treasure. Venturing out to find a universal plug adaptor in spite of the leaden skies, I took shelter beneath the yawning awning of a restaurant when the inevitable came to pass. Just like Mr. T used to love it when a plan came together, restaurant owners and shop-keepers love it when wet season presents its daily outburst: those caught out usually have no choice but to duck into whatever building is closest. Unless you're wearing minimal clothing and have zero possessions to hand, such rainstorms must be avoided: they saturate in seconds.

Accompanied by uprisings of thunder, the rain pulsed along the street, considering all drainage options. Inches fell within minutes, the majority of thoroughfares becoming dangerously inundated. I sheltered for an hour, allowing the cycle to relay the water to the next stage of its remarkably efficient system so it could drain back to the sea ready for the following day when the sun would reheat it again, causing it to evaporate and form clouds. In a similar vein to the circle of life, the water cycle heralded a deadly climax that deserved to be respected and embraced regardless of its intimidating nature. Once the worst part of the storm had passed, people proved eager to resume their routines, a sickening wave of bikes zipping through ankle-deep puddles, impatience shaking their compromised motors. Meanwhile, stalls selling heavy-duty umbrellas continued to make a killing, not by swiping potential customers around the heads with their handles, but by offloading them at what groups of naïve Australians believed to be genuine cut-price rates.

I followed the water every step of the way. It naturally led me towards the beach. Exiting Poppies Lane in the shadow of a gargantuan construction site, I was momentarily reminded of Vegas. Glancing further along the beachfront, four separate projects were in full swing, antiquated cranes reaching out over the beach, mimicking the 'grabber' in *Toy Story*, primed to pluck unsuspecting bathers from loungers. To all intents and purposes, Kuta's waterfront was in turmoil. An eyesore of unimaginable proportions, it certainly didn't represent paradise in my eyes.

The 'Sheraton' project was the largest and loudest. Very little could be seen of what was going on behind the high white fence surrounding the site. All I could glimpse was an earth-violating excavation so wide and deep it looked as though the hotel chain was more concerned with mineral mining than laying foundations. Springing out from behind a security checkpoint, a young boy prodded a handful of beaded wristbands in my face, jumping as high as his stubby legs would allow, perhaps conscious that the closer a product is to a person, the more inclined they'll be to buy it. Fearing that he was an orphaned street urchin who was nonetheless exceptionally gifted at producing traditional trinkets, I scanned the parched grass beyond the checkpoint, spying his young mother cradling a newborn. Aware that the opal-encrusted band would pose as a wonderful gift, I asked the boy, 'How much?' His face lit up in response to my interest. 'One-hundred thousand rupiahs!' he confidently yawped. Appearances could be deceptive after all. Instead of being a cute lad of about five, he was in fact a ruthless business-boy, working at his mother's behest to support the ever-enlarging family unit. 'Ten-thousand!' I bargained, stretching the band over my hand, trying it on for size. Without consulting his mum, he nodded with so much vigour that I unconsciously massaged my neck, experiencing 'sympathy pains' as part of the deal.

I handed over an appropriate note. Sultan Mahmud Badaruddin II's stern face caught my eye as the boy snatched the note bearing his image. The warning was too little, too late. I'd still been ripped off. The name of the

Sultan depicted on the ten-thousand rupiah note had captured my imagination, however. I pondered, could Rudd be a derivative of Badaruddin? If that was the case, perhaps I was in line for unspeakable riches. Buoyed by hope, I promptly wedged myself in the corner of an Internet café over-promoting daily tours to Mount Bromo. With the image of the moustachioed Sultan imprinted on my mind, I unveiled the genealogist in me. It was time to undertake a dash of research.

~

I'D BECOME EVERYTHING I DESPISED; I'D BECOME WOEFULLY PREDICTABLE. Even worse, I was apparently unrelated to Badaruddin. I should have been in Sanur, yet I'd based myself in Kuta for six days. Mind you, I had an excuse: my backpack had gone AWOL, and I was holding out hope that the airline might still be able to locate it, even though Achmad - with whom I'd been liaising - lamented that roughly one-hundred and fifty flights passed through KL every day. Chances of it showing up were slim. I thanked him for his fickle vote of confidence.

Annexed to 'Salon May', a beauty parlour of repute, the 'Taman Ayu' complex ironically didn't boast a single bungalow. What it did possess in abundance was a range of spacious apartments shackled to a bizarre pricing structure. A single room cost ninety-thousand rupiahs per day, while a double room (which was the same size) cost one-hundred and seventy thousand. Usually, single rooms cost almost as much as double rooms, so it made a change not to feel as though I was paying over the odds. Arranged around a central courtyard, the apartments wielded en-suite facilities and overhead fans, although I invested minimal trust in the latter 'perk' as I reclined to write. The central shaft wobbled to such an extent that the fan blades circled at bizarre angles. I dreaded to imagine what the net effect might be if the fan plummeted from the ceiling whilst revolving at top speed. Were it to land on my face, I doubted the consequences would be pleasant.

The three guys running 'Taman Ayu' were all in their twenties. Presumably the owner's sons, they lounged and larked about when not attending to the needs of guests. Giving the impression that they were Emo-expounding surfers, their interests were reflected in their fashion, with caps, black T-shirts, cut-off denim shorts, and a multitude of piercings on show at all times. Whenever I saw them together as a band of brothers, they reminded me of Sober, the resident rock band at the 'Hard Rock Café'. Proud of Bali, they were only too willing to extol the island's virtues, recommending a trip to the Batur area in the mountainous north to see the lake if nothing else. We chatted over breakfast, a tea and toastie-based meal that could be enjoyed in one's room or up on a pagoda-styled eating area set on two levels. Shedding my made-in-Mumbai sandals, I swung my legs onto the main platform, sheltered by a pointed wooden roof. Consisting of a painted expanse of wood, the platform housed a central table. Unused to dining whilst hunched in the Lotus Position, I concentrated just as much on maintaining my straight-backed posture as I did on the freewheeling conversation. Beside me, John from Mozambique munched on his toastie with menace, keen to explore Bali by bike. Between open-mouthed bursts of chewing, he confided that he was fresh from Thailand, having partied his way along Pattaya's infamous Walking Street on New Year's Eve. He then told me he was in the import-export business. I quickly changed the subject, unwilling to be embroiled in what could have potentially amounted to smuggling. I trusted him, but my guard nevertheless remained up - just in case. A burly man in his mid-thirties, he was kind enough to pass me his contact details. 'Call me if you ever make it to Mozambique. Where I live, it's easy to get into Malawi. South Africa can be reached by car in less time than you think. Then there's Lesotho: a country within a country.' I thanked him as he unfurled his legs and slid off the platform. Timing things perfectly, a young couple arrived as John sloped towards the street, fumbling in his pockets for his motorbike key. Having been deprived of travel talk for four days since Simon and Sheetha had flown east, I clinched every chatty gambit going. The couple introduced themselves whilst in the throes of enquiring about room availability. David and Anne, from Ireland and France respectively, had just flown in from Oz. As shattered as they were ravenous, they were disappointed to learn that all the apartments were full. Regardless, they stayed for breakfast, vying to get the low-down on Bali. I confessed that I'd not left the Kuta area once since becoming an honorary islander. 'I just can't seem to leave,' I chuckled, not overly worried by the fact I had less than three weeks to experience as much of Indonesia as I could before stampeding into Malaysia. 'I'm a self-made prisoner, dying to see more, but reluctant to edge into the unknown.' I didn't know what had come over me. It was as though somebody else was talking. By trade, I was a globe-pounding travel-writer, yet the motivation to move on had escaped me for the first time in a decade.

David and Anne proceeded to regale me with stories from their travels in South America, comically focusing on the eccentric toilet habits of certain Bolivians they'd encountered. While David dashed over the road to see if he could bargain for a room, I continued chatting to Anne. It transpired that she hailed from Poitiers. I told her I'd visited her hometown in 2006, going so far as to describe the hostel in which I'd stayed, on the outskirts, near a water tower. Judging by her vacant stare, she was unfamiliar with the grey suburbs. David returned with good news: accommodation was available less than twenty yards away. In the wake of reminiscing about fruit-picking in Queensland, they scooted to the far side of Poppies Lane to sign in, leaving me with the rest of the day to creatively slay.

Unearthing nothing on my mental agenda, I kowtowed to something of a routine which had established itself without me even noticing. As per usual after breakfast, I stamped down to the beach before negotiating the network of back lanes to a cheap Internet café. It had become a second home while I'd been in Kuta. There, I busily uploaded my latest clutch of stories. Avoiding the afternoon's cursed lashing of rain, I ventured along Legian, shaking my head every time shady guys delved into their pockets to proffer small boxes of 'Viagra'. I hopped over the road beyond 'Bounty Discotheque', only to fall foul of two bouncers stood outside the 'Engine Room' club. 'You want to dance or rock out?' asked the beefiest of the duo. 'Neither,' I revealed. 'I just want to get some food.' Next door, I was offered dreadlock repairs by a man who evidently assumed I was the most gullible traveller ever to have cultivated temporary roots in Kuta. 'I give you dreadlock repairs for cheap price, boss!' Had he looked up from his urgent pawing of the *Bali Advertiser*, he'd have seen that I barely had any hair on my head, let alone a tangle of dreadlocks awaiting urgent hands-on attention. Perched behind a glass counter, he prided himself on being as ignorant and rude as he was shamelessly crude. His counter was covered in a hodge-podge of mildly amusing yet often shockingly distasteful stickers, a selection of which capitalised on being more offensive than Ali G's sense of humour crossed with Dave Allen's penchant for sex-sensitive wordplay. 'EX-WIFE FOR SALE' and 'TOUGHEN UP PRINCESS' ruled the roost as two of the least-offensive slogans to raise a smile.

Shunning the man's shop, I tottered up to the nearest 'Circle K' store where I picked up my own copy of the *Advertiser*. Having been seduced by the island in less than a week, I considered searching for work in order to stave off bankruptcy. I asked the cashier how much the paper cost. 'No charge,' he grinned. 'It is free?' I double-checked. 'Correct, boss!' he shot back. It wasn't the only thing that was free.

~

AT LEAST THE VACATIONING FRENCH GIRLS CONSIDERED IT FUNNY. I, on the other hand, was literally being driven to distraction, around and around in circles, getting to know the impossibly narrow lanes of Kuta more intimately than I would have liked. For the past hour I'd waited patiently for a Sanur-bound shuttle bus which never came. Literary fodder came in the form of *Shantaram*. I gamely crunched through page after page as plumes of water poured over the eaves of a huge construction project unapologetically raging beside the beach-fronting 'McDonald's'.

The shuttle bus, when it eventually arrived, assumed the guise of a mini-van. Tiredly snatching a cursory glance at the so-called boot, it was obvious that my freshly-recovered backpack didn't stand a chance of being wedged into the gap between the stained back seat and the artistically dented door. The driver tried to fit it in nonetheless, ignoring my cries of protest. 'Please be careful... there's a "Netbook" in there,' I wheezed in horror as he slammed the boot against the front of my backpack. I was sure I heard a crack, but it was neither the time nor place to unpack my belongings to check.

We were trapped. As anybody who has ever spent time on Poppies Lane will be aware, it's a nightmare for drivers. Having spent over two minutes attempting to stow my pack in the back, trails of traffic had massed on both sides of the van, leaving the driver with no choice but to meekly indulge in a temporary stakeout in a random yard. Apologising for his lateness, he excused himself by lamenting that two of his drivers had let him down, hence why he had to resourcefully filter three routes into one. On the upside, Sanur was slated to be the first stop. However, he first needed to pick up a couple of travellers from an undisclosed location. Believing the couple to be residing in a guesthouse off Legian, he swung into the gaffe's courtyard... to be greeted by nothing but a cluster of gently swaying palm trees. Wrong place, it seemed. Cultivating a brainwave, he took his chances along a road running at a right angle to Legian. Distressingly, there was nobody at the second guesthouse either. As the driver grew increasingly impatient, the French girls slapped their right palms upon their mouths, ironically amused that he was going to so much trouble to locate the stray passengers-to-be. 'Ooh-la-la!' the girl beside me giggled, taking her time to frown upon my apparently unkempt appearance, panning her gaze back from him - the Luckless Driver - to yours truly: the Funky Buddha. I fired an unscrupulous look of withering ire in her oh-so-sophisticated direction, intimating that I was kidding by realigning my exaggeratedly arched eyebrows.

We'd so far exchanged mere pleasantries, the la-di-da-doting French girls and I. Sensing they would rather tumble down a well than speak English, I fused my lips together in a juvenile act of defiance that could only ever deepen hostilities. Not even a hearty blast of Pidgin English was going to sweeten their uptight tongues. That's why I did something very stupid indeed: I began to talk in French. It had been six months since I'd last exercised my lyrical license in the language as a result of staying in the beautiful Dordogne region of France. Homme, I was taking a risk, prepared to feminise the masculine.

'Ou habites-tu?' I asked the girl to my left. She could have been a robot sent from the future to kill me for all I knew. I still hadn't caught sight of her eyes; in spite of the overcast weather, she refused to remove her shades. They were so huge they resembled a pair of goggles. 'Mais Paris!' she responded. 'Why the "but"?' I countered, confused by her answer. 'La butte?' she replied, wrinkling her nose, subtly implying that she would prefer silence over small talk boasting scant substance. Deftly changing the subject, I went on. 'Sanur?' If my mind was honest with my tongue, it was at a total loss for words. It simply didn't have the willpower to craft meaningful sentences. Believing me to be asking after her name, she finally lowered her shades. 'My name is irrelevant,' she whispered, lurching into 'spy fantasy' territory with a distinct lack of accomplices. So she could speak English after all! Setting affairs straight, I confessed that I'd meant to ask her where she and her friend were going. 'Mais Ubud!' she sourly stated, pushing her shades back over her eyes before turning to face the tinted window. God, her world must have been dark.

We eventually located the missing travellers a few blocks from where we'd launched our search. So much for so many of Kuta's guesthouses sporting such similar names. As soon as the newbies had squeezed onto the back seat, we were off, bucking forward towards Sanur, roughly ten kilometres distant as the proverbial crow flew. Unsurprisingly, an uneasy silence blossomed, engulfing every inch of seat space. The tension only intensified at a roundabout when a man selling papers sprinted towards the van. Fearing some kind of reprisal, our driver activated the internal locking mechanism, preventing the man from opening any of the doors. But all he wanted to do was sell a paper or two! His intentions were entirely innocent, unless the man behind the wheel knew different. Driving the same route every day, perhaps he'd become privy to secret knowledge concerning the newspaper-seller's ulterior motives. His shoulder-heaped array of tabloids and spreadsheets was perhaps a front for underhand car-jacking exploits. If that was the case, we were lucky; we were in a van.

Signs for various resorts tore up the roadside, pointing down almost every alley known to Bali. There's certainly no shortage of accommodation on the island. I was eventually deposited outside a 'McDonald's' on the corner of a road intersection. Ironically, there didn't appear to be a single guesthouse in sight. In the hurried wake of bundling my backpack into the gutter, the driver told me to jump out and scoot on my way before he got fined by the traffic police. He'd halted in a 'no parking' zone.

In truth, I felt let down. Having spent thirty-five thousand rupiahs for my ticket, I protested that I'd only been given half a ride. The travel agent had sincerely looked me in the eyes whilst assuring me that the drop-off point was within a bottle's lob from the disembarkation point for ferries motoring over to the idyllic island of Nusa Lembongan. It was a tragic shame I never got to argue my point: the second I backed my pack and spun on my heels, the driver doffed his frayed cap, accelerating in crass 'Fast and Furious' style. Left for dust, and shaking from thirst, I trudged due east towards the beach, bustling past the hustlers, mentally manhandling my options. As pensive as ever, I wondered: should I stay, or should I row?

~

I WAS GOING TO HAVE TO DRAW THE LINE SOMEWHERE. Having traipsed around the outskirts of Sanur for two and a half hours, my back buckled in disgust at the way it was being treated. And I thought finding a cheap place to stay would have been easy... at least a little easier than it had been in Kuta. I knew I was wasting my time at the hotels. There were no rooms available for less than two-hundred and fifty thousand rupiahs per night: approximately eighteen pounds. As I grew increasingly disillusioned, I asked if a compromise could be embraced, begging each receptionist to surrender the smallest and grittiest room in their respective establishments for half the pre-quoted price. After trying my luck at every single hotel along three roads tearing away from the beach at right angles to the meandering boardwalk, I stumbled past a beleaguered Information Desk. For once, the cheerful man behind it harboured no intention of thumping me with the hard-sell about fast-boat trips to Lombok or diving options around Gili Trawangan. Perhaps he was the only person working within the tertiary sector not to be on commission. Failing that, he was simply a straight-up kind of guy, pleased to be of service regardless of the situation.

My stooped posture must have been the most obvious thing highlighting my plight. He could clearly sense I was desperate to find a room. I barely had the energy to greet him with a handshake over his leaflet-laden counter. 'You should ask for rooms at "homestays", my friend.' Taking his complimentary suggestion on-board, I paced the necessary forty yards beyond a 'Circle K' to a streak of gravel below a welcoming sign. Pointing to a 'homestay' along a lane, I turned and waddled forth, praying that a room would be ready and waiting for less than one-hundred thousand rupiahs. Shockingly, the prices of rooms at the 'homestay' were two and a half times the price I wanted to pay.

It was back to the drawing board. Having said that, I might have had more fun literally drawing the bored. Curiously, Aussie holidaymakers looked grumpy, in spite of being well-fed, watered, and bronzed. It was rare to clock anybody cracking a smile. I'd noticed the same on Kuta Beach:

foreigners of all ages trudged across the sand or buried their noses in novels, pained expressions plastered across their slowly-burning visages. I couldn't help but wonder why those reading were being so consciously ignorant of the beauty surrounding them. Had they not worked their fingers to the bone for the past year in order to save up for their holiday? Had the travel agent's brochures depicting blue skies, scintillating surf, and cute beach bungalows done the reality of the place a gross disservice? Had they not wanted to escape from reality, to iron anxieties upon lush acres of paradise? If that was the case, then why did they actively ignore the inescapable beauty, the fun-loving Indonesians, and the respect-anchored culture within eyeshot? Although they were baking upon plastic loungers 'in body', some men evidently preferred to be fighting for their lives with Chris Ryan in gun-battling spirit. Women, meanwhile, seemed happy - or unhappy, as the case may have been - to compare their lives to those lived by characters polluting throw-away chick-lit. 'Look!' I felt like imploring. 'Look at the bounty in every direction - and then look even closer.' Nature never failed to awe me. I was staggered by its variety and the way its delicate ecosystems nurtured life, be it in animal or plant form. Even though I was flagging, I still invested time in observing the minutiae, paying as much attention to detail as ever, longing to be able to reach 'rambutan' from wall-shielded trees as I pursued the main road around an invitingly curvaceous corner. At the far side of the concourse, a 'homestay' shared its premises with a massage parlour. Having unwittingly stayed in similar places in Thailand, I was sceptical about the potential set-up, but I carefully cut through the motorbike-dominated traffic to launch enquiries about room rates. Treading a path between three teen-aged masseuses, I hastened to find the proprietor. A lady promptly emerged from an agency promoting cruises to Lombok. It transpired that room prices were considerably cheaper within the accommodating grasp of 'Lila', so I booked in after bargaining the nightly rate down from one-hundred and ten thousand rupiahs to the far more attractive figure of one-hundred. As with most rooms in Indonesia, two beds came as standard. A heap of 'Chippendale' furniture was also included in the price, although I had no idea what use I might have for the intricately carved dressing table.

Famished, I threw my backpack onto the nearest bed and hit the streets of Sanur in search of food and drink. Avoiding pricey restaurants serving steak and chips, I bowled up to a dark cellar of a roadside dwelling, egged on by its chalkboard menu. Steamed rice cost just three-thousand rupiahs. Even better, I could order a steaming bowl of 'chicken foot soup' for just six-thousand, or 'fish head soup' for seven. Faced with such a conservative menu, it was a tough call. The startling lack of choice reminded me of a sun-drenched weekend spent on the svelte Croatian island of Korcula: the sole budget-friendly café didn't even have a menu, for it served nothing but cheeseburgers. Craving a punchy fix of protein, I made my order before reaching the greasy chef hogging the serving hatch. For once, unruly decisiveness took over. 'Sorry, but we do not cook until later,' echoed the reply to my plea for chicken feet. Now where had I put that drawing board?

I followed the road around another corner. Grand entrances to beachfront resorts assaulted my vision on the left. To my right, a money-hungry parade of tour operators, bar girls and shop-owners began to unfold their stool-planted bodies, greeting me with a diet of fake smiles engineered to dupe me into pandering to their generic sales pitches. One unit offered 'Complimentary Therapies' around the clock. Indulge? It would have been rude not to: it's not every day complementary therapies are free, owing to a lethal spelling mistake on the business owner's head. Astounded by the amount of 'Absolut Vodka' for sale in roadside racks, I wondered if many people got busted by traffic cops for drinking and motoring. Fancying a slurp of raw spirit, I asked how much a bottle cost. 'Thirty-thousand,' replied a female rack-supporter. 'You have bike?' she went on to ask. 'No - I just want a drink.' If only I'd known the vodka bottles contained fuel, such vessels playing their part in the recycling process with consummate flair. It's just fortunate that alcohol was still present, albeit in a less drinkable state. Coughing up a shot, I dreaded to imagine how my head might feel in the morning. But that would be the least of my worries. My liver would surely be incommunicado.

~

'HARDY! I'M LOOKING FOR A HARDY! I DON'T SUPPOSE YOU KNOW A HARDY, DO YOU?'

Suan had specifically said he would 'be with Hardy at eight,' but the rest of his message had been somewhat vague, akin to instructions received on USS Alabama in *Crimson Tide*. I'd only just arrived in Sanur a few hours beforehand. I didn't know a single person in the area, let alone a guy called Hardy. I didn't even realise that my friend Suan lived just outside Sanur until he informed me of such a fact via 'Facebook'.

I proposed to catch up with him for a cold 'Bintang' or two. He suggested we meet 'with Hardy,' even though I'd have preferred to have hooked up outside where I was staying. But he knew best. That's why I wound up frantically pacing around the car park of a 'McDonald's', hoping that the fabled Hardy was a prominent shop or well-known restaurant instead of a random person who could be anywhere. 'Is there a Hardy close by?' I asked a man outside a walk-in ATM. Shocked to have been verbally accosted by a foreigner, he stepped back, almost flooring his at-ease motorbike. 'Well there's "Hardy's" department store,' he replied. As optimistic as I was ever destined to be, I pleaded for directions. Unable to relate them via language, he relied on gestures alone, pointing at the moon before punching his right arm over the nearest banana tree. Such directions were open to misinterpretation to say the least, but I could only presume that he meant for me to walk straight before hanging a right. If that was the case, it meant the store was back in the direction from which I'd marched... way, way beyond my guesthouse.

I glanced at my watch. It was a quarter to eight. Curses, I stammered to myself. I hated being late and letting people down, so it was time to get a shift on. Within five minutes, I was retracing my steps past 'Lila', feeling as guilty as ever for shaking my head when the demure masseuse outside politely asked if I desired a massage. I raced around the corner, past the dive of a restaurant which sold little more than 'chicken foot soup' and instant noodles. Wheeling up to a sun-kissed surfer, I begged for location-specific confirmation that I was heading the right way. 'Sure thing,' he drawled, 'just keep on going.' A few corners further on, and there it was: a shopper's utopia. There was no mistaking the neon sign out front of the complex, just like there was no mistaking the absence of Suan. My watch sorely whispered: eight o'clock on the dot. I ducked into the car park, past the security box. In a 4X4, a woman sullenly removed makeup from her face, subliminally admitting defeat. Reflecting in her rear view mirror, her eyes were the saddest I'd ever seen.

A sleek black motorbike chugged across the forecourt. Judging by the way its front wheel made a beeline for my defenceless shins, it knew me - or at least its rider did. 'Steve!' It was Suan all right, armed with his usual grin-heavy greeting. 'Sorry I'm late, mate. My friend was supposed to come down too, you know - but he can't make it because he's ill.' Forgiving him his belated appearance, I hopped on the back of his bike as instructed, psychologically preparing myself for a neck-snapping burst of sheer acceleration from the get-go. 'You got a helmet, man?' he shouted back. I didn't even have a bike, so why would I be in possession of a skull-saver? 'No, but perhaps I could borrow one from my guesthouse. I think they have spares,' I offered. 'Cool! We'll stop there later. Let's find a bar first!'

In terms of bars, we were positively spoilt for choice. Sanur rivals even Kuta for the quantity and quality of watering holes at its disposal. Choosing one of his favourite haunts, Suan led me into 'Lazer Sportsbar', a spacious joint at the heart of which a rowdy family of Aussies salivated over the size of the steaks they'd just been served. Football was playing on one of the big screens to the left of the stage. Suan and I slid onto a couple of bar stools while I ordered a large bottle of 'Bintang' each. Arguably the tastiest beer in Indonesia, it's a household name, immortalised through the excessive amount of vests bearing its logo which are aimed at booze-addled tourists. Adapting to the bar's laid-back rhythm, I asked Suan: 'So where's the best place in the country to catch a football match?' Although he was mid-gulp, he laughed heartily, unintentionally spurting beer out the side of his mouth, amused by my interest in Indonesian football. 'The best place to see a good game is on the beach!' he beamed, offering me a cigarette whilst phone-juggling.

'There's a girl I want you to meet. An old friend who lives on the Sanur outskirts with her Kiwi husband. She's a writer, too.' This followed ten minutes of silence during which time Suan's concentration had been compromised by texting. Fortunately, a rock band had struck up. Jack-knifing their way through a crossbred set of pop and rock tunes, their funky fashion sense supported their musical prowess. Aching for a game of pool, Suan and I edged closer to the table in the corner to see how a ten-year-old prodigy fared against his father.

They were still playing thirty minutes later, by which time we'd treated our palettes to two beers. 'Let's go, man!' Suan yelped. It was seemingly time for a ride into the unknown.

En-route, we stopped at my guesthouse to grab a helmet. In spite of confusing the proprietor, he eventually let down his guard, having accepted that I had no desire to hire a bike for fifty-thousand rupiahs. A lone helmet would suit me fine, with or without a visor. In truth, it didn't suit me in the least. It didn't even fit. Was my head bigger than the average Indonesian's? Accepting that the answer was beyond both myself and non-judgemental laws of the universe, I resaddled, trying in vain to adjust the helmet's strap before Suan gave the burgeoning breeze a run for its money. It was illegal to ride without a helmet upon a bike of his calibre. On scooters, it was fine, but his bike roared into a different, faster, scarier gully of injurious contention.

'You ready?' he asked, glancing behind to search for an opening in the labouring traffic. My 'no' was evidently whipped away, for he revved and rolled without double-checking to see if I was sat tight with my hands gripping the tiny rail crowning the back of his bike. With the useless helmet still in my hands, I couldn't have been any less prepared. But it was too late. Cutting into a wildly eddying stream of cars, scooters and bicycles, I forced the helmet down over my head as far as it was willing to go. I then gratefully gained purchase on the handhold. Sucking back on the dragonfly-pitted air, I looked ahead. Chewing up the miles, we zipped north, gallantly acquainting ourselves with The Dead Zone.

~

'NOW IT'S YOUR TURN!' I shook my head vehemently in response. My fingers had forgotten how to play, how to work together under pressure. They had, in fact, shrunk in awe in the wake of having heard Suan's friend play. A budding singer-songwriter, he'd just treated his buddies to a raw, spirited, deep and meaningful song penned the previous night. With his eyes closed, he sung from the heart. Instinctively, his mates proffered perfectly pitched harmonies, making me feel guilty for contributing nothing more than my attention. To use the excuse that I'd forgotten how to play guitar was admittedly lame. My confidence on the instrument had significantly dwindled, though. So much for my plan to release *A Vagabond's Vices* before turning thirty: another dream to have tumbled by the wayside for one reason or another. Suan's friend, meanwhile, was on the cusp of forming a band. Voicing my support, I jokingly told him that I could be the lead singer. 'Why not?' he curtly countered. Investing trust in my confidence, I could tell he was being serious.

Suan had met me a little later than expected owing to an untimely thunderstorm. The rain had washed the Sanur roads clean of life in all its forms during the hour it raged and wrecked havoc. He knocked on my door at quarter-past the hour. I answered it in style, slipping on the rainwater that, unbeknown to me, had crept beneath my door, making the tiled floor treacherous to the sandal-lacking foot. My elbows computed the danger level long before my brain acquired the hard evidence. Slamming down upon the floor with no grace whatsoever, I told Suan that I'd be right with him. 'You okay, man?' he called back. 'Sure, mate. I'm just checking out the print quality of the floor tiles, but thanks for asking.'

He'd brought along a friend. In reality, he was a relative, albeit a distant one. 'I don't even know how many cousins I have,' Suan confessed when I'd asked about his family. Intrigued by his family's heritage, I learnt that Suan had been born on Bali and knew the island intimately. Assuming that he would be as knowledgeable about neighbouring islands, I asked him where I should stay on Nusa Lembongan. 'Never been,' he quipped, as proud as a man holding his firstborn. 'But it's only about ten miles away across the Badung Strait,' I commented. He thought for a second before replying: 'I know, but there's nothing on that island that won't be on Bali!' His mischievous grin oozed primal conviction.

I invited Suan and his friend into my home-from-home. It wasn't anything flash, but it was enough. I had a bed more than I required for a start. The oak chair beside the window looked as though it might generate a wad of handy cash were it to be auctioned. The huge mirror, meanwhile, did nothing but mock my traveller's beard. Whichever way I glanced into the wall-mounted monstrosity, the emphasis of my reflection routinely fell upon my facial hair, subtly giving me a hint. I duly picked up the scissors.

Eager to broker a deal with a Japanese man over his house, Suan paced out of my room, his beloved 'Blackberry' giving him an earful. Apparently the man was interested in renting Suan's place. It constituted great news. Momentarily distancing his psyche from the phone, Suan encouraged me to talk to his dubiously distant cousin. 'He needs to improve his English, so just keep talking. He might not understand, but it'll be good for him.' So I talked. I asked questions. I used gestures when my strongest method of communication failed me. Conscious that my monologue and barrage of questions might have been alarming, I injected humour into the situation, laughing at myself, struggling to comprehend my own shortfalls. I asked him his age. He stared back. Not one muscle on his face twitched. I pointed at myself then held aloft my hands. I balled them up then unfurled them, before re-balling and repeating the finger-explosion twice. It was meant to convey the fact I was thirty years old. The silly nature of my actions provoked a knowing smile. Fortunately, he understood, proceeding to open and close his fists, prior to opening them once more. That made him twenty by my reckoning.

Suan promptly confirmed my suspicion. He'd re-entered the room having arranged to meet the Japanese man the following day for a house-viewing. I just hoped everything was in order at his place, and that his house would be clean and tidy enough to impress the man into shaking Suan's hand and signing relevant paperwork, if indeed any formal documents were necessary. It seemed that trust-anchored agreements of a verbal variety were the order of the day in Indonesia, making the country far less bureaucratic than India. The previous evening, I'd asked Suan about laws related to driving as we peeled towards his friend's secluded villa. 'Do you take driving tests in Indonesia?' I asked. Suan choked with laughter. 'No, we just teach ourselves or learn from our parents and friends. There's no test.' That partly explained why so many boys and girls zooming around on motorbikes looked no older than thirteen or fourteen. So long as they deemed themselves 'safe' and 'of no risk to others', they effectively had free rein of the far-reaching road network. However, foreigners should exercise caution: spot-checks by 'polisi' are common. Two days beforehand, I'd sauntered past the rear entrance to the palatial 'Hyatt' complex where six officers randomly whistled at scooter-abusers. One female Australian traveller had been told to remain seated upon the kerb while her shaken boyfriend returned to their guesthouse to grab his International Driver's License. Without it, they would have inevitably faced a fine. It's also important to hold insurance documents closer than partners.

We drove north out of Sanur, though the lane-littered landscape didn't alter in essence as we edged into a different town. Ultimately bound for his friend's house, or his parents' abode at the very least, we snared our priorities by crawling around a desolate labyrinth of back roads in search of spirits:

not of the otherworldly variety, but the alcoholic strain. Scouting for a sacred bottle of 'arak', his friend slid out of the car and strode over to an open-fronted building. He was noticeably armed with a greater deal of hope than cash, confident he'd be able to score a bottle for approximately sixteen-thousand rupiahs. He returned brandishing a smile as gigantic as the bottle resting in his palm. A fair deal had been struck. Arak-nophobic or not, I was rumoured to be in for a neat treat.

~

IT WAS A TYPICAL 'LADS NIGHT' IN, INDONESIA STYLE. There were six of us in all, spread around the atrium of a friend's stately house. The pumping heart of the abode appeared to be its reception area, just beyond the porch, from where the rest of the building's deceptively spacious and high-ceilinged rooms radiated. There were no chairs: just a mat upon which we sat cross-legged. The TV was initially tuned to 'Indonesia's Got Talent', but Suan remembered that football was on: Manchester United versus Liverpool, live and direct from the UK. How ironic, I thought. I'd travelled halfway around the world to suffer a match beamed from a too-close-for-comfort neck of England I knew well. It was an FA Cup engagement, the battle featuring familiar faces in the form of order-barking Kenny Dalgleish (who gurned his way through much of the first half once Man U. gained a lead) and 'old faithful': Ryan Giggs.

Suan was delirious with fury because he'd neglected to pin a bet on the game. Gambling is big business, not to mention a revered past-time in Indonesia. People throw money on all manner of sports fixtures, along with supremely violent cock-fights. I'd been told that such fights were not a pretty sight. Unfortunately, they're an integral part of Indonesian culture.

While some folk enjoy watching 'Legong', traditional Balinese dancing, others flock to see beaked showdowns. It's not particularly hard to source them: that afternoon I'd rumbled a suspicious gathering of boys and men whose ages roughly ranged between five and seventy-five. Having indulged in what was quite possibly the tastiest noodle soup for thousands of miles around in a roadside restaurant (chunky slices of carrot, cabbage and runner beans had been laid upon the egg-infused tangle of noodles, the entirety of which had been freshly prepared and cooked to boiling point), I bolted down the adjacent road towards Segara Beach, often referred to as Sanur's South Beach. It was uncommon to see so many motorbikes lining one particular stretch of road, except on Sunday afternoons when an exceptional number of courting couples and families head onto the beach to picnic and party. Dangerously consumed by intrigue, I ducked down a side lane, deepening my morality-hinged investigation. An explosion of jeering and clapping provided the ultimate giveaway as I rounded a blind corner. There, in a scrubby walled enclosure, fifty or more males encircled two cocks. When written down in such a manner, it understandably sounds dreadful; the reality was even more disturbing. The filthy, sweaty, depraved guys were placing bets on which cock they thought would win based on criteria related to speed, strength and killer instinct. The secretive affair wasn't privy to spying eyes of random passers-by, hence why the location was a fair way from the main road. When I'd asked Suan about the legalities surrounding cock-fighting, he'd shrugged his shoulders with embarrassed flair. 'It is and it isn't legal, if you know what I mean. A lot of things are like that here. The authorities sometimes ignore certain events or situations if they think money can be generated for their own ends. It's true: there is corruption here, and there are gangs, but it's not much different to anywhere else. England is corrupt, too. Dirty dealings are just swept further under the carpet in the UK, to a point where fewer people can see what's going on, and even fewer care.'

At the house, we did what an unhealthy proportion of folk do every Saturday night without fail. Fortunately, we'd come prepared. Suan's friend had scored a large bottle of 'arak' that we were going to mix with a ginseng-flavoured drink to soften the spirit's brutal aftertaste. 'Arak is like vodka,' I'd been assured by the twenty-something friend of Suan's playing cosmic guitar across the shadow-streaked hall. He poured half a glass of the clear liquid from the pitcher he'd made, instructing me to down it without qualm. 'Brace yourself for the deadly bite a few seconds later,' he laughed as soon as I paid lip service to the glass with a well-camouflaged wince of trepidation. I'd never been much of a spirit-drinker. The last time I'd hit spirits with considerable gusto was in the Thai town of Kanchanaburi. Shamefully, I'd wound up in bed for two solid days, paying for my stupidity. But that was then, and whiskey had been to blame, and this was now, and 'arak' was visibly game. So I necked it, slammed the glass on the mat, and faked a smile. 'You like?' Suan asked. 'I could get used to it,' I ruminated, fortifying my opinion too soon. It was only then that the poison set my throat ablaze. I did eventually get used to it, though - much to everybody's surprise.

We spent four hours relaying the pitcher around the tight circle of friends that had formed. Although Suan's friends weren't as confident when it came to conversing in English, they were desperate to learn. The guitar-player and wannabe pop star in our circle had the most competent handle on the language. 'We learn English in school, but I work on cruise ships, so that helps,' he stated. I asked if many Indonesians felt the need to head further afield to find work. 'A lot of young Balinese go abroad for employment. Things have never really been the same since the 2002 and 2005 bombings.

Tourism has recovered to a large extent, but the bombings in Kuta destroyed a lot of people's confidence. I think there are fewer tourists now than there used to be.'

Captivated by the romantic notion of setting sail on epic voyages, I wondered where he'd been whilst working as an assistant waiter. 'Brazil. Italy. South Africa,' he mused. 'On the twenty-sixth of this month I will go back to Brazil. I'll fly from here, to Jakarta, and then to Rio via Hong Kong.' The flight alone would be an adventure in itself by any Indonesian's standards. Suan and his travels notwithstanding, he was the best-travelled Indonesian I'd so far met. 'Of all the places you've visited, where's your favourite?' I ventured, reeling from my sixth shot. He formulated a funky response before I finished posing the question. 'Italy, boss! Ah yes! It's so sophisticated, the girls are stunning, the food is divine. It's somewhere with as much substance as style.' He went on to chat about various cruise liners run by 'Bounty' and 'Quicksilver', quick to add that working upon them was tough. Fifteen or sixteen-hour-long shifts were the norm, hence why staff on-board such ships rarely got much time to explore cities upon striking land for a day or two. 'Just because the ship docks, it doesn't mean work stops. Passengers can come and go as they please, but food and drink are served around the clock whether we're moving or not.' The conversation awarded a compelling insight into what it must be like to toil within the potentially claustrophobic confines of a seafaring liner. A part of me even fancied the idea of hunting for a ship-anchored job in *The Bali Times* or *The Jakarta Globe*, not necessarily as a quick-footed waiter, but a resident writer. Trusting my instincts, I picked up the fresh glass of 'arak' that had been set a hairsbreadth from my knee. Glancing around at my expectant friends, I thanked them. I subsequently swallowed the contents. Then the lights went out.

~

THE DAWN CHORUS WAS AS UNBEATABLE AS IT WAS UNREPEATABLE. An uplifting symphony of birdsong, it clambered through my open window. It was promptly followed by a different call of nature.

The 'homestay' owner's son vaulted up the steps to my room at half past the hour. 'Morning! Hot water!' he called, stood on the dark side of the door, brandishing a flask. Rushing to retrieve the vessel, I'd been craving a hot drink since the crack of dawn. Luckily, two sachets of 'ABC Plus' had been left on my dresser. Arguably the strongest coffee known to Asia, its granule-based kick is notorious. I chased the coffee with two cups of herbal tea, sugared to the brim.

I'd become so hopelessly accustomed to the 'homestay' life that I couldn't envision myself ever leaving 'Lila'. I didn't understand why some people were seemingly content to pay a fortune for hotel accommodation when a room in a 'homestay' could be accrued for a dazzling fraction of the price. Crucially, all the same mod cons were included. The proprietor even dashed up to change the bedding and sweep the floor every morning, restocking the tray of coffee and tea supplies underlining the room's hardwood-framed mirror as he toiled. Truth be told, I'd never felt so at home.

All of a sudden, I was running out of time, though. Having squandered almost a week in Kuta whilst waiting on my backpack, I was guilty of spending too long in Sanur, another of Bali's most popular beach resorts. There were so many other wonderful places waiting to be discovered throughout the diverse archipelago of islands. As a result, I borrowed a map, engaged my mind, and belatedly started plotting. A sucker for making things up as I went along, I'd foolishly avoided formulating a subject-to-change itinerary. Instead, I'd been winging my pan-Asian travels, yet I was fully aware that thirty days in Indonesia would never be enough. My friends were already on the cusp of flying to Borneo, their ever-evolving plans depriving them of the opportunity to return to Bali. Ironically, my long-term plans seemed to change on a daily basis, even though I had no short-term objective in sight.

Promenading along Sanur's beautiful boardwalk, I gazed longingly across the serene Badung Strait upon which bright boats lazily bobbed. On the horizon, the distinctive profile of Nusa Penida captured my imagination, though the island cowered behind a heat haze, forcing me to wonder if the image my eyes had registered was really a humpbacked mirage. Less than fifty yards further along the boardwalk, a testosterone-weighted office sold a variety of tickets to the castoff teardrop of land, the confrontational male ticket vendors refusing to let anybody 'pass go' without them first agreeing to cruise the strait and narrow with 'Super Scoot'. A fast boat could have me touching toes with Nusa Lembongan within thirty minutes. The public boat was cheaper but slower. Once I gained a modicum of purchase upon Nusa Lembongan, it would be quick and easy to head northeast to the far more imposing island of Lombok. Stealthily giving the office the slip, I vowed to return to North Beach at eight in the morning. Passage on the public service blew into my good books at just eighty-thousand rupiahs per person.

In the meantime, there was more of Sanur I aspired to feast my eyes on, starting with 'The Diamond'. Resting on its side, the diamond-shaped structure doubles-up as a wedding venue of the most extraordinary order. Time has not served it well, however: its once well-defined edges have succumbed to the ghastly build-up of dirt amidst general disrepair. Instead of acting as an awe-inspiring beacon, it looked tacky and under-used, as though couples preferred to take one another's hands in marriage upon the infinitely-more-inviting sand rather than inside a structure that might have once been fit for inclusion in 'The Crystal Maze', neglected to a stage so far beyond love it could barely be recognised.

The main stretch of Sanur's boardwalk extends for approximately three miles. Having vaulted into the habit of walking along the multi-purpose pathway every morning between intense writing sessions, I knew which hustlers to avoid. I wasn't the only person traversing the path to be sick of hearing the 'You want transport?' questions or 'Look at my shop' demands which seemed to be projected every few yards. One elderly American could no longer contain his anger at being disturbed. All he desired was a hassle-free stroll beside the sea. The taxi-driver between us had evidently pushed the man too far. 'NO! I DO NOT WANT A TAXI! I DON'T WANT TO LOOK IN ANYBODY'S SHOP! AND I CERTAINLY DON'T WANT A MASSAGE! I AM ON HOLIDAY AND WANT TO RELAX! NOW LEAVE ME ALONE!' he bellowed for the benefit of every desperate-for-custom driver, shopkeeper and masseuse within a ten-mile radius.

Making the most of the free Wi-Fi offered by a '7-Eleven' whilst supping iced coffee, I asked the bearded twenty-something opposite me where he'd been. Introducing himself as Hendog, it transpired that he was a German traveller, fresh off the boat from Lembongan. Warning of an approaching downpour, windswept branches clattered upon my 'Netbook' as we conversed, prompting me to gently shut its black jaws, wisely guarding against injury. Had its screen been smashed, I would have struggled to cadge a replacement. Compromised software had already begun to plague the technology's practical essence, its so-called 'International Warranty' unrecognised by Indonesian dealers.

I'd been frequenting the same food-stall for three days. Whenever haughty hunger pangs hammered at my stomach, I marched towards the modest stall with just one word loudly serenading my taste buds: 'bakso'! An integral part of any Indonesian's daily intake, 'bakso' is essentially noodle soup topped with meatballs. Unable to resist modifying my midday snack, I ordered a bowl of 'bakso ayam', the 'ayam' literally playing chicken. Serving my soup with a sneer-tarnished flourish, the man stole a container of blended chillies from a different table. At the end of the day, he was only stealing from himself: both tables belonged to him. Though no ceremony was required, I made a scene of slowly dipping a plastic spoon into the 'masala' of chillies, spreading a spoonful over the opaque surface of my soup before duly stirring them. Copious amounts of soy sauce and tomato ketchup followed in the wake of the chillies, serving to provide my uninitiated taste buds with a story to tell the grandkids - or so I hoped. Disappointingly, no fuel had been added to the proverbial fire: the addition of chillies didn't make any difference to the bowl's spiciness.

To my dying day I shall use the excuse that the heat of the sun made it impossible for me to think logically. The disturbing truth should be commemorated, for I continued to stir more of the chilli mixture into my 'bakso', willing to run the gauntlet if it was prepared to materialise. I treated myself to a follow-up taste-test, confident that two more spoonfuls would award the liquid base something of a sweat-spurring, eye-watering kick. I was dumbfounded when it still tasted the same. I was all for calling the stallholder over to make enquiries about his pathetic excuse for the chilli-plugged accompaniment he'd decided to leave lying around for the spice-loving community to turn its nose up at. But I held my tongue, stabbing each of the six balls of chicken, twisting the noodles around a fork, slurping up all that remained. And then it hit me: the taste I'd been missing. Hot enough to permanently scorch my throat beyond recognition, the chillies did have a debilitating kick to them after all. It was then, as I wrapped my hands around my gullet in shock, that I made a brief 'note to self' which could potentially benefit you, too, as a discerning reader: chillies rapidly sink to the bottom of soup, making it increasingly spicy the deeper the diner boldly delves. Given that it's common sense, my abominable pitfall beggared the question: what on earth had I been thinking?

Never one to fritter food, I wound up scooping the trace elements from the bowl's bowels with tears spurting from my eyes, sweat flooding my forehead. Even my poor earlobes were sweating, and that had only ever happened once before: in Miami, on the hottest day of 2006.

Yes. I was bound to miss Sanur. Killer food-stalls and all.

~

'WHAT DO YOU MEAN THERE'S NOT A SINGLE BANK MACHINE ON THE ENTIRE ISLAND?'

Not only was I experiencing a crisis of conscience, but a fear of bankruptcy had also threatened to compound the anxieties coursing through my stress-riddled mind. But there was no turning back; not for an ATM. We were in the choppy grip of the Badung Strait, slicing through waves within waves on our way to the tinier than tiny island of Nusa Lembongan. Attached to the even smaller island of Ceningan, Nusa Lembongan constitutes an integral part of 'The Tropical Triangle', with Gili Trawangan one of the most popular destinations for ardent island-hoppers and wildlife-spotters.

I should have done more research about the facilities available on the island before hopping onto the early morning public boat from Sanur's North Beach. My mind had been elsewhere. In truth, it had been in England with my beautiful girlfriend as I'd hastily booked a succession of flights: a one-way slog from KL to Stansted in the UK, plus a return flight from there to Bergerac in France. My itinerary had changed once again. I was now looking forward to returning home in order to make plans with Sarah instead of ducking south to see The Wizard, the wonderful Wizard of Oz.

Two public boats leave Sanur for Lembongan every day. I made haste to be on the first boat at eight, necessitating a seven-thirty arrival at the ticket office. I was instructed to wait on the concrete sea wall while five men clad in blue T-shirts sought to load all manner of essentials onto the upper deck of the vessel. Ten-litre bottles of water, canisters of gas, and containers of hydrogen peroxide were relayed from the northern reach of the boardwalk. Two of the men got to grips with flexible shafts of wood from which four bottles of water could be strung per trip. Heaving the wood onto their strongest shoulders, off they marched, down the steps, over the flotsam-strewn sand, straight into the water, wading through the dirty swell in knee-high shorts which somehow managed to stay dry. A jovial bunch of muscle-bound heroes, they subsequently assumed the guise of porters in exchange for tips, offering to carefully convey backpacks and suitcases. We tentatively pranced into the shockingly cold water after them, climbing aboard as best we could, between four motors raring to go at the rear.

Embracing the no-frills integrity of the bench-marked lower deck, I hopped over six benches to the front, calming my nerves adjacent to a slightly elevated sleeping area made of slatted wood. There were another twelve passengers, making me 'unlucky thirteen'. Keeping time with second-counting accuracy, we motored into the unknown at precisely eight o'clock, amassing considerable distance between us and the 'bakso'-consuming public on the boardwalk within a bundle of minutes. Half an hour later, we seemed to be no closer to Lembongan than when we'd departed. High-rise waves walloped our boat from all angles. Now I understood the need for stabilisers on Indonesian boats: three multi-coloured arms extend to long white poles which help to maintain essential balance in all excuses for weather. Assaulted by a nightmare of a daydream, I recalled a pivotal scene from *The Perfect Storm* at the worst moment imaginable, powerlessly observing a wave of punishing proportions sweep in from our starboard side in tune with a swell, giving dramatic rise to our port. Swooping through a blinding, lashing, vindictive wall of spray, the boat mock-lurched before nose-diving into a trough. The wood from which it was constructed had never seemed so flimsy, so insignificant, so downright vulnerable. The young child protectively cradled in the arms of his father behind me began to cry, literally sick of the uncontrollable turbulence afflicting the strait.

We docked on Lembongan seventy-five minutes after pulling away from Bali. For the money we'd saved, it had been worth taking the public boat instead of the fast ferry. Armed with nothing more than a clothes-stuffed backpack, I blundered ashore to be greeted by a grinning tout. 'How long you stay? Where you from, boss? You want motorbike? You talk to me if you want motorbike, yeah?' I told him to slow down, to hold his hogs. I needed a moment to relax, to smile, to pay homage to the goddess watching over folk who foster a penchant for travelling in order to live, learn and educate. The tout was getting restless, peering over my shoulder, scouting for easier pickings. He trained his beady eyes on a twenty-something mademoiselle struggling with her rucksack. 'Be right back, mate,' he sniggered, injecting a note of sarcasm into proceedings, having pegged 'moi' for an Aussie backpacker. When I made a move and began traipsing along the beach, he bolted back to my side. 'I show you cheap accommodation, my friend.' I came clean about my tighter-than-Scrooge budget, confiding that I could afford to splurge no more than eighty-thousand rupiahs for a room.

Sympathising with my financial status, he led me around a corner, down a side lane to a complex of cheerless rooms set around a central courtyard. I hated the room I was shown at first sight, but at seventy-thousand per night, the price was most definitely right, wholly reflective of its dark interior and laughably makeshift shower. I snapped it up without hesitation as a couple of Finnish girls entered the courtyard. They, too, had been on the boat. We chatted whilst committing our vital stats to the ledger, exchanging information about where we'd been and what we had on our agendas for the coming week. I confessed that I had no guidebook, my plans vaguer than an uneducated no-mark from Loserville. Out of the blue, I asked them if they knew where the nearest ATM was located. They glanced at one another before shaking their heads. I assumed they were as clueless as me... but it was worse than that. It's not that they didn't know where the nearest automatic teller machine could be found; the simple truth related to the spine-chilling fact that there wasn't a single ATM for miles around. My face must have been a picture as my brain processed such news.

I had enough money to pay for my lodgings, for sure, but how in Neptune's name was I ever going to get off the island when the cheapest ticket back to Bali cost sixty-thousand rupiahs? What was I going to do for food? Would I have to resort to drinking dirty water from the rust-wrapped tap in my room? I'd noticed countless signs pointing along narrow alleys to money exchangers, but the only cash I had stashed in my wallet consisted of practically worthless Cambodian and Vietnamese notes. They'd have been impossible to trade. One hotel boasted that payments within its gecko-spotted walls could be made with 'MasterCard'. If only 'Visa' had staked a claim on such premises instead. Cursing my luck, I sloped into my room. I wanted time to think; I needed 'Western Union'.

~

'GET A BIKE, YOU LOSER!'

It's always good to ingratiate oneself with the locals. Shame the 'locals' in this instance were Aussie louts, overly keen to prove their supposed worth by being disrespectful to those of less fortunate means. What I'm trying to say is this: they were on holiday, probably charging motorbike rental costs to their parents' credit cards, while I was attempting to travel as far as I could on as little as possible. Even so, I didn't begrudge them their spirited freedom of speech. I knew they meant nothing by what they said; they were just having a laugh on their way south to Dream Beach, surfboards secured to the sides of their road-hogging scooters. Nyoman, the tout who'd guided me to my lodgings, had offered me a bike for fifty-thousand rupiahs. I had no choice but to back away from the deal. Put simply, I had no money left owing to my oversight. It was true: not a single ATM blessed the tropical paradise. Similarly, Internet connections were few and far between. Those in existence were painfully slow to the point that it would have been quicker to write a longhand latter and dunk it in the post rather than compose and send an e-mail. As a direct result of there being so few places where access to the net could be gained, the few 'cafes' that did offer browsing sessions duly charged the earth. For example, it cost me thirty-five thousand rupiahs to 'surf' for an hour. It cost less than eight-thousand in Kuta for the same length of time. I felt like stuffing my feet in my mouth as the counter on the dust-collecting computer ticked towards the sixty-minute mark. I'd invested the last fifty minutes passionately writing an epic and frankly essential love letter to my girlfriend, telling her that I'd be coming home after concluding my travels in Indonesia and spending a 'chaser' week in Malaysia. I clicked on the 'send' icon in the dying seconds of the hour, only for 'Internet Explorer' to unkindly inform me that it didn't feel like responding. A spinning hourglass icon surfaced to taunt me. I waited in vain, hoping the PC's processor might eventually catch up with itself. To be fair, my frantic speed-typing couldn't have been easy for the system to compute when it was probably used to dealing with slower typing speeds. Sighing my soreness, I paid my dues, vowing never to return to 'Ryan's Internet' unless psychologically prepared to waste a pocketful of money.

Upon learning that a fresh wad of money wasn't going to be an easy commodity to come by on the island, I executed a couple of essential calculations to see how much money I had to survive on before returning to Sanur. Retiring to my room, I conspiratorially shut my curtains, unprepared to expose my embarrassing lack of money to prying eyes. I switched on the lamp, provoking a tiny umbrella of light to penetrate the clawing darkness. I'd never rated zero-watt bulbs. In spite of the light-deprived circumstances, I whipped out my wallet, consequently putting aside seventy-thousand rupiahs for my room, plus sixty-thousand for the boat ticket back to Bali. That left me with precisely seventeen-thousand rupiahs on which to survive until my feet reclaimed Sanur's sand and I was able to sprint to an ATM. As any seasoned traveller will know, seventeen-thousand measly rupiahs won't buy you much, especially not on an island of Lembongan's disconnected standing. Since almost everything is imported from Bali and beyond, prices are inflated across the board.

Having not eaten since... well, since the last time I'd pushed food into my mouth (I'd gone almost thirty-six hours without a bite), I scanned the disproportionate wealth of menu-boards on the beachfront. There were no meals for less than thirty-thousand rupiahs. Hoping food would cost less on the back roads, I cut inland via an uneven lane, past the secretive might of Puseh Temple, around the corner to a couple of roadside restaurants facing one another. Spotting a couple of familiar faces from the boat ride, I took a seat at the nearest family-run gaffe, ordering the cheapest dish on the menu: egg-topped vegetable fried rice. An accompanying glass of hot tea brought the bill to twelve-thousand rupiahs in total, leaving me with just five-thousand for the remainder of my time adrift.

To take my mind off food-affected outlay, I walked, striking north towards the lighthouse. To my left, a series of tree-shaded lanes bumped towards the beach. Such lanes petered out the further north I marched. The road hooked a sharp right near the lighthouse, leading me between a tight cluster of wooden abodes. Outside them, large mats had been laid upon the parched earth. Freshly harvested seaweed had been left out to dry. Aged men and women tended to such mats, separating entwined strands to decrease drying time, the weed's golden colour and stringy texture reminding me of spaghetti.

I was trampling due east, keeping an eye out for Sakenan Temple as I made a beeline for the must-see Mangrove Forest in the crescent-shaped neck of Lembongan's lush northern reaches. Cursing the growling dogs in my path, I hesitated, stealing sustained glances over the water. Bali's coastline could be seen on the far horizon, beyond which a towering mountain reached into a grey streak of clouds. Although scrawny, the three dogs sure knew how to yap, intimidating me to the point of retreat. Rabies is endemic on many Indonesian islands, so I reined in my common sense, backtracking to the village where a charismatic shopkeeper greeted me with a smile more menacing than The Joker's ear-to-ear beamer. 'Hey Beppe!' he sang, raising his arm with a view to high-fiving me. I'd never seen the man before, yet he was adamant that he knew me. Disturbingly, he knew where

I was staying. Lembongan is such a small island that one's privacy is bound to become somewhat compromised when your business has the tendency to become everybody else's by default. Because only a handful of boats dock at specific times each day, it's simple for native islanders to ask around in order to find out the names, nationalities, and temporary lodgings of all those who have waded ashore for one reason or another. Coming to terms with the aforementioned state of affairs, I lowered my guard, confirming that I was indeed residing at 'Johnny's Losmen', prior to correcting my name. 'Oh… you're Steve! Hey hey – sorry Beppe! I didn't realise you were a Steve, boss!' The inexcusable integrity of the conversation ripped apart at the seams. 'Anyway, Steve, Beppe, whatever your real name is. Would you like to rent a bike? You look like a surfer. I bet you'd love to see Mushroom Beach and Sunset Beach. They are too far away to reach on foot, especially this late in the afternoon. That's why I'll give you my bike for fifty-thousand.' I shook my head, lamenting that I needed an ATM before I could even think about hiring any mode of conveyance. Heartily patting my shoulders with a genuine look of sorrow creasing his features, the Beppe-lover wished me luck.

The road wheeled into a run of unforgiving corners as the gradient increased, gaining ground between tightly packed stands of palm trees and bushes. Cacti could also be spotted. After slogging my way over the rise, two backpacking girls approached, having already hot-footed it down to Dream Beach and back. Thankful not to be the only bike-lacking doofus in a five-mile radius, I asked them if the beach was much further. The sun had begun its fabled descent; it would be dark within the hour. I decided to turn back upon learning it would take another forty minutes to catch sight of the sand. Cutting my losses, I strode back through the village with my last five-thousand rupiah note burning a hole in my pocket.

Feeling more ravenous than ever, I had two options: kick back with a simple bowl of steamed rice for four-thousand, or pluck a bunch of five bananas for the fairest of exchanges. I settled for the latter option, the bananas representing true value-for-money. Had I been better endowed, I'd have purchased fourteen curlers for fourteen-thousand rupiahs: the equivalent of a round British pound.

A pronounced sinking feeling consumed me as I handed over my very last note. With not one spare rupiah to my name, and with no hard currency to exchange, I wished upon every single star glinting in the night sky that passage on the public boat to Sanur would cost no more than the sixty-thousand I'd thoughtfully stashed under my pillow for safekeeping. If the ticket cost any more, I'd be swimming.

~

REUNITED WITH BALI, I SLUNG MY BIKE INTO A U-TURN, charging across both lanes of traffic to kerb the central embankment, negotiating the flow of vehicles on the far side of the highway. It was all I could do to avoid being stung. I'd sensed that I shouldn't have been on Highway 1 from the moment my bicycle and I had wobbled onto the beast. Diurnally pulverised by vehicles travelling at breakneck speeds, it constitutes the busiest and most dangerous road on Bali.

Fatigued by the quiet back lanes serving Sanur, I'd decided to head south in search of better beaches. The only way to reach the southernmost part of the island was via the highway. Initially willing to risk being caught if it meant paying foot service to Nusa Dua, an overhead sign detailing destination distances promptly hammered things into perspective. I was only a third of the way there: Nusa Dua was still fifteen kilometres distant. The sight of 'polisi' up ahead also put me off. Persistence had never seemed more futile. Truck-trawling highways are no place for meek men on crossbar-lacking bicycles. As the traffic dodged past, it was clear that I was out of my depth. Fearing retribution from the yellow tabard-sporting cops for not wearing a helmet or having oiled my chain, I ruled that a measure of avoidance needed to be actioned before I was fined or flung into the no-nonsense confines of an Indonesian jail. Neither form of punishment appealed.

Prior to cutting across the highway, I had to swerve off the hard shoulder into the nearest clump of bushes for the sake of slowing down. Neither the front nor back brake was in working condition: another reason to be fined. With my bicycle freshly embedded in the Indonesian equivalent of Japanese Knotweed, I turned to face the traffic rushing forth from behind, secretively scouting for attractive gaps to enable me to scoot over to the middle of the perilously wide tongue of asphalt.

My chance came ten minutes later when a slow-moving vehicle in the fast lane accidentally obliterated the onslaught. Seizing the opportunity with both feet, I began to peddle furiously towards salvation in the form of the raised reservation which conclusively divided lanes of traffic speeding in opposite directions. Just as I regained my balance, I shot a last-second glance to my right. To my horror of horrors, a school bus was in the process of pulling out from behind the slow-moving truck, under-taking its wealth of sitting-pretty pupils to an early grave if I didn't whip out of its way within the nervous twitch of a nose. Had my chain snapped, it would have been velvet curtains for each and every one of us. Fortunately, I bounced to relative safety, out of the danger zone, into the fast lane. The truck was still over twenty yards away, allowing me enough time to bunny-hop onto the reservation between two proudly-pruned bushes.

The bush to my left blocked my view of oncoming traffic, forcing me to nose my bike forward so I could crane my neck around the darling buds of January. And that's when I spotted him: a fellow maniac pedalling north on a grin-inducing wreck of a borrowed bicycle. I waved in recognition of shared circumstances. He turned away as soon as he spotted me, perhaps wary of stranded, sunburnt foreigners travelling on a bicycle best suited for women. Okay, so there was no crossbar to speak of, and the gear-shifter lacked style, but I'd been assured by the sweet lady who'd loaned me the bike that it was the best hunk of mobile metal a man could get in the prevailing climate. But of which climate had she spoke? The economic, or tropical? Whatever she'd referred to, it no longer mattered.

Desperate to make the other side of the road, I suddenly felt like the ridiculed chicken at the heart of the timeless playground joke. 'Why did Steve Rudd risk death by crossing the highway on an antiquated bicycle?' Was it really to get to the other side of the road as per the simple but effective rib-tickler? Was my train-of-thought becoming too existentially offbeat for my audience's liking? Grounding myself, I edged out, wrenching the bike into seventh gear. Clocking an opening between a slack duo of blue cabs, I spun off the kerb at a perfect right angle to the traffic, praying that I'd be able to announce my arrival to all fellow road-users by easing into the flow. Having gained more momentum than I ever thought possible, I willed my bike to turn before smashing through a fence and rumbling down the far verge into a weed-smothered moat. I somehow managed to pull the bike parallel to the grittiest of hard shoulders in the nick of time. If only I could have patted myself on the back. I needed to concentrate, the Sanur-bound traffic heavier than the amount streaming south. Spying a sign which announced that Denpasar was ten kilometres away, I crunched through the gears until one stuck. In spite of it being a twenty-one gear bike, the largest cog took precedence, rendering any gear higher than seventh useless. Making do, I chased the man in front for no good reason. He evidently saw me coming a mile off, for he slowed and allowed me to pass... straight into the hands of a tree-obscured policeman.

Protesting my incontestable innocence before I'd even manhandled the two-wheeled contraption from beneath my aching thighs, I could tell the policeman courted a hidden agenda. 'I know I should have a helmet, I know... but, but, but,' I dared to stall, hoping he might take pity and void the fine he was liable to ink upon an unofficial document of shame. 'I honestly thought it was okay to ride on the highway. I've seen other people on bicycles. Just look behind me,' I pleaded. Removing his crash-helmet with achingly slow authority, the traffic cop smiled with arresting sincerity. 'Don't worry. I don't want your money. It is perfectly fine to ride here on your bike,' he assured, peering down his nose at my spoke-buckled wonder. 'All I want is enlightening, boss.' I couldn't believe my ears. Did he really expect me to expose the meaning of life to him at the side of a fume-stricken dual-carriageway? Even if I knew the meaning, I'd be hesitant to unveil it at his behest. I dreaded to imagine what he might do with such knowledge. 'I think you misunderstand my bad English,' he continued. 'I need a light... a lighter for my cigarette. Mine dropped from my pocket onto the road. It got crushed by a car.' He then apologised for stopping me in such a manner. I uncharacteristically cackled in response.

It was all part and parcel of a traveller's work, rest and play.

~

THE FINEST EATERIES TEND TO BE THE MOST SECRETIVE. Sick of paying over-the-odds for authentic

Indonesian fare, I was grateful to be pointed in the direction of a marvellous place to dine amidst the shadows of an inconspicuous lane. Having been shown the proverbial light by a strange German woman, I couldn't get enough of the 'restaurant'. Its popularity had evidently grown on the back of personal recommendations. Ninety per cent of restaurants on the main tourism-driven road, Danau Tamblingan, had waiters or waitresses taking it in turns to hand out leaflets bearing menus. By and large, such restaurants appeared overwhelmingly opulent, style burning the substance of meals served. The average price of Indonesian staple 'nasi goreng' was thirty-thousand rupiahs in the swankiest eateries, yet the place I'd just discovered produced the same simple dish for just five-thousand. 'How can the owners of this place afford to offer dishes at such low prices?' I asked myself. By eliminating 'middle men' and clamping down on overheads, that's how. The place was essentially a house, four oak tables furnishing the shaded courtyard. Their 'helping people to save money' motto was adhered to from the second I muttered my initial order. In addition, they were helping people to taste the very best that Indonesian cuisine has to offer.

For just over the equivalent of fifty pence, I was brought a plate overflowing with fried rice, along with a mug of sweet hot tea, within three minutes. There was no dilly-dallying; no pretension; no unnecessary flamboyance. The focus was on delivering great food for a greater price: quickly, efficiently, and with pride. Impressed, I noticed my feet making their way back to the courtyard a few hours later. The matronly owner of the house kindly took the time to explain the menu, painstakingly translating each and every dish. I learnt more Indonesian words in those five minutes than I had in two language-packed weeks, thanks in no small part to her admirable patience.

'Makanan' means food. Drinks, meanwhile, gather beneath the far-reaching 'minuman' umbrella. Craving a random fix of meat, even though I'd surprised myself by morphing into a full-blown vegetarian in India, I enquired about 'bubur ayam', aware that any dish with 'ayam' would be dominated by chicken. She paused to consider how best to describe the dish. 'It is porridge with chicken,' she grinned, performing a dance with her hands. It sounded too outlandish to miss, so I nodded my head in earnest. I nodded with even more enthusiasm when I saw it cost just three-thousand rupiahs. She returned almost immediately, reverentially laying to rest a bowl ablaze with steaming rice porridge blended with appetising slices of chicken breast. I half-expected her to say 'bon appetit' until I remembered where I was. The lady hadn't exaggerated in the least. Chicken strips floated atop a despicably oily mound of porridge. Attacking the feast with a fork, then a spoon, I was in my element, savouring its succulence whilst glancing around at the homely environs, absorbing all-round authenticity. To my right, beyond the arrangement of tables, the elevated walkway to a gold-embossed temple triumphed in being the best place to sit and watch international football. A TV had been planted beside the door of the shrine. In front of me, a working area presented a cloying muddle of personal possessions piled high in a towering glass case. Composed mainly of childrens' clothes, neither rhyme nor reason could be applied to the manner in which such clothes had been entrapped. It seemed as though somebody had been told they had twenty minutes to fill a time capsule of twenty-first century garments. Topping a different case, a line of cigarette packets glared at me, evidently for sale. In spite of not smoking, the lady offered me a cigarette on behalf of her chain-smoking husband who was drowsily engrossed in the football. Seeing that I had my work cut out with the food, she backed away, leaving me in peace as I dug into clumps of rice grazing the bowl's base. Stealing a glance to my left, I noticed an elderly lady delicately weaving strips of banana leaves around flat bases to form the trays upon which offerings are made to countless gods and goddesses at all hours. She worked with silent diligence, modestly injecting passion into crafting such trays by being so precise, perhaps enjoying the meditative quality of working without distraction. The only sound to be heard emanated from my quarter of the calming yard, unhinged cutlery musically pinging against porcelain. Curiously, the TV had been muted. Birdsong was unheard-of.

I was the only person to dine there in the hour that I loitered. Transported by the soundless environment and astounding hospitality of the three women pandering to my food-related desires, I saw no reason to greet the main road where hassle would swoop in my direction as I strode home. I'd been searching for precisely the kind of experience I was in the throes of cherishing since first touching-down in Indonesia. It would have been churlish to purposefully taper its refined edges by returning to a cruel street upon which money was king, and where little else appeared to matter.

My bill fluttered from a pad onto the table without any added tax. I grinned my gratitude as I relayed a five-thousand rupiah note. The lady then rushed over to the adjacent table, grabbing a photocopied menu. She must have known I was a writer. By sheer coincidence, I'd been about to ask if I could take a photo of the food list. Charmed by my interest, she once again talked me through the menu in its entirety, showering upon me another invaluable language lesson.

'Goreng' means fried. Thus, 'nasi goreng' is fried rice. 'Capcay' is a fried vegetable dish shot through with meat, while 'ikan' poses as fish. Prematurely deciding to sample 'ikan goreng' (fried fish) later in the day, I had just one question to ask. Sustaining simplicity, I said, 'pisang goreng'?

Cocking an eyebrow whilst allowing her amusement to convert her otherwise tight-lipped expression into a face-brightening smirk, she confided that it was nothing more than fried banana. Reflecting on the sickly nature of the last banana fritter I'd downed on an Indian train, I privately dry-heaved before upping to leave.

Everything about the atmosphere, the people, and the food had been a stomach-pleasing eye-opener. When I told the lady I'd be back for seconds, albeit not in the form of a deep-fried dessert, my sincerity was guaranteed to hold sway.

~

'OH, MR. STEPHEN, WHY YOU NOT STAY WITH US ANY LONGER?' We were at an impasse, the 'homestay' owner and I, shuffling upon the threshold between my room and the frond-fronted balcony. Laden with retro flasks full of hot water, he suddenly seemed reluctant to pass mine over. I felt like a traitor, as though I should have forewarned him of my plans to ditch Sanur in favour of culture-enlivening communities at the heart of the island. He cocked his head around the door jamb to make sure everything was still in its place: the dressing table, the mirror, the twin chairs. Begrudgingly nodding consent, he passed me a chipped flask. It reminded me of meadow-staked picnics on childhood holidays in the Yorkshire Dales. 'I really hope you've enjoyed your stay here, Mr. Stephen. You have been a valued guest.' My heart began to bleed.

The owner knocked on my door again an hour later. 'Your driver is here!' he remarked. 'My driver?' I baulked. 'Yes, the driver of the shuttle bus to Ubud.' For a second I feared that some kind of secret society had sent me a personal chauffeur for reasons best known to the megalomaniac backing whatever shady operation had been authorised. I'd been getting ready on 'Indonesian time', yet the more time I spent observing the level of efficiency on Bali, the more it became obvious that if you need to be ready for something, it's better to be early. Fortunately, I'd packed and tidied the room, ever-conscious that any mess I made would have to be cleaned by somebody else. 'Maybe we'll see you again, Mr. Stephen?' queried the owner through gritted teeth. Fate would tell, but it was far too early in the day.

There was only one other person kicking back on the shuttle bus operated by tour company 'Perama'. Japanese, she was also bound for Ubud: an extremely reassuring fact when I thought about it. Pulling away from 'Lila', I spotted a mobile 'bakso' cart doing the rounds, feasting on people's fixation with devouring the Indonesian dish alfresco. Such 'mobile' carts are easy to push at the side of roads. In truth, they do a roaring trade, cart-operators cooking meatballs to order. Then, as if to further taunt my taste buds, a mobile ice-cream seller whipped past, dispensing scoop-topped cones from a small icebox strapped to his bike.

The Japanese woman and I were dropped off at a meeting point in sight of a 'Dunkin' Donuts' outlet. The van driver proceeded to make a ghastly meal of turning around in order to speed to base. A larger bus beckoned with doors wide open. Not only was it scheduled to stop in Ubud, but it was also primed to drop passengers off at Candidasa, a Lombok Strait-overlooking resort on the east coast. As we waited for other van drop-offs to duly increase the size of the collected backpacking fraternity, a French girl edged over to chat. I'd seen her somewhere before, yet it took me a moment to recall specific details. A random synapse-founded slideshow of images soon soothed my anxiety at not knowing where I was, let alone where I'd just been. 'Lembongan, right?' Her shrill laugh made me doubt myself. 'I'm Anne... but yes - we spoke on the boat to Lembongan.' She went on to relate how she'd detested the disconnected nature of the island. She'd stomached it for one night before ferrying herself around to Lombok, upon which better facilities existed. Her next port of repose was destined to be Candidasa, in spite of having just landed in Sanur. 'Ah, I detest Sanur. It's too up-itself. Nusa Dua is even worse. If you don't want to shop until you drop, have every single crease massaged out of your body, or drink until you're dead, then Sanur will struggle to hold much appeal to anyone for longer than a few hours. It all seems so superficial, so style-orientated and lacking in real Balinese culture. Even the "Legong" dance performances seem contrived, as though the costumed dancers are puppets in an outdated play.' The way in which she lambasted Sanur sent me reeling, her cynicism defining every word she heatedly huffed.

We sat apart on the bus, primarily because I wanted to embrace a sustained bout of positive thinking. I sank onto a seat behind a fellow Brit in the process of bemoaning how he'd had to leave Oz due to his visa expiring. 'I didn't even want to come here,' he grumbled, 'but Denpasar Airport was the nearest international airport. I figured I might as well see a bit of Bali while I'm here.' No need to force yourself, I thought, unable to understand why some people always wanted more: something bigger, or better. Seemingly incapable of appreciating the beauty and opportunities for spiritual growth in their present grasp, they transposed their thought patterns, wishing themselves away, denying reality a fair chance of survival. As an ambassador for Professional Eavesdropping, I tuned deeper into his tale of woe as he related it to a female Australian backpacker. She, on the other hand, adored everything about Bali, joyously taking not a glimpse of the island for granted. Gradually zoning out of his dichotomy-etched drone, I deflected my attention to, through, and beyond the window. Unspeakably stunning swathes of greenery bowed beneath a cloudless sky whenever release from the labyrinthine road network was bestowed. Nosing our mortal bodies north whilst ushering our knotted mindsets forth, we ricocheted between the built-up confines of Tohpati, Batubulan and Celuk, rising above the monotony inspired by the visual similarity of roads darting off at every angle conceivable. Underlining the dizzying blue forever, a bedazzling tapestry of rice fields fought to attune my consciousness on all levels, deftly accentuating the priceless worth attached to terra firma. Submerged in ankle-deep water, men and women surveyed crops, perhaps making small talk with the green strands of life poking up through the muddy undertow. Their lives and allotments flashed by within seconds, never to be polluted by my prying eyes again. Still, I sought to communicate and commentate, not alienate; to be opinionated without allowing my deep-rooted beliefs and passions contaminate those held dear by strangers into whose path my trajectory barrelled, for better or worse.

I alighted in Ubud on the periphery of contentment. Subconsciously, I recognised the folds of ground surrounding the town; I warmed to the sound of sizzling meat; I smelt the soil's fertility through the moisture-rich humidity hovering above it. My feet might not have previously made tracks around Ubud, but my soul had been there before. Intuitively 'conversing' with the energy, I willed it to liberate itself once more.

~

THEY WERE CLEARLY NOT 'AU FAIT' WITH THE INEVITABILITY OF SPINAL COMPRESSION. Balancing two breeze-blocks on their heads as they swayed towards a hotel in-the-making, three women worked beneath the midday sun as though the heat didn't bother them. Softening the cutting blow with circular cushions placed upon their flattened crowns, they sallied back and forth with unhurried grace. Further along the same road, a group of women were digging a trench, putting the men staring across at them from their 'taxi-rank' to shame. Indeed, Indonesian women are nothing if not hard-working.

I was on my way to the fabled 'Art Zoo' of Ubud, a lively building inside which an explosion of art creatively assaults the senses. The town of Ubud has long been renowned as a cultural hub where creativity positively blooms in every sense of the ever-so-vague term. Painters galore have their work for sale. It's not uncommon to be assaulted by bold designs in Abstract, Modernist and Classical styles within the same shop. The district of Ubud consists of eight villages in all, boasting a combined population of over sixty-thousand. Basking five-hundred metres above sea level, the district is over forty square kilometres in size.

As soon as I was dropped off at the 'Perama' agency on the southern outskirts, I was reminded of Luang Prabang in Laos. It had something to do with the exquisitely chilled-out vibes permeating the air up there; the way hassle from taxi drivers was non-confrontational; the manner in which gifted artisans courteously conducted themselves inside and outside their stores. Ubud also bears much in common with Chiang Mai in Thailand, not to mention Santa Fe in the American state of New Mexico. Acting as a magnet for art-lovers, food connoisseurs, traditional dance-devotees, massage-addicts, and spiritualists wanting to heal and be healed, the town waits in danger of becoming a caricature of itself if district planners aren't careful. 'Starbucks' has already snagged a prime cut of real estate within sugar-spilling distance of a staggeringly beautiful temple. Compromising the traditional integrity of Balinese culture, 'Starbucks' appears to be spearheading globalisation's slow but sure invasion of Bali. However, all is not lost, for the majority of coffee-shops and restaurants gracing the settlement are owned and run by locals, though a percentage of such establishments seem keen to dish up Turkish and Italian cuisine instead of focusing on what Ubudites know and cook best.

'You want motorbike to see paddies? A cheap "homestay" with hot water and fan? An elephant ride through Monkey Forest?' In truth, I just wanted a minute to myself in order to think clearly. 'How much for a room in a "homestay"?' I asked, unsure where to begin with my search for cheap lodgings. Without giving me much choice in the matter, the travel agency-affiliated tout led me to his motorbike. In spite of inelegantly rocking around corners due to the undignified bulk of my backpack, we steadily motored north for a mile before the middle-aged Indonesian man swerved to a stop outside 'Wayan Family Homestay'. Guilelessly assuming the role of tout, personal escort and 'homestay' promoter rolled into one, he hurried past the owners, straight to a vacant room. 'It's yours for one-hundred thousand rupiahs.' Admiring the floor-scraping double-bed and bamboo-strapped wardrobe with a deliberate air of indifference, I tried to barter the price down. I'd already told him that my budget wouldn't be prepared to err above seventy-thousand. 'I'll pay eighty, final offer,' I said. 'One-hundred and ten,' he argued, cutting loose all sense of logic. 'You're supposed to bring the price down, not put it up,' I clucked in aggravation. 'But you get a free breakfast for such a special price. Toastie, fruit, tea. All good, good.' Half-tempted to introduce a last-minute bid of ninety-thousand, I'd already mentally conceded to his annoyingly persuasive sales pitch. 'One-hundred thousand rupiahs. No more,' I politely fumed, detesting the thought of being ripped-off, yet elated to have found somewhere half-decent to lay my head for a couple of nights. 'Done deal,' he guffawed, delightedly shaking my hand as though he'd just offloaded an unmarketable haunted house with a scrapyard-doomed car.

I hit the streets sprinting, desperate to see if Ubud justified the hype. I marched up Hanoman Street towards Main Street, walking on the road as much as possible to avoid steep dips in the pavement which allowed rainwater to rush into the offering-blocked gutters or grate-covered black holes as and when necessary. Innumerable temples flanked Hanoman, a couple of which had hoardings outside advertising the coming evening's 'fire-dance' performance. If it wasn't 'Legong dancing' being promoted, it was 'Barong', arguably the most popular dance on the island. Distilling an age-old 'good versus evil' morality tale into a visually stunning show of theatrical movement, the dance features a smorgasbord of masks deemed so sacred that they're routinely sprinkled with holy water before being worn.

Awarding 'Starbucks' nothing but a wide berth, the lure of the aforementioned 'Art Zoo' beckoned me in a rough westerly direction along Main Road for a mile. Beyond a scintillating gash in the land where two streams converged to create the brownest of rivers, the vegetation-embellished banks of which were sewn together by a soaring bridge, 'Art Zoo' served to please art-lovers of all kinds. Within spitting distance, the much-admired 'Blanco Museum' also proved to be worth a visit.

Back on the dreamy streets, craft stores galore displayed shelf after shelf of grotesque masks, coolie hats, bamboo wood chimes, two-dimensional shadow puppets, leather-laced drums, more Pop-Art prints than Warhol could have hoped to 'copy' in one lifetime, butterfly-shaped kites, baskets woven out of palm leaves, trays of bracelets ravaged by bright flower patterns, and wall-suited woodcarvings. And then there were the independent clothes boutiques, a smattering of them proud to sell eco-friendly garments which had allegedly been produced without affecting the environment in any harmful capacity. All consumables considered, it was a fashion-conscious souvenir-hunter's interpretation of heaven on earth.

Nevertheless, it was the raw nature languishing on Ubud's doorstep that interested me more than anything, not to mention 'Sjaki-Tari-Us': a centre for mentally handicapped children run by a non-profit organisation. Eschewing the temptation to ride down to the rice paddies on the edge of town, I walked to the 'S.T.U.' centre, ideally situated within a football's throw from the south-eastern corner of the playing field that attractively borders Monkey Forest Road. Armed to the legs with an afternoon to spare, I knocked on the door and strode in. Help, in the form of Steve Rudd, was at hand.

~

'CAN YOU HEAR THAT, OR IS IT JUST ME?' I wasn't sure if I was hearing things or not. Convinced my instincts could still be relied upon, I motioned for Jenny - an Irish girl with whom I'd been travelling - to quietly edge away from the hut. At first sight, the building had appeared to be unpopulated, yet a clap of noise from within had inspired us to actively remain on guard. We'd seen too many grisly horror movies, pessimistically anticipating an 'alternative' ending for ourselves were we to hang around to see who or what lurked inside the remote mountain refuge. I half-fancied the possibility that a lonesome mountain lookout was reposing inside, mincing his way through Jack Kerouac's *Desolation Angels*: a profoundly moving novel in which he whimsically recalls his time as a lookout in America's Pacific Northwest when employed to scan the horizon for outbreaks of fire. Perhaps Jenny and I were letting our impressionable imaginations gallop away with themselves. Maybe it was just a buck in the breeze that caused the corrugated iron roof to reverberate as we innocently shot a reel of panoramic photographs. Squeezing the wooded slopes beyond Lake Batur into frame was no easy task; the placid lake dominated the view-finder, its sacred sheen easy to appreciate from our altitude-levied vantage point. Not a single person could be seen on the lake. It was a sanctuary, and certainly not suited for water sport enthusiasts with penchants for ripping across still water on jet-skis or speed-boats. Having said that, at least one of the lakeside hotels brazenly offered banana-boat rides. Nevertheless, there was minimal noise pollution affecting the district, a fact that contributed to making the mountainous northern region of Bali all the more relaxing and alluring.

Discreet plumes of smoke rising from the volcano's crater assured us that Mount Batur was indeed active. Unforgivably using ignorance as an excuse, we'd naively dismissed all warnings awarded, believing Mount Batur to be dormant or extinct. It goes without saying that locals always know best. We'd been fools to shrug off their advice about refraining from climbing the high-rise beast without the knowledgeable expertise of a guide well-versed in first aid just in case one of us took a tumble. Stealing uncouth glances at the crater behind and the lake in front, the noises to our right tickled our worst fears. A hundred yards further around the serrated edge of the crater, another hut could be seen through smoke without mirrors. Voicing the most common line aired in movies since the golden era of Hollywood died a death, Jenny couldn't help herself, an unusually high pitch accompanying her wish to descend. 'Let's get out of here,' she repeated when I failed to respond, mesmerised as I was by the steaming interior of the circular crater.

By no means were we anywhere near the highest point of the volcano, but we were high enough. Strapped in anti-climbing sandals, our feet had seemingly been ripped beyond repair; we were dreading going back down, hence why I hung back to admire the sweeping view from one end of the lake to the other. On the literal upside, if the weather happened to suddenly deteriorate, we couldn't have been in a better place, in spite of balancing on the woefully exposed side of a belittling and smoking volcano. The hut would provide adequate cover had rain descended faster than we were able to retreat to 'Hotel Surya' a couple of miles away. Comprehensively covered by a well-designed and tightly-fitted roof that was bound to deflect any type and amount of precipitation with ease, the hut also came complete with a timber yard's worth of benches, not to mention a cubbyhole in which one or two people could comfortably bunk down if the worst came to the absolute worst, and they became stranded up-top for a night or two. Venturing into the rear abyss of the hut to further my unsolicited investigations on tip-toes, I heard a couple of groans. Again, the source of such unsettling noise couldn't be identified. Either they were emanating from the ever-flexing roof, or they were seeping through the gaps in the door. 'Please, let's go,' Jenny quietly wailed. Terrified we might be reprimanded for scaling the sacred mountain without assistance, or a signed and stamped permit, we duly scrammed, sacrificing further photo opportunities by returning to the top of the rock-strewn trail up which we'd just breathlessly clambered. The groaning continued, accompanied by a sound that could theoretically be blamed on a form of restrained shuffling. We mutually raised our eyebrows, slaying the need to mouth words. Had somebody already fallen foul of the lonely lookout and been imprisoned against their will, or were primal fears duly making a mockery of our common sense, quashing bravery whilst amplifying paranoia?

I knocked on the door. It was padlocked from the outside. Hearing no acknowledgement of my greeting, I knocked again, pounding my fist against the cold steel. Jenny had by this point braced herself for the descent, stowing her camera in her backpack, showering a brief pep-talk upon her bruised and blistered feet. 'Hello,' I chanced, half-expecting to hear and recoil from an explosion of confidence-rattling clawing on the dark side. I focused on the padlock, fumbled it into my shaking hands, then surveyed the violated keyhole. It sprung open unexpectedly, awarding me the chance to see what sparkled beyond my jitters.

Jenny could no longer be seen for tumbling scree, a grey stream of loose rock conceding to the force of gravity. The wind was whipping up, announcing the imminent arrival of a storm. 'Is anybody in there?' I called to nobody. The tiny room was the size of a cupboard. It openly appeared to house nothing more than a generator-backed refrigerator, presumably full of drinks for summit-attaining tour group members. Satisfied that everything was in order, I shut the door, only to hear a scratching sound. My attention turned to the ground, my eyes tiredly scouring the deepest recesses of the hut for floorboards. Concluding that some kind of vermin was preying on our fear-sheathed vulnerability, I bolted after Jenny without succumbing to the temptation to race towards the lip of the crater. Entertaining flashbacks to a time when I'd been obsessed with the Tom Hanks-starring movie *Joe Versus the Volcano*, I fought valiantly against the adrenaline rush that threatened to consume me, turning my back on the crater's lip before charging towards and over it. The day had been altogether too beautiful to ruin it by indulging in a one-way trip to Hell.

The only way down was via the same winding and mercilessly steep trail we'd previously negotiated on our ascent. Directly below us, a blackened shrine soured the sight of the sun which was daring to illuminate the foreboding darkness of the hardened lava field less than a kilometre distant. The tang of uprooted onions broached our nostrils. Desperate to get back to our hotel before being soaked, we speedily wound our way down to lake-level as though Satan was clipping our heels, surprised and disgusted at ourselves for being so boldly stupid in risking all that really mattered.

~

IT LOOKED LIKE THE END OF THE WORLD; IT FELT LIKE IT, TOO. Perched on the edge of a damp and dirty step, I had nothing but ugliness staring back at me. Over the road, a huge restaurant appeared to be totally deserted, akin to the gaffe in which Jack Nicholson's character horrifyingly secreted himself in *The Shining*. To my right, a middle-aged woman whose forehead had been scarred by overexposure to the sun hurried to deconstruct her mobile 'bubur ayam'-vending stand before rain intervened and washed it away. Depositing her cooking utensils, a vat of rice, and plastic bags full of chicken balls into the back of a car, she wasn't going to risk hanging around a minute longer. To my left, a parade of shuttered-up stores fell into a bend on the main road to the northern coast. Behind me stretched eternity in all its poverty-stricken glory.

I'd rode up to the mountainous environs of Kintamani primarily to catch up with Suan. His aunt owned a house in the area. Trading messages via 'Facebook', I'd promised to let him know when I arrived, unaware that there were no Internet connections for miles around. If I'd realised as much before being abandoned on a ridge overlooking the enchanting expanse of Lake Batur, I would have made a note of his mobile number so I could have got in touch with him that way. Frustrated at being disconnected on all levels, I resorted to asking dumbstruck locals in shops and on the roadside if they knew where his aunt resided. My queries drew unambiguous blanks. I even asked the old man serving 'bakso' for the bargain price of five-thousand rupiahs on a quiet road brushing the lake's south side. He struggled to understand my request for 'bakso' as it was, so I unintentionally caused him supplementary confusion when I started flinging names through the incense-scented air. 'He's called Ketut Suantika,' I said. And then I said it again, hoping his name might provoke a positive response, sensing the community to be so tight-knit that everybody would know everybody: not only as a matter of fact, but also as a matter of principle. However, owing to the language barrier, I think he thought I was hungrily hankering after a follow-up bowlful of noodle-smothered meatballs.

As I casually allowed a couple of sauce-streaked meatballs to liberally cartwheel around my mouth, a female shopkeeper ambled over for two reasons. First and foremost, she desired a bowl of 'bakso' as much as the bearded traveller beside her. Secondly, she'd overheard me mention my friend's name and was confident she could help in tracking him down. She confessed that she had school to thank for her respect-worthy grasp of English. 'So you say his name is Ketut Suantika?' she checked as we retired to a bench fronting her banana-steeped store. Still clutching our respective bowls, we aspired to work out if the guy I'd befriended in the UK was the same thirty-something man she knew. 'He's known to his family and friends as Suan for short,' I elaborated, flinging the fact that his aunt owned a guesthouse in Kintamani into the blossoming riddle. 'Well there are a lot of men and women called Ketut Suantika all over Bali, not just in our district.' My ears pricked up when she said that women could be called Ketut as well. Unadulterated puzzlement must have manifested itself in my expression because she went on to explain that the fourth-born male or female child of the 'Sudra' caste in a Hindu family is called Ketut by default. Since Bali is Hindu-dominated, many islanders' names routinely depend on their caste, with four different castes recognised on the island. The 'Brahmana' caste shields priests; the 'Ksatria' caste kowtows to rulers and warriors; the 'Wesia' caste refers to merchants and officials; and the 'Sudra' caste salutes farmers. Although Suan hailed from the farming caste, he'd recently invested in an all-terrain vehicle so he could take tourists 'on tour' around the inspirational highlands of northern Bali, honourably going some way to usurp tradition, purposefully marking distance between him and his heritage. If only I could find him so he could show me around…

Chastising my intuition for not having thought ahead and scrawled Suan's number on the back of the last bus ticket I'd balled in Ubud, I accepted that the likelihood of him wheeling past on his motorbike was slim. All I could do was move on to Lovina and inform him of my relocated whereabouts from there, Internet permitting. So, in the wake of climbing Mount Batur with a friend before she returned to China to continue studying for her degree, I was ready to edge even further north, out of the mountains and down to the sleepy seaside settlement of Lovina, via the relatively bustling town of Singaraja. 'Hotel Surya' had catered to our requirements admirably, having awarded us with a single room each. The fact I'd had to sit on the toilet to write due to insufficient light in the main room notwithstanding, I'd become unseasonably attached to the twin-bedded cell in the nine hours I spent there after dark.

I agreed to meet Jenny outside at seven in the morning, keen to wrestle the hill behind the hotel with a view to reaching the ridge-based point where we'd been dropped off at Penelokan. Adamant that the taxi ride to the hotel had taken no more than five minutes, we were astonished to discover that the distance took more than an hour to overcome on foot. Merrily humping our backpacks uphill at a spirit-crushing rate of less than one kilometre an hour, we were offered no end of lifts from passing drivers. The most common vehicles using and abusing the road were mineral-conveying trucks replete with spades and labourers digging their heads and heels into the raw material. Otherwise, it was mainly waves of black Mitsubishi Colt pick-up trucks belching toxic fumes into our faces as they wheezed past, immaculately-dressed groups of men, women and children sat in the back of them, tickled by the sorry sight of two flagging backpackers with too much pride to surrender. The eyes of one truck driver in particular amazed him to such an extent that he conspicuously slowed to a crawl in our presence, comically jutting his misshaped head through the window to loudly snicker. Clearly the shock factor of seeing a couple of foreigners struggling beneath the weight of their backpacks was too much for his vocal cords to deal with.

Jenny and I decided to walk at our own pace. Without meaning to leave her for gravel, the gap between us gradually widened as I took the lead, pace-setting a treat. Determined to make things harder than necessary for herself, she pointedly refused to let me take one of her three pieces of luggage in transit. Constantly glancing over my shoulder to make sure she was okay, I stopped and waited wherever sharp corners took hold of the road, or whenever dogs nervously barked.

An hour after trudging out of the hotel's forecourt, I heard my name being called. Believing my ears to be hearing impossible things, I continued walking, my peripheral vision expanding to incorporate the priceless view unravelling beyond the right-hand edge of the road, the smoking might of Mount Batur presiding over its liquefied counterpart in the glistening lake below. I would have halted to snap a couple of photos were it not for a familiar face seeking to drag me into a Land Cruiser. It was Jenny, cunningly cadging a free lift with a French guy she'd met on the island of Java over a week beforehand. Reeling from the fated coincidence as much as her, I was tempted to remark that Indonesia is a small country. To have made such an inane statement would have surely cost me dearly. Given that Indonesia consists of thousands upon thousands of islands spread over an enormous area of the earth's surface, the country is a water-surrounded beast to say the least.

In spite of being in sight of the ridge, I acquiesced, not wanting to appear rude by turning down the best travel-orientated offer I'd had in minutes. Feeling marginally guilty for cheating on the home-straight, I sat back and thought of England - if only for a second.

~

IT COULDN'T HAVE BEEN WORSE TIMING. A bus was about to stream past, and I had a bowl of 'bubur ayam' in my hands. Placing it on the step behind us, I shot forward into the road, attempting to flag down the speeding blur of blue. The driver saw me, that much was certain, but he had no intention of stopping to pick us up. Just as I was about to return to my breakfast, another bus steamed around the corner into view. Instinctively, I backpedalled, waving my left arm to no avail. Disregarding the speed at which he was travelling, I saw the driver smile, perversely happy to see foreigners left by the wayside. His passengers consisted mainly of men sporting white headbands on the way to a religious festival further up the road. Only ten minutes beforehand, a 'bemo' driver had taunted us, insisting we had no chance of staking a ride on any of the public buses frequenting the high road strung between Ubud and the north coast. Paranoid that he was feeding us lies, we stood our ground, adamant that at least one public bus driver would take pity on two bedraggled backpackers.

Before arriving in the vicinity with Jenny, I had no idea that the Kintamani district would be so cut-off. Public buses were few and far between; Internet was little more than a virtual buzzword; and not a single travel agency existed to help backpackers move on once they were through with scaling Mount Batur and admiring the unruffled beauty of the lake. We were at a loose end because the only way we were guaranteed to reach Lovina for lunch was by hopping into the back of a 'bemo', one of the many converted pick-up trucks which ply the roads on Bali and beyond. It had just gone eight o'clock in the morning, so time was on our side. Patience, however, stamped upon our dreams. The dreadful state of the weather was no incentive to hang around. The low cloud cover became suffocating. Coupled with the lashing rain and low temperature brought on by the high altitude, the quilt of moisture maliciously pressing down from above proposed that Jenny and I seek sanctuary on the northern coast before the rain started to really pelt its fury upon the bleak ridge where we were slumped: waiting for salvation in the form of a bus with two vacant seats and a personable driver who gave a damn. 'And breathe,' cautioned the wordsmith within.

The quiet seaside town of Lovina was purported to possess black sand. A popular place for visitors to base themselves for a day or more, it's common to see dolphins at play a few kilometres out from shore in the Bali Sea. Diving and snorkelling opportunities are also abundant. Meanwhile, for those who prefer to keep their bodies above water, Sing Sing Waterfall is only a short drive west. Such delights seemed to be a world away from the primitive hell to which we'd been banished. Barely anyone dared to venture onto the streets owing to the shocking nature of the weather. The only advantage of the forsaken street was that Jenny and I would stand out even more to bus drivers. The first 'bemo' driver we'd spoken to had been right, though. All of the buses were packed with people aiming for the celebrations at Batur Temple. Two more buses fishtailed past in quick succession, provoking yours truly to collapse on the pavement in resignation, identifying misfortune, acknowledging self-pity. Then, by rousing coincidence, the same driver who'd told us about the Hindu festival raced out of the rain-thrashed murk, U-turning over to us in front of honking cars and beeping bikes. I groaned in disbelief, reluctantly being honest with myself: the maniac was our last resort - or so it would seem.

Assuming the guise of the unlikeliest hero in Balinese history, the driver convinced us that he'd transport us to Lovina for only a fraction more than it would cost on the bus. 'I take you direct, too!' he beamed, optimistic that we were on the verge of kowtowing to his sales-pitch, knowing he was sat in a position to fleece us of everything including trust. I asked Jenny how much she was willing to pay for the privilege of being shaken around in the back of a van that hadn't been touched by a mechanic since first leaving the manufacturer's factory some twenty years beforehand. 'Seventy-five thousand each,' she whispered, intent on avoiding confrontation with the man who refused to stop revving the vehicle unless we bundled our gear into the tarpaulin-covered rear. Initially, he'd protested that it wouldn't be in his best interests to drive such a considerable distance for less than three-hundred and fifty thousand rupiahs. A master at bargaining, I slashed the fee to two-hundred thousand. 'It's still a lot of money,' I argued. Jenny nodded in agreement, a fellow slave to a lacklustre budget. 'How about you take us for one-hundred and fifty thousand?' I asked. He spat out of the window before bellowing in my face: 'Do you know how much it costs to run my van? The offer of one-hundred and fifty is an insult! I state the price, not you!' Clearly upset by the stand-off, he released the handbrake and sadly rolled down the hill towards the swamped southern extremity of the puddle-blitzed lay-by. Keen on conserving fuel, he had no intention of igniting the engine for the sake of removing his reddening face from our sight. Fearful we'd blown our only chance of fleeing the increasingly dull district, I asked Jenny if she thought it might be wise to reconsider, to effectively supply what he demanded. But there was no need. In the wake of an unscheduled toilet-break behind a fence, he got back in his van, fired it up, and reversed to where we were still stood. 'Okay. One-hundred and sixty. My last and final offer. So that's eighty each, yes? The best bargain you'll get.'

We scrambled in without further argument, positioning our backpacks side-by-side so they wouldn't roll out. Bidding adieu to the bleakly beautiful refuge of Kintamani, we hoarsely laughed in the face of fate, shivering on account of the penetrating rain, uproariously elated to be moving again.

~

'IT'S NOT FUNNY. I HAVE BRUISES ALL OVER MY LEG.'

For some strange reason, the driver had commanded us to hop out of the back of his truck and sit up front with him. As the only passengers, there was no obvious reason why we shouldn't make the most of the benches beside our backpacks. Perhaps he was simply lonely. We'd already covered at least ten kilometres since leaving Kintamani, so why did we have to suddenly alter the seating arrangement?

Outside, rain continued to lash out, provoking motorcyclists to don unfashionable ponchos. Mist reduced visibility further. If only our driver had the common sense to use the windscreen wiper. Instead, he allowed droplet after droplet to hurtle against the windscreen before they coalesced into a confusing liquid dream, forcing him to fall back on guesswork when it came to negotiating potholes and the ill-defined road edge. As the rain became heavier, I pointed to the wiper, mirroring its theoretical trajectory with my hand. 'No work,' he confessed with a disturbing chuckle. It didn't surprise me, especially not when I took into consideration the appalling state of the 'bemo' from a chassis-wide point of view. He'd instructed me to sit beside him, with Jenny squeezing in the gap between my left knee and the passenger door. All three of us wound up being shoulder-to-shoulder, hip-to-hip, knee-to-knee. The only obstruction was the gear lever. Each time he needed to change gear, he dead-legged me by ramming the lever into my right thigh, hence why I had so many bruises. Intimating that I had to shuffle even further to my left to grant him a tad more leverage, he shoulder-barged me into Jenny. She barely had any breathing space, yet she still managed to tell me how 'Facebook' was banned in China. What's more, her e-mails were censored. Some never even reached intended recipients. 'I once tried to send an innocent e-mail that happened to mention Tiananmen Square as part of the content. When I hit "send", the screen froze, suggesting that "Tiananmen" and "Square" had been tagged as disallowed buzzwords. I had no choice but to turn off my computer and restart it. There was no trace of the e-mail when I rifled through various folders on the off chance it had saved itself.' Cramped in equally as uncomfortable positions, we prayed for a 'Welcome to Lovina' sign to rear its redemptive head. As expected, we were way off.

Surrounded by mountains, we approached Batur Temple, in the grounds of which a religious festival was swinging into action. Stalls at the side of the road sold a curious mixture of offering-inspired artefacts and kitsch toys for kids. Even though it was only nine in the morning, a gargantuan crowd pulsed along the road fronting the temple. The scene put me in mind of the madness associated with Pushkar Camel Fair. Unable to see pedestrians or other vehicles in front of us, our driver combined two fail-safe techniques by extending his head out of the window (in the zany style of Ace Ventura) whilst punching one of only a couple of things that still worked: the horn. The intensity of the festival was too much, though. Peeling past at warp speed wasn't an option. Doing the one thing he hated more than anything else, he eased off the accelerator, giving the mass of Hindus decked in white just enough room to glide into the temple without blood coming to stain random body parts.

A chronic fidgeter, he couldn't keep still, constantly reaching for a comb to restyle his hair, opening and slamming his door to make sure it was shut properly, and flipping over the time-worn compilation of Indonesian Pop music jammed into the cassette deck. Amplifying an intoxicating fusion of Western and traditional melodies, electric guitar solos and progressive keyboard refrains clashed with tuneful flute flurries and haunting Kate Bush-esque vocals. Such music saved us from sitting through an uncomfortable silence. In one of his dangerously distracted moments, he scraped against another car without bothering to stop. Consumed by guilt, he was too scared to confront the other driver, worried that his precious nose might be crushed by a quality right hook. It was unlikely that either vehicle was insured. Moreover, there was a strong possibility that our driver was physically and psychologically unfit to be behind the wheel. Incidentally, the steering shaft belonged on a clown's car in a circus. No joke. Every time he aspired to turn left, it was necessary to shunt the shaft to the right, the slack nature of the turning circle crowning an extended list of 'Causes for Concern'. As for the dashboard, nothing remained of it. In its place, a compact whirlwind of wires chased a couple of cable-ties from the ignition across to the gear lever. The dials didn't budge in any capacity for the entirety of the journey, rendering it impossible to get a handle on our cruising speed, or the number of kilometres we'd killed since rumbling away from Penelokan.

As we gradually wound our way down to sea level, leaving a surprisingly unappealing concoction of grubby mountainscapes in our wake, the sun emerged, shedding light upon the Bali Sea as we struck the coast at Singaraja. It was like returning to civilisation after spending a pronounced period of time in solitary confinement. Inviting Internet cafes advertised fast connection speeds on prominent hoardings as we nosed our way towards the bus terminal.

'I drop you here,' our driver dryly announced. 'No way! You said you'd take us all the way to Lovina. That was the deal, and the only reason we agreed to come with you,' I retaliated. Lovina's stretch of black sand-glazed beaches lay approximately eight kilometres away. He abandoned the left-turn he was midway through executing as soon as Jenny chimed in her support, swerving back onto the main coastal road ringing the bulk of the island, much to the detriment of cars and bikes behind us. 'What is the name of your hotel?' he mumbled. Splurging our energy on being spontaneous, neither one of us had booked anywhere to stay. 'Take us somewhere cheap,' I remarked. 'I don't know where that hotel is,' he responded. 'No - you misunderstand. We do not have anywhere to stay. We would like two single rooms in a hotel or "homestay" that are very cheap,' I clarified. Belatedly unveiling his kindness, he bounced us down a multitude of lanes in search of accommodation. We eventually decided to stay at 'Puspa Rama', scoring two rooms for the reasonable price of one-hundred thousand rupiahs each.

Swatting an aerial assault of mosquitoes towards the nearest wall as I strode into the room, I barely allowed myself time to relax before booking an onward ticket out of Lovina. I had just nine days remaining on my thirty-day Indonesian visa. Having so far spent time on no more than two islands, I shook my non-existent itinerary into being. I needed to get onto the island of Java without delay so I could meet a friend in Jakarta come the weekend. How I was going to reach the country's capital in two days was beyond me, especially since I was prepared to tackle the epic journey by using achingly slow bus and boat services alone.

~

THE ONLY ELEMENT MISSING WAS TUMBLEWEED. I felt like Marty McFly, engaged in a Wild West stand-off at midday; trapped between two rival travel agents, I didn't know which way to turn. I knew which way I wanted to turn, but the agent selling the most expensive ticket to Jakarta gazed at me as though he'd break both my legs were I to defect and purchase a ticket from the cheaper establishment behind me. Tourism really can be a cutthroat business, not just in Indonesia, but in countries all over the world. Everybody wants a slice of the money it harbours the potential to generate, hence why competition to sell tickets and promote tours can be so fierce. It's common sense to buy any kind of product from the place selling it at the lowest price, yet the man flogging combination tickets to Jakarta for four-hundred and twenty thousand rupiahs still couldn't understand why I was prepared to skip over the road to buy the same ticket for three-hundred and sixty-thousand. For some reason, it didn't make sense to him. If he was willing to compromise and duly lower his price, I might have considered relaying my hard-earned cash over his counter, but the gulf between prices was too large. In spite of my obvious persuasion, the rip-off merchant beckoned me over to his agency in the same breath that the ticket-seller boasting better prices urged me to retreat to her bureau. I suddenly felt obliged to split myself in two so I could offer them both a piece of me. Whatever happened to freedom of choice? I resented the pressure heaped upon me. All I desired was a value-for-money passage to the Indonesian capital. Risking a torrent of abuse, I turned and accompanied the lady to her desk where she signed and dated a generic scrap of paper. It sported the illegible name of a bus company. She told me to wait outside her bureau at six o'clock the following morning. Desperate to know the name of the bus station at which I would arrive in Jakarta, I dug for details. 'I'm only an agent,' she remarked, excusing herself. 'There's a strong chance it will be "Puspa Sari", but I'm not certain.' I thanked her for her help whilst psyching myself up for the walk of shame past the agency I'd betrayed. I should never have bought biscuits and bottles of water there after all. Sometimes no trade is better for all concerned. I'd only asked the price of the ticket to Jakarta out of interest, keen to collate and compare quotes like any seasoned traveller is liable to do. It was too late now, though. A deal had been struck over the road. The opposition would just have to 'man up' and accept that he needed to lower his prices in order to make more money - as ironic as such a concept sounded. A dash of market research would have benefitted his business enormously, for there can be no allowances made for bully-boy tactics in a sector fraught with so much healthy competition.

I was still in Lovina, having fought my way north through Bali from Kuta, via Sanur, Ubud and Kintamani. As much as my eyes ached to see the island of Lombok, my clockwise intuition suggested it would be wise to leave the islands east of Nusa Lembongan for a future trip. Fortunately, one of Indonesia's most fascinating islands lay immediately west of Bali in the form of Java. Back when I'd considered all options concerning onward travel, I'd enquired about the cost of flying from Denpasar to Jakarta. Even though it would have meant backtracking from north to south through Bali, the hardship entailed might have been worth it if an inexpensive flight was rumbled. As expected, a range of 'Air Asia' deals tempted me to rush straight back over the mountains: the lowest fare flew in at just over four-hundred thousand rupiahs. Since it took just thirty minutes to fly between Surabaya and Denpasar, I estimated the flight time between Denpasar and Jakarta to be roughly ninety minutes. In gross comparison, the only other way to reach Jakarta from Bali would necessitate at least two buses and one ferry ride... or a bus, a ferry, then a train. By land and sea, the trip would obliterate the meatiest morsel of twenty-four hours. Depending on the condition of the vehicles involved, not to overlook the weather, it could potentially take longer. Nonetheless, my days as a traveller who enjoys doing things the hard way were far from over. More importantly, the scenery en-route to Jakarta was tipped to unveil an awe-inspiring succession of gasp-inducing surprises. Diligently sweeping aside the cons of my plan, I focused on the pros, justifying my decision to spontaneously travel by any means without allowing images of emerald runways and airport terminals dominated by free Wi-Fi to stream through my mind.

Lovina had less going for it than I'd hoped it would. Its necklace of black sand proved photogenic in its own right, but it wasn't a place that could comfortably be tolerated for longer than a couple of days owing to its small-village feel and the hassle it inspired. One masseuse in particular was on to me, tailing me every time I exited the hotel grounds. The previous day I'd told her that I might consider having a massage 'tomorrow'. Now she wouldn't leave me alone, unwilling to accept that I'd said what I had in jest to stop her from hassling me further. Therein bloomed the ragged extent of the irony.

The beach appeared to be perpetually patrolled by ownerless dogs on the lookout for fresh flesh in which to sink their teeth. Having read that an average of eighty-five dog bites were reported every day across the island, I refused to take chances, wading into the sea - in spite of my jeans and leather shoes - if any canines strayed within a five metre radius. Territorial by nature, they hated to see foreigners suppressing sand on their patch, often silently springing from beneath moored boats to sharpen the surprise element involved in attacks.

As I tripped east along the beach, I pondered. I was due to fly home to England from Malaysia in less than three weeks, yet I was still a long, long way from KL. The next stage of my journey was destined to be beautiful and brutal in equal measure. Nobody enjoys being subjected to stuffy, bumpy and exhausting bus rides, yet the prospect of hitting the road for such an epic ride excited me beyond measure. The priority was to reach the Balinese dock at Gilimanuk via the coastal road. It would see me pass through places such as Seririt, Gondol and Pulaki, the latter village from which it is sometimes possible to glimpse sea turtles.

Directly south of Pulaki stretches the West Bali National Park, an expansive bounty of mountains ranging between Mount Kelatakan's squat profile and the one-thousand five-hundred and eighty metre-high brute known as Mount Patas. However, all of the mountains in the protected region pale into relative insignificance when compared to Mount Agung, situated southeast of Mount Batur. Over three-thousand metres in height, Agung is indeed the daddy of Balinese peaks.

Beyond Gilimanuk, I'd be relying on the ferry to guide me.

~

I KNEW IT WAS GOING TO BE A LONG HAUL, but the bus ride was getting out of hand. Where were we, and was there any chance of reaching the sprawling Indonesian capital by nightfall as promised? Harbouring a barrage of doubts, I returned my attention to the grimy window, casting my gaze across the plain of paddy fields stretching to the far horizon and beyond. The flat landscape was otherwise featureless. Not a single hill roamed into view. Such fields were still a sight for sore eyes. For the past ten hours there had been little more to look at than litter-choked roads trailing off from the main highway that dissects the colossal island of Java.

I should have flown. It would have been much simpler, and only a tad more expensive. The adrenaline-addict in me had hastened to book a combination bus and boat ticket from the reserved resort of Lovina, though. The journey had started well, its shuttle bus-based rush to the busy port of Gilimanuk allowing my eyes to smart from the majestic beauty of northern Bali. In spite of initially detesting Lovina, I'd come to adore the place in the wake of discovering a certain stretch of its black sand a mile west from my guesthouse. Indeed, the beaches in the Lovina area trail the photogenic coastline for approximately twelve kilometres.

A disquietingly tranquil alternative to the southern beaches of Bali, Lovina's charms are undeniably subtle, but once they've worked their magic, you'll be detained at their mercy until you regrettably force yourself to abscond. Dismissing the advances of the aforementioned masseuse, the majority of locals were non-intrusive. They didn't get overly upset if you strolled by their shop or restaurant without showering a glance in their attention-expecting direction. As a result, guilt failed to edge into Eden.

Keeping my distance from the beach-hugging slew of restaurants, I marched towards the main coastal road upon which I found two family-run eateries within a kilometre of one another. Neither of them had been previously patronaged by a foreigner, yet both cooks obliged my desire for steaming plates of 'nasi campur' and 'nasi goreng' within two minutes of such traditional fodder being requested. Supping 'Frestea' as I ate, I wisened up to the area's delights, becoming even keener to keep company with the road to observe the various processes involved in rice harvesting.

Paddy fields sandwiched the ribbon of asphalt in spectacular style, their flooded environs brown due to the mire of mud oozing underfoot. I would say that such fields came in all shapes and sizes if that had been the case, but the majority of fields were almost perfectly square in shape, of roughly similar sizes to adjacent plots of stunningly fertile land. Tended to by bent-backed men and women shaded by the conical might of coolie hats, the rice fields assumed lives of their own as farmers stooped to assess the latest crop. Meanwhile, a lonesome farm worker on the outskirts of Singaraja resorted to employing an antiquated aid in the cumbersome form of a seed-planter, heaving the wheeled contraption up and down the field in straight lines. Careful not to invade anybody's sacred privacy, I faced south to shoot an explosion of photos framed by the eastern extremity of the West Bali National Park. Atmospherically backed by a range of mist-devoured mountains, the scene was literally set for a photo-shoot of breathtaking proportions as school-bound children on motorbikes weaved behind me, hurling good-natured sarcasm over my head. The spread of fields was interrupted only by the road itself, along with its eye-stinging array of motorbike repair shops which intermittently supplied racket-laced vigour to the sumptuous lay of the luxuriant land.

I retired to my favourite roadside café for food, scuppering the sun's wish to singe my forehead. Not noticing a dog stealing shade beneath a table, I accidentally brushed against its hind legs as I sat, duly rousing the canine into an unbecoming frenzy. I should have been more observant. I'd spotted the dog in repose there on previous occasions, so I would only have had myself to blame had the skeletal brute seen fit to munch on one of my legs, potentially relaying rabies in the most bloodcurdling fashion. My saving grace presented itself in the café's owner who shooed the dog away, launching a meat-coated bone towards the road, hoping the shady crossbreed might take the hint and scarper to leave me in peace. She couldn't help but proudly unveil the smile of the victorious when the dog fled, the stray's gaze meeting the bone halfway as the projectile's trajectory became prematurely compromised by a roadside collision with a signpost. It was my cue to eat, so I did, honouring the silence brought on by a rare break in the traffic. All that could be heard was the sound of the owner's obese daughter meditatively chopping onions primed for inclusion in upcoming spreads of 'nasi campur'. She hadn't looked up once since I'd eased my legs beneath the sauce-heaped table. Swivelling around to cast my ever-expanding field of vision towards the Bali Sea, I wondered what the sullen girl might have been thinking, conscious that she could have been wishing she was elsewhere, living a different kind of life entirely. Ironically, a shred of my essence envied her seemingly innocent existence. It might have been impoverished by degrees, yet I could imagine myself engaged in the simple life, preparing vegetables day-in and day-out amidst the scenic splendour of a seaside settlement on a tropical island disconnected from the depressing trappings of contemporary society. An eminently adaptable master of reinvention, I would intuitively look upon any change of scenery as an embraceable blessing, going out of my way to seek truth in the purity of innocence.

Suddenly, I was glad of the mistake that had been made. Nine hours earlier, an unrepentant knock on my door had threatened to splinter the wood from which it was composed were I not to answer the person on the other side. As it was, I'd just shouldered my misshaped backpack with the intention of leaving, hoping a six a.m. bus would be waiting to convey me to Gilimanuk.

'Mr. Stephen... are you still alive?' hollered a faceless woman. 'Yes, yes,' I stalled, stumbling, rifling through a landslide of outdated magazines in search of the door key. 'I'm stuck,' I called, neglecting to elaborate about the whys and wherefores of my apparent entrapment. 'Yes. You are, Mr. Stephen. I was wrong about the bus.' In spite of uncovering the key beneath a week-old copy of *The Bali Times*, my heart sank. 'It leaves from outside my place at three in the afternoon, not six in the morning. Please accept my apology.' Burdened with a further nine hours to slaughter in Lovina, I thanked the travel agent for letting me know before I returned to bed. Daylight might have begun to seep skyward, but there was only one place I wanted to be: in a land far, far away.

~

'ARE WE NEARLY THERE YET?' It was arguably the most overused question in the history of travel, yet my thirst for knowledge had so far drawn blanks from everybody I'd asked. Then, two seats in front of me, a man cocked his head, tuning his hair-stricken ear into my plea for the truth and nothing but. 'We should be there in about eight hours,' he stated, butchering my chance to respond by slipping on a pair of headphones before I formulated an answer. As if to re-iterate what the man had said, a roadside sign flashed by. It read: 'Jakarta 470'. Implying in no uncertain terms that the city was still almost five-hundred kilometres distant, the dented hunk of steel (a.k.a. the bus) undermined my resolve to sit still. I'd been hunched beside a petite Indonesian lady for the past twenty-two hours. The only time we'd spent apart had been on the hour-long ferry ride from Gilimanuk to a starlit port on the eastern edge of Java. She'd even opted to sit beside me when we'd pulled up for breakfast and dinner, perhaps seeing me as some kind of alien guardian angel, however bedraggled I appeared.

I'd been warned that the journey by land and sea from Lovina to Jakarta could take up to thirty-five hours if fate was particularly unkind. Having endured and somehow survived a succession of epic bus and train rides elsewhere in the world, I'd prepared myself for a day and night of unquestionable hardship on a bus with a fiery driver at its helm. Nevertheless, a part of me wished that I'd held my proverbial horses in Gilimanuk and stayed there the night before easing over the placid strait holding the islands at bay.

The two-hour journey to the very edge of Bali's north-western extremity had seen us plunge between lush forests of vegetation and the wave-massacred Bali Sea. Although I failed to glimpse any sea turtles or dolphins en-route as I trained my eyes on the water, I came to realise that Bali seduces each and every sense more than is seemingly possible. A feast for one's eyes, ears, mouth, nose and hands, its palette of spectacular landscapes dilates pupils to straining point, its ever-present thrum of birdsong making you long for an ear-candling session so you can better appreciate such lilting music, its divine range of authentic food inviting taste buds to attend foam parties, its earthy aromas and never-far-away incense sticks stimulating one's nasal cavity to "Scratch 'n' Sniff" heaven and back, while the mountains, forests and sea uniformly beg to be touched, to be felt by one and all in order that they can duly feel.

Left to our own devices outside a café, we had to wait for an hour before a connecting coach whisked us onto an awaiting ferry. It was geared up to transport cargo and vehicles as much as it was foot passengers. The approach to the ramp was strewn with middle-aged men aspiring to sell wrapped-up pouches of 'nasi', transparent bags of cracker-like sweets, and unbranded bottles of water. One guy even managed to bustle halfway down the gangway before being turfed off. Brandishing a ukulele, he sang and played a wistful Indonesian song before stamping towards the door with his right paw held out, begging in the wake of busking. As soon as the driver wedged the vehicle in a corner of the ferry's lowest deck, passengers piled off with a view to charging onto one of the two upper decks above the wealth of cargo, cars and coaches being manoeuvred into position by trained personnel. I sunk into a chair on the middle deck, struck by the sight of what I wrongly presumed to be men sorting laundry. Three men could clearly be seen sifting through mats before they accosted one each, easing themselves onto their knees. Little did I know they were Muslim men ensconced in the fine art of praying, the cabin behind a wall-mounted TV playing host to a mobile mosque of-sorts. A café at the rear of the middle deck roared to the sound of people demanding glasses of hot tea and packets of biscuits. Shielding my stomach from food, I surveyed the strait. Light was failing, darkness was falling, and the world had never seemed to be so at peace. Though an inconsiderate armada of boats prevented us from easing away from the dock, I embraced the formidable feeling of being back at sea as the far mountains of eastern Java dematerialised before my eyes, the shroud of night stealing them away from sight, substituting a paltry silhouette in their place until the dawn of a new day could hanker after regaining lost ground. An international football match blared on TV, but nobody was watching; by and large, the twittering mass of fellow passengers was either preoccupied with consuming food, or equally as taken by the quality of light playing on the water's surface.

The winking lights of Gilimanuk waved us off with an anticlimactic flourish, the surge of another power-cut on land making us suddenly thankful that we were primed to escape for a brighter shore. The slow speed of the ferry had to be experienced to be believed. Just when I hoped another gear might be metaphorically engaged, the rusting rectangle of metal lurched straight around the Cape of Pointlessly Projected Hope without stopping, its mechanical indifference humming a painfully melancholic ode to acceleration.

Tired of overhearing small talk that I didn't understand, I loped up the steps, expecting to stumble into a toilet, but instead finding an upper deck built around an open-plan viewing area on which people milled, smoking the dying day away. There was nothing stopping people from smoking anywhere else on the ferry, least of all on the kid-packed middle deck, but the majority of smokers ironically warmed to the chill of the open deck, iconically leaning against railings as though they belonged in a cult art-house flick.

Spotting the token foreigner in me, and a non-smoker to boot, an Indonesian man ambled over to talk. His spiel about him being involved in the import and export trade failed to unnerve me. I stood my ground, listening, watching the sky slide into a darker shade of purple, the water reacting to the celestial transition by reflecting such eternal magnificence. It transpired that the man had been working in Nusa Dua. He was returning to his family home in Jakarta, openly confessing that he'd never before seen a foreigner making the journey over to the Indonesian capital by bus and boat. 'You must be crazy,' he smirked, assuming I smoked by shoving a cigarette beneath my already offended nose. 'And so must you to be smoking the way you do,' I responded, having seen him suck back on three nicotine sticks in alarming succession. He took both the hint and himself back to where he'd come from. Minutes later, preparing to dock, he accidentally nutted the top of the door as he passed through it. I, meanwhile, bolted, vying to locate my AC-cursed coach before it rumbled off with my clothes.

~

HE WOULD SURELY BE AWAKE for the next forty-eight hours, the ten-year-old 'Ovaltine' addict leering over the seat. We were still aiming for Jakarta. The parents of the boy regarded his behaviour as normal. It was anything but. He was eating the powder from an 'Ovaltine' sachet, perhaps oblivious to the fact that hot water should be added to such powder first. He ripped open two sachets within five minutes and licked the lot, grinning mischievously after discarding the empty sachets on the otherwise clean gangway. Surprisingly, the coach was in a shockingly sound state of repair. For the first time in three months, I'd actually boarded the kind of bus that I'd been promised at the travel agency. It was a luxury mode of conveyance, right from its reclining seats which actually worked, all the way down to the DVD-playing TV up front. The sole downside blasted headwards in the form of its centrally-controlled air-conditioning. Cranked down to the coldest setting possible, the AC conspired to inspire colds in even the most well-prepared travellers. I'd wondered why some passengers who'd boarded at Gilimanuk were layered-up to the nines in jumpers and jackets. All had subsequently become clear. Sporting little more than a T-shirt, I had no choice but to shiver my way across Java, wrapping the blanket provided around me as tightly as possible. In a gesture of unexpected kindness, passengers were awarded complimentary boxes of food and drink once settled. It was just a pity that the size and heaviness of the box belied its meagre contents. Inside, a sealed plastic cup of water had resolutely pulverised the poor excuse for a chocolate-filled croissant. To have dubbed the pastry 'pain au chocolat' would have done a gross disservice to the French equivalent's lusted-after reputation.

Nevertheless, I ate what remained of the pastry as we continued to bumble west.

Having initiated our jaunt across Java at six the previous evening, we were midway through one of the longest hauls I'd so far undertaken. The same driver had been shifting gears for the past nine hours, surely wishing that he had a buddy who could take over whenever bursts of tiredness overtook. Given that it was three in the morning, I should have been asleep, yet the discomforting demeanour of the mobile icebox prevented my eyes from staying closed. In theory, they should have frozen shut. Scoping out the various states of repose elicited by people around me, I was in the minority. Hoping that reading a few more chapters of *The Choice* by Nicholas Sparks might bore me to tears and then slumber, I fished in my satchel for the copy I'd been given. To the contrary, it kept me awake, its lovelorn plot setting my heart ablaze. Three hours later, as a new day encroached, I was thumbing my way towards the end of the novel, the watery state of my eyes attracting an unwarranted amount of attention from two men sat on the other side of the bin-pocked gangway. Mocking my sensitive nature, they laughed and pointed as a cavalcade of tears made a beeline for my cheeks. Determined to prove that I was in no way embarrassed to have been so profoundly moved by a three-hundred and seventeen page-long tract of romance-drenched prose, I glanced over at the men as I closed the book. 'You are in pain?' the youngest man asked. I shook my head whilst tapping my shirt's left breast pocket, attempting to imply that my heart lay in tatters as a result of such a beautifully penned story. Such a gesture made them laugh all the more.

We stopped for breakfast at eight. Holed up in a restaurant that existed solely for the use of coaches travelling long-distance, it oozed all the trappings and charm of a truck-stop ingloriously set adrift in the middle of nowhere. Apportioned thirty minutes to get our fill of the free food and drink, the majority of passengers pushed and shoved towards the self-service area as though Armageddon threatened and The Last Supper awaited. They duly procured a plate each before shuffling along in line, helping themselves to precariously heaped mountains of white rice which they surrounded with curry, pickled cabbage, leggy fried chicken, and dabs of unbearably hot chilli sauce. At the end of the line, a trolley of mugged tea persuaded fans of the sweet beverage to indulge. Unsure about the protocol involved, I stepped aside to observe. I noticed that every passenger surrendered a specific section of their bus ticket; representing a redeemable token, the tear-off section reminded me of the vouchers that students used at school if certain circumstances entitled them to free dinners. When I thought about it some more, I actually felt as though I'd been spirited back in time to Driffield School's canteen. Perhaps it was the spine-chilling sound of scraping chairs and the scent of reheated food which was to blame. Then, suppressing my school-based memories, I imagined that I was in prison, namelessly falling in line to receive the only meal of the day. Fearing the worst, I ladled as much food upon my plate as those who'd waddled before me. Two guys had already rejoined the queue, greedily clamouring for seconds.

I'd been warned that the scenery en-route to Jakarta wouldn't necessarily be something to e-mail home about. Having been seduced by the bountiful beauty of Bali, I'd hoped that Java might wield a similar strain of awe-inspiring diversity when it came to ushering forth its landscapes. Our course took us nowhere near Mount Bromo, though. Nor did we sweep past any ancient temples of note. For the most part, the dull road was sandwiched by an endless parade of shops, motorbike repair joints, and 'nasi goreng'-promoting restaurants. A succession of toll roads were also encountered, allowing our driver to floor the coach like never before, indecisively hogging both the slow and fast lane, unwilling to let any vehicles wider than motorbikes overtake. A self-appointed road hog, he evidently wanted to lead the way to the Indonesian capital, an unsubstantiated uprising of pride preceding the fume-spewing passage he'd spawned with professional flair.

If only Jakarta was upon us. If only its skyscraper-clad CBD could be glimpsed. If only I knew what I was going to do when I arrived. If only I'd done more research about the twelfth most populous city in the world that had once been known as Batavia.

~

THROUGH WITH A WHIP around Jakarta's National Monument and its atmospheric harbour with Geography teacher Amy, I returned to a home from home in Singapore. Although I reacquainted myself with the city by way of Changi Airport's cold floor, it didn't take long to get into the city centre via shuttle bus. Singapore is notoriously well-connected in every respect, both in terms of its transportational capabilities and the extent to which it's hooked up to the rest of the world via technology. Efficiency - if not value for money - is key.

Clearing Immigration with arresting ease, I was escorted to a parking bay on the frightfully clean doorstep of Terminal One. Though the terminal was the victim of renovation, the spectre of potential inconvenience couldn't have been more blurred. For just nine Singaporean dollars, I was whisked to Arab Street via the coastal road which stalks the east side of the island. I'd requested to be dropped off in the Kampong Glam area, but the driver had demanded a specific hotel address. Fully prepared to trawl around the city in search of budget accommodation, I told him that I'd walk from Arab Street to better scope out the options. 'If you don't have an address, I can't take you,' he warned. 'Arab Street is an address,' I argued. His frown suggested that I better fathom a more specific address. 'Okay... take me to "Sleepy Sam's Guesthouse" on Bussorah Street,' I said, ever-keen to please. He nodded and engaged first gear, glancing in his rear view mirror to make sure the other passengers were comfortable.

Traffic lurched into 'heavy' territory on the periphery of the finance-orientated CBD as early as eight. Cruising around its eastern edge, we struck Beach Road and rolled in a rough northerly direction, halting to let go of a backpacking girl at 'The Little Red Dot' gaffe. The conveniently located hostel coolly made reference to one of the country's nicknames. I was half-tempted to hop out after her; it looked to be a funky place to stay. Instead, I sat it out, leaning in to a left hook that was determined to pummel Middle Road. We duly fought our way along Victoria Street, eventually righting ourselves on Ophir Road. Given Bussorah Street's admirable predilection for favouring pedestrians over vehicles, the driver stopped and pointed his finger. 'Down there,' he gestured, his index finger brushing the tip of Sultan Mosque, a trick of perspective fooling my eyes into believing that the photogenic place of worship was closer than it really was.

The receptionist had been expecting me to roll up nine hours beforehand. Having reserved a bed in the backpacker-heaped guesthouse via Internet, I'd estimated my time of arrival to be around eleven p.m. the previous evening. As it was, I'd succumbed to Singaporean 'Chinese Whispers' at the airport which suggested that the guesthouse locked its doors at ten. Without the door's security code stowed in my mind, I would struggle to ingratiate myself with the building's interior without waking guests within.

No stranger to crashing in rigid seats at airports the world over, I fancied that I'd score at least a couple of hours sleep. Before closing my eyes, I placed a foot through one of my backpack's straps. That way, if I did nod off, nobody would be able to steal my gear without first lifting my dead-weighted leg to gain purchase. Unless they came equipped with a sharp knife, of course. Planting my body near a window, I caught sight of something befuddling. Conscious that my eyes were prone to pick up orbs in the strangest of circumstances, I tried to blink away my disbelief. But yes... levitating sparks of light were shifting back and forth on a perfectly horizontal plane. I didn't know what to make of them. I later realised that what I'd seen had been the internal carriage lights on a low-speed skytrain conveying people between different terminals. Reassured that I hadn't been hallucinating, I inelegantly slid off the chair and onto the freshly polished floor, aching to lie down. I subsequently stretched out until a security guard intimated that it would be in my best interests to inconspicuously relocate my inert body. His superior had the power to imprison me if he classed my apparent crime as serious. Anxious that I could be locked up if I didn't comply, I moved, reminding myself of some of the silly things deemed illegal in Singapore.

Importation and distribution of chewing gum is against the law for a start, with fines often imposed on folk complacent enough to spit gum on the streets. Smokers aiming to quit by using nicotine gum are fortunately spared; the chewing of gum for medicinal purposes is permitted. Surprisingly, jay-walking is not strictly illegal, unlike in Canada, where bored cops routinely siphon as much money out of nonplussed foreigners as they can. I'd been caught in the act whilst strolling through Calgary. A car-bound officer beckoned me over to his vehicle before threatening me with an on-the-spot sixty-dollar penalty. Be warned, though: if you're traversing the wrong road at the wrong time in The 'Pore, you could still get fined. It's even been known for first-time offenders to be stung with penalties to the tune of one-thousand dollars: approximately five-hundred British pounds. The act of riding bicycles through underpasses isn't for the fainthearted either - for precisely the same reason.

What else is illegal in Singapore? I willed my brain back into action, in spite of the late hour. Drugs were definitely to be avoided. Dealing, distributing or 'doing' them was bound to badger serious repercussions. Few exceptions would be made, and even fewer excuses would be entertained. For those caught with hard drugs, a hanging could well wind up being the death of them. Drug dealers disposed of, the 'Lion City' is certainly no country for litter-bugs. Cynically thinking outside the box, I half-expected trees to be felled were they to shed a leaf, even if a passing breeze was to blame and the barked beauties were innocent. Pursuing such an outlandish train of thought, I dreaded to imagine what would become of copses come autumn. Deep down, I knew it was going to be difficult to re-adapt to a country ruled by regime, but I was ready and willing to take my chances.

The male receptionist was neither sleepy nor Sam. I never did catch his name. Annoyingly, he rejoiced in using my unabbreviated Christian name, purposefully making me feel guilty for not arriving earlier. Fresh-out-of-bed guests dreamily squeezed behind me as I checked in. A mouth-watering breakfast consisting of fresh fruit greeted each and every one of them. I, meanwhile, was left to hunt for food on the streets. Unable to stake a dormitory bed until midday, I stood my backpack in a rack overflowing with left luggage. On the streets, beyond the streamlined profile of Sultan Mosque, I allowed my nose to guide me to Chinatown where I grabbed a plate of fried vegetable balls served with a saucer of spice. At three dollars, the so-called meal was a blatant rip-off. The photo-laced menu had promised a plate of ten balls or more, drowned by an ocean of appetising salad. My dish was served without the slightest whiff of a single lettuce leaf, yet I was still charged full price. Never mind, I mused. Little India was a short walk away... and it would soon be lunch-time.

~

BOASTING AN ENVIABLE BLEND OF ARCHITECTURE from different periods and in varying styles, the tropical island city of Singapore is certainly a sight for ruralised eyes if you've been away from civilisation for a prolonged period of time. Aesthetically-pleasing from every angle, it presents some of the most extraordinary and dizzying buildings the world has ever seen, going so far as to give the forward-thinking likes of Dubai and Vegas a run for their gazillions.

Encouragingly, it's not just in the skyscraper-outlined Financial District where you'll find the latest and greatest feats of engineering. Some of the oldest buildings in the city remain the most impressive, the truly beautiful nature of 'Raffles Hotel' triumphing in capturing one's imagination as soon as steps are taken past the immaculately attired doormen. Paying testament to the opulence of a bygone era when Sir Stamford Raffles fortified his designs on the city, the hotel is a marvel. The sole downside to a trip inside is the price of food and drink. A friend called Leigh from my hometown had warned me that a 'Singapore Sling' was likely to cost as much as forty dollars, or twenty pounds, not least because the gin-based cocktail was born in the hotel's Long Bar. At least it cost nothing to peruse, unless I was populating a league of my own when I swept through on a whim. A short distance away, 'Raffles Hospital' can be found. This time around, I breezed past the junction-abutting building without a care in the world. It was a far-cry from when I'd visited the hospital in 2006 for a post-bite rabies jab.

Trundling onto Victoria Street, I aimed my feet towards the nearest bridge over the Singapore River. En-route, I wound up walking past St. Andrew's Cathedral, a stunning place of worship a font's hurl from the waterfront. Washed in white, it acts as a central beacon of purity and hope. In a similar fashion, the city at large leads by example in many ways, its strict laws suggesting that everything's dandy. However, if laws applied to any given town, city or country become progressively stricter, it doesn't always mean that crime is gradually reduced as a result. What happens instead, more often than not, is that crime plunges deeper underground. So, while Singapore might appear to be almost crime-free and exceedingly safe even in the darkest and most far-flung districts, the smokescreen effect can only ever fool so many for so long.

I fancied a walk towards Sentosa, a smaller neighbouring island suffused with all the fun of the proverbial fair. An adrenaline-activating playground for children and adults alike, there are numerous ways to let one's hair down, whether by commandeering a Segway, zip-lining over a swathe of jungle canopy, communing with nature within its Butterfly Park and Insect Kingdom, or learning about the history of Fort Siloso by exploring its old tunnels.

Spying no slip road over to the island, I headed in the direction of the train station as a rainstorm swept through the CBD's soulless urban canyons. Careful not to get fined for jay-walking, I followed the masses, waiting patiently for cheeky green men to flash at the busiest intersections. If I came to a point where there was no pedestrian crossing in place, I either dashed over the road, hoping for the best, or I swung left or right and followed the pavement until it yielded a light-aided place to cross, safe in the knowledge that there was absolutely no chance I could be fined. Unless my feet happened to overstep the white lines marking the road, that was.

Ironically, as soon as I began crossing a large proportion of roads, the light-contained green man began flashing faster than ever, suggesting that I better get a move on if I didn't aim to be, a) flattened by traffic, or b) chased by a cash-hungry cop. One sign I couldn't help but notice read: 'Vehicles parked here will be referred to the Traffic Police'. Was 'referred' really the most appropriate word that could have been used? It seemed altogether too ambiguous, potentially implying that such vehicles were going to be awarded a gratifying reference. In reality, they would no doubt be taken to a compound and then a crusher if the owner failed to pay the levied fine. Anyway, where was I? Ah yes... that's where I was! I was pondering if I could get fined for crossing a road if the green man was flashing with greater regularity than a pervert. It was a distinct possibility. Granting my mind space to somersault in contemplation, I took a moment to breathe, clocking a man rooting in his ear, digging for wax. A second later, he extracted his finger and flicked a nub in an arc towards the gutter. 'Noooooooooooo!' I felt conditioned to scream. I even half-considered propelling my body into the type of horizontal position made famous by Superman. Summoning The Good Samaritan within, I couldn't let the wax fall to the ground in case The Earwax Police had set their sights on the man. It was a moral obligation to help prevent a fellow foreigner from getting fined a fortune for something he perhaps didn't even realise was a crime. But that's the thing. Could flicking earwax in public be construed as a crime, or was I being overly cautious? Pouring yet another vat of fuel upon my burgeoning paranoia, Michael, a friend from the UK, had just messaged to highlight another faux-pas that could wind up being costly: 'Not flushing the toilet after you've used it can come with a fine of up to one-hundred and fifty dollars. Many toilets have infra-red sensors, so it can be easily detected if someone's been lazy and just walked away without being considerate enough to do their part in helping to keep the city as clean as can be.'

Michael had lived in Holland Village. He'd worked in and out of Singapore for the best part of five long years. Employed in the media industry, the country had provided a sound base for him. Keen to get an insider's lowdown on the city, I asked him about the best things to see and do. In response, he mentioned the obvious, along these straight and narrow lines: if money's no object, head for Orchard Road in order to shop yourself silly; should you possess a head for heights, take a ride on the world's largest observation wheel, The Singapore Flyer; if you aspire to drink amidst an atmosphere of sophistication, pay a visit to 'Hacienda' in the Dempsey area. Meanwhile, if you fancy catching sight of animals during your stay, a visit to the zoo or a ride on the Night Safari should cater to your needs. For sure, you're unlikely to see much wildlife on the streets of the city other than in the form of unassuming cats. Singapore's certainly no country for stray dogs. Replying to Michael's message, I asked him if he still had any friends kicking back in the city. I was surprised when he said he didn't, until he elaborated. 'They all got bored and left,' he remarked, which forced me to wonder how much longer I might stay.

~

WHY DID THE CHICKEN REALLY CROSS THE ROAD? Because it was cooped in a liberal country where it could! I, on the other hand, stalled every time I attempted to cross, living in fear of being fined beyond my limited financial means. Vying to admire the soaring Singapore Flyer from its base, I needed to somehow traverse Esplanade Drive. Stuck at a crossroads, the only way to reach the far side was to negotiate three other roads in turn; it was just one of those junctions, summing up Singapore perfectly in light of it being so frustrating. I'd spied something that resembled an underpass, but it merely granted access to the nearest MRT station. Three security cameras hung their heads high, capturing every speck of action in the vicinity. Twenty yards further along the same road, another set of three cameras monitored passers-by. Being brazen for once, I threw a smile at the pack of cameras, toying with the possibility that I'd be arrested. Indeed, Orwell's 1984 had nothing on modern-day Singapore. Even if a casual jay-walker or serial litter-dropper isn't nabbed in real time, there's a strong chance they could be tracked all the way back to wherever they're staying to be fined subsequently. There really is no escape. Given its island status, Singapore could be compared to a colony, under constant and unfairly invasive scrutiny. Freedom of speech might be all the rage, but if you step out of line, you're bound to be cornered and punished accordingly. As bizarre as it may sound, people can even be reined in and fined up to one-hundred and fifty dollars for feeding birds from pavement-punishing restaurants. Stray crumbs could be deadly - but evidently not half as deadly as the risk incurred by treating cute sparrows to hardy crusts of bread.

It took me fifteen minutes to cross Esplanade Drive in the end. Incredibly, it had been easier to traverse the busiest roads in Ho Chi Minh City. And that was saying something.

The Singapore Flyer felt no closer. I marched forward regardless, brushing past a fellow traveller who looked to be just as bemused by the road system. The skyline-dominating Flyer bears much in common with The London Eye. Fitted with twenty-eight pods, each pod boasting a capacity of twenty-eight people, the one-hundred and sixty-five metre-high wheel ever-so-slowly inches around in fine style, awarding passengers the ultimate panorama of one of the world's most impressive skylines. The 'flight' takes thirty minutes, the whole experience buoyed by elegance. It's even possible to hold conference meetings and champagne-toting wedding receptions in the pods.

Beyond such a wheel of fortune, the mighty 'Marina Bay Sands' complex lured my feet in its direction. One of the most jaw-dropping structures to grace Planet Earth, the outlandish nature of its sleek design has to be applauded. Consisting of three towers topped by a connecting crown, the hotel is straight out of Vegas… literally. Designed and constructed by the same company behind the 'Sands' complex in America's self-styled 'City of Sin', it undoubtedly represents a masterpiece of contemporary engineering. As I duly gave the hotel the slip, a man approached a security guard, wondering how to cross the road. Had I just heard right? What had become of the man's common sense? Then all became clear as I tried to reach 'The Shoppes'. There was no obvious way over the road other than via a pedestrian crossing some two-hundred yards distant. Indeed, there's a significant risk you could waste half your life waiting for little green men to appear in Singapore. Believers in aliens need not apply.

'The Shoppes' section of the complex was like nothing I'd seen before. Quite possibly the most overblown shopping mall in the world, it houses a staggering range of designer outlets. As an army of credit card-swiping financiers and captains of industry strode in and out of stores as though their vacuous lives depended on blowing thousands of dollars on a jewel-encrusted watch or bespoke suit, I wondered if my maturing career as an offbeat travel-writer would ever grant me enough money to be able to afford a regular bottle of water. Surprisingly, the ambience in the mall was depressing and seriously lacking in substance. To what extent do the attitudes of shoppers affect such vibes? Asking myself unanswerable questions on a lower level, I wondered if the sterile environment was to blame for the sullen expressions carried around by the style-conscious clientele sashaying between 'De Beers' and 'Vertu'. There was even a skating rink inside the mall, not to mention a stretch of fake canal that reminded me of 'The Venetian' in Vegas. Running with such comparisons, 'Marina Bay Sands' boasts a casino of its own, along with a couple of theatres. One happened to be advertising an upcoming solo show by none other than Elvis Costello, along with the 'in residency' musical, *The Lion King*.

Undeniably out of my depth, I knew I was being watched. The security guards knew I was out of my depth, too. I was reminded of a story that one of my uncles had once told about how he'd been prevented from entering 'Harrods' in London on account of his biker clobber - not that the guard working the door had judged my uncle by his ripped jeans and oil-stained boots, or anything.

Sporting a shirty patch of sweat between my shoulder-blades, the manner in which I was dressed made me stand out. The only person in casual wear, I proved to be a walking target for questions. 'Hello, Sir... can I help you?' Strangely, I was the only person to be greeted by many of the guards. Clearly they harboured suspicions about me, in spite of the passion with which I affirmed that I was simply curious about the interior of the mall and its stunning architectural merit. I confessed that I was looking, not buying, yet the truth couldn't be bought. To them, it was obvious that I wouldn't even be able to afford a slice of cheesecake, but I walked on regardless, staring in rapt awe at the dazzling window displays. Sensing that I was being watched from all angles, I felt as uncomfortable as when I'd traipsed around the perimeter of the Capitol Building in Washington D.C. four years previously. Not knowing what to make of the mall's elitist extravagance, I surmised that it was hiding something terrifyingly obvious: the death of the soul, the extinction of spirit. Despairingly trapped inside the air-conditioned vision of a future that couldn't have been colder, I could feel my sense of self being compromised as the wealth of shoppers around me bought into the latest trends like mindless robots, unaware they'd already forsaken their individuality in the name of sickening materialism. Reminded of when I resided in Rotherhithe, London, and tirelessly trekked across to King's Road to observe how hard cash was splurged (read 'wasted') without a second thought, I couldn't understand why some folk believed that personal happiness levels might increase if they filled their fingers with diamond rings and their houses with 'priceless' homeware. Nobody really owns anything, the pointlessness of possession representing liberation from consumerism. Tired of the dollar-damned charade, I tried to find an exit. But I searched in vain, tracing circles larger and faster than those I'd stamped out upon getting hopelessly lost in a similarly unsettling mall in Minneapolis. I desired nothing but liberation.

Give me a bustling market bazaar any day. The mall-life wasn't for me. In my eyes, 'The Shoppes' complex was frequented by the dead: zombies that had suffocated the capacity to think for themselves. It was evidently time to escape while I still could, before I lost my mind.

~

I COULDN'T GET MY FILL FAST ENOUGH. I'd just sat down inside one of Singapore's busiest soup kitchens on the edge of Chinatown, a prawn cracker's flick from the market-orientated madness of Pagoda Street. Having queued patiently for ten minutes, I was politely informed that they were no longer serving the soup of my choice. Sensing a wave of restlessness behind me, I needed to decide on an alternative dish pronto. I glanced up at the menu board, blindly opting for 'laksa'. Three dollars lighter, I shuffled through the tiniest of gaps to a no-frills table in the corner. It was midday, and the claustrophobic eating area heaved with a mixture of market traders and sharp-dressed business-folk. Never before had I seen people eat food with such a vengeance. In their defence, a large proportion of them would have been riding out their lunch hour. Wasted time would represent lost money were they to return to their office-based workstations late.

Focusing on my food, I inventoried the soup's contents, attacking the noodles with a pair of chopsticks. A little rustier with such utensils than expected, it seemed I needed a bit more practice before I could competently let myself loose in a restaurant if I didn't seek to splash fellow diners with oily collateral. I was a menace to myself, dipping into the soup with trepidation, careful not to send stray noodles flying out of the eating area, onto Amoy Street. I wanted to dine, not get fined.

Ironically, a shop selling T-shirts next door had a black beauty on display, coolly lampooning the city's notorious obsession with penalising people. 'Singapore: it's a fine city!' it read. The sentiment couldn't have been truer. Abandoning the sticks, I abducted a fork before the owner of the soup hall and I came to blows about the mess I was making. It had been less than eighteen months since I'd last used chopsticks on a daily basis in Vietnam and Cambodia, yet my fingers acted as though they'd never touched a pair before. Either that, or the integrity of the sticks was to blame. The soup itself tasted divine, the sheer heat of the concoction remorselessly burning my lips and tongue, along with the inside of my cheeks. A middle-aged Singaporean woman sat opposite me, apologising for the disturbance. As it was, there was literally nowhere else to sit. Office workers were pouring out of the surrounding skyscrapers, rapidly conversing in 'Singlish': a cute hybrid of the obvious. The woman smiled, unloading a feast fit for five people from her cutlery-heavy tray. Armed with chopsticks, a fork and a spoon, she swooped into her food as though competing in a world record attempt to eat as much rice as possible in sixty seconds. From where I was perched, triumph seemed inevitable. A sucker for sampling all and sundry, I was still recovering from a spicy take on 'mee remus' that I'd sunk the previous evening.

Cheap food isn't always easy to find on the streets. For example, even in Amoy Street's colossal Food Centre, an unembellished plate of 'nasi goreng' demanded three dollars. Two days beforehand, back in Jakarta, I'd been picking up the same dish for a third of the price. But beggars can't be choosers. The stress I'd been under had made me hungry. Such stress stemmed from the conniving way in which Singapore seems geared to catch people out. As if paying homage to America's abominable compensation culture, the despicable amount of fines attributed to so-called 'offences' in the country made my blood run cold, not least when I strolled past the high and mighty Ministry of Information building in the Civic District. There's only so much pillaging one person's wallet can take; for the Singaporean authorities to nonchalantly dole out astronomical fines for the silliest of supposed crimes, I couldn't help but cynically conclude that something was amiss. On the gum-free surface, the city comes across as being positive in every respect. But it's a façade. The more I pondered, the more I realised that the 'Pore is negative by default. It's hard to be a 'Yes Man' in a place where so many signs are strangled by the word 'No!'

Craving a dab of solitude, I moseyed out of Chinatown, but not before pausing for reflection at the end of Smith Street. Such a street once played host to a parade of brothels back when males in the city far outnumbered females. The majority of such flop-houses were Chinese-run, although two of them had been Japanese. It's alleged that conditions within the brothels were so bad that suicide amongst working girls was common, a number of women feeling so trapped and depressed by their circumstances that they resorted to throwing themselves from roofs. In addition, opium overdoses were rife. These days, the street's abuzz with comparative innocence. As I passed, it thrummed to the racket inspired by excited Chinese men and women preparing for the New Lunar Year.

My soles soon made contact with Hill Street, duly conveying me to the alluring edge of Fort Canning Park, a beautiful expanse of woodland and greenery at the heart of the city. In the mood for presenting myself with a comprehensive history lesson, I bounded up a series of steps to stumble onto 'Raffles Terrace'. Having gained a surprising amount of height within the space of a minute, I spun around, hoping that a view to die for might assault my eyes. Were it not for the ancient trees crowding the natural vantage point, the scintillating skyline would have looked a picture. On the upside, the bulk of 'Marina Bay Sands' could be seen perfectly, its three towers standing directly opposite the terrace, engaged in an architectural stand-off. I much preferred the humble nature of the whitewashed building timelessly presiding over the terrace. The adjacent lighthouse harked back to when the fort area fronted the water, prior to the point at which land south of the hill was reclaimed and developed. Cherishing the tranquillity that my heart craved, I knuckled down to write in the shade of heritage trees galore. Beside the lighthouse, a photographer artistically orchestrated a shoot with an impossibly skinny model that appeared to resent every second of pose-throwing whilst role-playing. What was arguably the most important reservoir serving the city reposed beyond a security fence. Signs guarding the

perimeter warned wanderers that it was a protected area, a
graphic picture of a man holding a gun to a trespasser's head
re-iterating such a point with spine-chilling authority. In
glass-fronted notice-boards, a flurry of posters advertised
upcoming events on the hill. Shows by Faithless and Deftones
were both scheduled to take place in the coming weeks. A
music festival featuring nine bands was due to be staged at
the weekend. By sheer coincidence, I'd blagged a coveted
ticket, having promised to interview The Temper Trap,
Warpaint and Foals before reviewing their much-anticipated
sets. Although I somehow resisted the temptation to play air-
guitar as I trundled through the Spice Garden, I felt
compelled to admit that I was ready when they were.

~

WHAT RIGHT DID THEY HAVE to throw a life-threatening
U-turn on a whim? 'Hypocrites, the lot of them,' I sneered.
The police cruiser spun off down the opposite side of Beach
Road. In it, two buddied-up officers joked as though the act of
serving and protecting wasn't an option so long as they were
laughing. A couple of minutes later, I caught up with the car
on North Bridge Road. Parked outside the National Library,
the black and white vehicle had nosed its way into place
behind two red 'Special Operations' trucks. With red and blue
neon lights blazing, their presence denoted a serious crime.
Perhaps somebody's book was overdue and a country-wide
investigation was in the bureaucracy-lashed process of being
launched. But no... that was impossible. It was a reference
library. A prominent sign declared as much. That in mind, no
books should have left the confines of the multi-tiered
building. Heaven forbid, it was entirely possible that the
authorities were dealing with a theft.

Earlier, as I'd made enquiries at the Golden Mile Complex,

I'd witnessed something out of the ordinary: a horn-honking driver. Dismayed at being cut up, he floored his car whilst thumping the horn, only for the driver who'd done him such a disservice to slow down. Such rapid deceleration on the initial offender's part caused the man behind to rear-end the vehicle, an accident that constituted the first smash I'd seen in Singapore.

The Golden Mile Complex is well-known to budget travellers as the most common place to be picked up and dropped off should they be overlanding to or from Malaysia and beyond. I remembered the place well from when I'd left the 'Lion City' to travel into Thailand in 2006. Nothing had changed other than the faces behind the travel agency desks. The Chinese New Year was looming on the near horizon; it was essential that I be decisive in formulating a get-out clause so I didn't get stuck in The 'Pore. A trip to Melaka appealed. At least stopping there would break the journey to KL. Had I been able to muster the energy required, I was in a position to bus my way back to Bangkok for the sheer thrill of it. A friend and fellow poet called Veera lived there. It would have been wonderful to meet.

I hustled a haphazard course in front of the agencies, demanding prices, collating quotes. The cost of tickets to destinations in Malaysia and Thailand can vary widely, so it's always best to undertake a spot of forward-thinking research. On average, direct coaches to KL cost thirty dollars, depending on the time and date of travel. Prices inevitably increase around Chinese New Year, hence why I needed to be careful. There was so much that I still aspired to see and do. Downtime in the glorious Cameron Highlands also teetered at the top of my mental agenda. Three days on the island of Penang would ultimately crown my stay in Malaysia.

Sloping away from the complex, I hastened to explore more of Singapore prior to committing myself to a departure date.

A girl in the guesthouse had assured me that a lift up to the Skypark at 'Marina Bay Sands' was cheap enough to take. Conscious that the view would literally be out of this world, I skulked along Ophir Road, hitting an overpass in due course. Each step was accompanied by posters advertising the upcoming 'Chingay' celebrations, due to take place below the Singapore Flyer, near the river-fronting Youth Olympic Park. Tickets for the event were alleged to be selling fast. Promising a dazzling parade, a feast of sumptuously decorated floats, the spectacle of 'flying dragons', and an event-climaxing show featuring over four-thousand performers, the New Year was destined to be embraced with eyes and ears wide open. Once again, it was up to the humble rabbit to usher forth good health and prosperity.

Weaving my way around a couple of golden rabbits unwittingly forming the entrance to a fairground, I sunk underground in hope that a subterranean mall might help to quicken my step towards 'Marina Bay Sands'. As I descended into the air-conditioned bowels of the city on an escalator, a man making an ascent hollered over the divide: 'You are a lucky man!' Perplexed, I asked him why, the distance between us gradually increasing once we'd passed each other. Wondering if it would be worth my while to chase the light and find him, I decided there was no need. I knew I was lucky; moreover, I realised why.

In spite of having just been offered a writing position on a new arts magazine in Australia, I was poised to return to England to be with my girlfriend who'd patiently waited for me so we could start making plans for our future together. If such plans involved me upending my globe-trotting sandals for good, I was prepared. As inspirational and educational as travelling can be, the excitement generated by the act of constantly moving has nothing on the hopes borne out of love's greatest possibilities. What had once been Van

Diemen's Land could wait; my best friend couldn't. As a radical partnership, my girlfriend and I had come far... much further than I could ever dream of going as an impressionable backpacker. Since striking thirty, I'd felt the essence of my priorities alter significantly. My ambition had once been to visit as many places and to meet as many people as one lifetime would permit. At the time, I'd never suspected that the gradual realisation of such an ambition would leave me feeling deflated, my high expectations consistently rendering my mission futile on too many multifaceted levels to detail. What had I really been trying to prove for the past ten years? The one thing I'd been searching for in over seventy eye-opening countries and thousands of extraordinary friendships had finally presented itself in the formidable form of a woman who was my equal, my soul mate. At the end of each day, all I wanted to do was to love and be loved: provisionally, unconditionally, truly.

It was almost time to go home... but first I had a score to settle - with an overpriced lift.

~

DASHING IN FRONT OF THE BLOOD-RED 'SPECIAL OPERATIONS COMMAND' TRUCK WASN'T THE WISEST MOVE I'D EVER MADE. It was a desperate case of 'do or die'... or at least a desperate case of 'do or get soaked'. Willing to risk a fine of up to one-thousand dollars if it meant saving my 'Netbook' from being destroyed by water damage, I splashed my way over the road, aiming for the gates of Singapore's Botanic Gardens, one of the most refreshing and captivating jewels in the city's crown. An unforeseen midday storm had already flushed the pavement clean of fellow pedestrians. Not for the first time, I was the last man standing, semi-prepared to be consumed by a downpour the likes of which my satchel had never before intercepted. Upon reaching the far side of the road, I glanced behind at the purring truck. Its windows were so heavily tinted that it was impossible to see inside, fuelling my intrigue. Beneath the truck, a line bore the brunt of its front wheels, praying for a green light to give the vehicle the go-ahead before the paint turned a paler shade of white. Menacingly, such trucks always seemed to steam around as part of an intimidating duo, parking outside buildings within inches of one another, proud of keeping a united front. Fearing that I would somehow be tagged, tracked, and fined for my jay-walking, I fled Cluny Road, bursting through Tanglin Gate in search of camouflage.

Knowing that tropical thunderstorms weren't to be messed with, I shot beneath an information-laced shelter until the ferocity subsided, at which point I aimed for the rainforest. Skirting the edge of the gardens via Swan Lake, I noticed two Dutch swans gliding across the water. One of them subsequently tried and failed to flap its way up and over a small waterfall below a wooden bridge to claim scraps of food shed by visitors. Either such visitors had refused to take heed of the signs, or they thought good fortune would favour them. The truth is, feeding any of the swans or fish puttering around the three lakes is strictly forbidden, unless they're being fed specific types of food purchased from official vendors within the sprawling grounds. Theoretically, the health of the swans and fish should benefit as a result; in the past, idiotic visitors have been known to discard all manner of food into the water, naively assuming that the native wildlife would be capable of stomaching anything offered from their potentially kind-to-be-cruel hands.

Hooking a right towards the iconic bandstand, I whipped around the edge of a photo shoot. A freshly-married bride and groom swooned at its stunningly choreographed heart.

Glancing across the grass, I clocked another two couples under the proverbial spotlight: further proof that the Botanic Gardens provide the perfect place for a romantic rendezvous. It was just a pity that both grooms, with slicked hair and dapper suits, looked disinterested, yawning when protocol dictated it to be time for their brides to have a slew of individual portraits composed and committed to a digital format. Rather than admire their respective partners from behind the photographers, they toyed with their iPhones, thumbing through applications more stimulating than the sight of their partners in all their eyelid-fluttering finery. Perhaps such men were just trying to act cool, downplaying the degree of their attraction. Maybe they didn't have time to gaze on adoringly at the loves of their lives, indifferently portraying themselves as card-carrying ambassadors for 'The Post-Romantic Movement', eager for the photographers to get their jobs done so they could 'do one', get changed, and party.

Surrounded by Yellow Rain Trees, the simple but insanely elegant bandstand still acts as the focal point for many post-wedding photo opportunities. However, secluded spots of sheer beauty litter the grounds. Although the rainforest might not be deemed the best place to propose in light of its dark mystery, it's arguably the most fascinating section of the gardens, if not the city at large. Unaffected by human development, it stands true to itself, spreading its wealth of trees over six breathtaking hectares. Over three-hundred species of plant are waiting to be discovered therein. It's amazing to think that the majority of trees have been present and erect since the founding of modern Singapore, back when Sir Stamford Raffles landed on the Singapore River in 1819 and had a dream. A walkway runs through the middle of the lush microcosm, allowing visitors to appreciate everything that the pristine environment has to offer. Suitable for wheelchairs and strollers, the walkway is wide and flat, attractively meandering past walls of vegetation so thick that barely any natural light penetrates the moist foliage. Twisted liana branches trace extraordinary patterns of life around gnarled tree branches and ancient trunks. Awestruck by the sky-reaching canopies, I found myself enchanted: totally and utterly spellbound by nature in its dehumanising glory. I even imagined myself to be hacking a haggard course through the Amazon basin, tickling the traits of Indiana Jones. Allowing my imagination to take flight, I sauntered out of the rainforest in a trance, a cleansed victim of rebirth.

Not wanting traffic lights to have all the fun, most Singaporean toilet cubicles come complete with LEDs. Acquaint yourself with a vacant cubicle, and there's a strong chance that a red light will promptly trade itself for a greener sibling, proclaiming it safe to proceed. A multitude of public conveniences also pander to the phenomenon of 'teaching on the go', explaining why plaques of fascinating facts often adorn cubicle walls. For instance, I learnt that a certain orchid thriving amidst the Botanic Gardens was the largest in the world, wielding the capacity to grow so large it could weigh a tonne once through with expanding. Pursuing the cute Sarka Stream to the nearest gateway, my feet slapped their way back onto Orchard Road, Singapore's overblown equivalent to London's Oxford Street. With blatant consumerism the order of every day, it's not uncommon to weave one's way through crowds of bold and beautiful socialites with more credit cards than charitable perversions.

As I eased my way towards the city's CBD, an ice cream vendor snared my attention. 'You try sweetcorn-flavoured ice cream?' Hopeful that I might be a guinea-pig on the verge of testing a new kind of dessert, I approached, optimism bubbling at the corners of my mouth. 'Okay, yes, sure,' I nervously laughed. 'Sweetcorn-flavoured ice cream!' I should have conjured something better to say, yet I was desperate to wrap my tongue around what I secretly feared would taste disgusting. Sandwiched by two wafers, the ice cream only just made it past my lips before surprise engulfed the essence of my being. In truth, it tasted sensational. If only I'd had a mug of Antelope Tea with which to chase it.

~

'WHAT ARE WE DOING? WHERE ARE WE GOING?' spat the American woman to her map-studying husband, evidently twice-scorned by his ignorance. 'These are just buildings,' she dryly added, mauling the skyline with her unappreciative gaze. She was correct in the respect that they were 'just buildings', but what buildings they were!

As a rule, prowling around Singapore's Civic District rarely fails to astound the casual visitor, even if architecture doesn't interest them in the least. It can't have any other effect: its tight cluster of extraordinary skyscrapers conspires to present an upwardly-mobile skyline like few others.

Less than twenty yards away stood the Armenian Church, a small yet dazzling building that's stood the test of time in bold style. Its humble nature reminded me of the beautiful churches gracing New York; it's always inspiring to see places of worship set adrift amongst skyscrapers. They are precisely the buildings that keep everything else grounded, reminding one and all that while making money might be the religion of some, the cultivation of a strong community reaps more rewarding results than any amount of cash ever can. Over the road stood an iconic fire station; operational to this day, it sought to serve the Civic District long before the first skyscraper was a glint in the most visionary architect's eye. Sporting red doors in a familiar British-style, the station became crucial in the wake of Sir Stamford Raffles seeing the potential of the island. 'Entrepot trading' led to the Singapore

River becoming ridiculously congested and repulsively polluted. As the Civic District developed on the back of such trade, fires became increasingly common, hence the need for a fire station in close proximity to the area. Given its pivotal role in supporting the district, it's fabulous to see that the station's been preserved.

History buffs are advised to indulge in a stroll around Fort Canning Park, undoubtedly the best place to learn more about pre-colonial Singapore. The city's name is said to have resulted from a Sumatran Prince spotting what he suspected to be a lion in the city. He went on to dub the island 'Singa Pura': The Lion City. In spite of there being no lions in Asia, the name surprisingly stuck. Excavations on the slopes of the park have unearthed a remarkable cache of artefacts. Deeply buried glass and gold have been found, supporting evidence which suggests that the island had been populated for centuries prior to Stamford landing in the early nineteenth century. Long before the British began to exert an influence, present-day Fort Canning Park was known as 'Forbidden Hill', a sacred place literally to be looked up to.

Raffles is widely cited as the man who founded modern Singapore. Recognising that the island was strategically positioned, he set about persuading the British to establish a colony there, conscious that the trade of spices (to name but one commodity) could potentially generate an excessive amount of revenue. In line with such expectant investment in the city, trade fortunately exploded in an exponential fashion. On the downside, the sinuous nature of the river struggled to cope with the huge quantity of 'bumboats' flanking its banks. Chinese labourers - or 'coolies' - overran such banks, loading and unloading, loading and unloading, hour-in and hour-out, day-in and day-out. Sun-bleached photographs proffer a shocking impression of the waterway when trade peaked. As it became more difficult for boats to negotiate the overburdened river, docking operations were gradually transferred to Keppel Harbour, allowing the river to inhale a rare gulp of fresh air. It was far easier for cargo to be deposited and loaded at Keppel. A greater degree of access and better facilities saw to that. The river's worth declined as a result, its progressive abandonment leaving it in a grotesque state of repose. Incredibly, it wasn't until the early nineties when the authorities spied the river's potential to appeal to visitors. Though Singapore initially appeared to be an unlikely tourist destination, vast numbers of people began staying for longer periods of time. It wasn't just the ex-pat community that savoured what the 'Pore had to offer. Having established itself as a major hub for international flights, Singapore morphed into a popular place for travellers temporarily suspended between leaps to Malaysia, Indonesia, and Oz. Keen to capitalise on swelling visitor numbers, a full-scale clean-up operation was instigated: a mammoth venture by any government's standards. Like Raffles and his colonising cohorts, city planners recognised the power brandished by the river. Envisaging a relaxing place where people could stroll to admire the skyline prior to eating and drinking their evenings away, they wisely invested a vault of dollars into making its banks infinitely more presentable. Today, such riverbanks scream with high-class bars, restaurants, and shopping malls.

Marking time with space as I strode away from the 'Merlion', I strode around the back of 'The Fullerton Hotel', the most majestic building to grace the high-rise Financial District. Along with 'Raffles Hotel', it pays its respects to an era in which opulence ruled. Compared to the futuristic spires overshadowing the relatively squat building, 'The Fullerton' is arguably the most beautiful building of all on the waterfront.

Crossing the oldest bridge abutting the CBD, I walked upriver, awed by the appeal of the boardwalk. I soon left

Clarke Quay for rain, its parade of eateries unwilling to provide shelter if I wasn't prepared to fritter a fortune. Abiding by water falling from above as fast as it flowed by my side, I stepped up my pace towards Robertson Quay, stunned at how soon the bars and restaurants petered out, making way for classy apartment blocks in what was predominantly a residential zone. Beyond 'The Quayside' complex, an indie festival raged into the evening on the northern slopes of Fort Canning Park, giving trembling 'laksa' leaves in the nearby Spice Garden a metaphorical earful of music. Beguiled by the melody of life, I reflected on the way in which water is key to everything, returning to base with a shimmering skinful of plans.

~

IT WASN'T THE TYPE OF DAY TO BE PRANCING ABOUT OUTSIDE. The snug interior of the guesthouse was far more appealing, not least because I'd just fallen into conversation with a Frenchman called Quentin. Half a year younger than yours truly, all evidence pointed to the fact that he'd puckered up to an amazing thirty years, mainly by way of the type of work he'd done. Having toiled on a series of documentaries sold to independent TV companies on the continent, Quentin had lived and laboured in Greenland, Iceland, Myanmar and Papua New Guinea. Unsurprisingly, he had more than his fair share of jaw-dropping tales to recite.

Though he should have been packing in preparation for catching a bus out of Singapore to KL, he excitedly told me about his time in Myanmar, confirming that it's one of 'those' countries which is extremely difficult to explore under one's own steam unless you aspire to attract suspicious government officials. Nonetheless, he'd had an amazing time in what used to be Burma.

Exploiting every single train-of-thought we boarded, our topics of conversation proved to be far-reaching beyond logic. First and foremost, we chatted about his stay in Greenland. Naturally leading affairs, he told me how he'd lived in a small community on the east coast. 'The population was just three-hundred and twenty,' he lamented, as though such a low number was in some way detrimental to the settlement's existence. I confessed that my vision of Greenland resembled a form of utopia in which everybody lived in perfect harmony without the trappings of technology to distract them. Quentin shook his head, sending half-hearted 'tuts' bouncing onto the table. 'You'd be surprised by the suicide rate, my friend. The popular consensus is that the smaller a community, the happier it's likely to be, but that's far from the case. Three people killed themselves while I was there. Drinking is a social issue that needs to be dealt with. Incidences of domestic violence are also high. In that respect, there really is trouble in paradise, even though the landscapes can hardly be construed as paradise. SAD can be a killer, too.' Taken aback by the gloom that had descended upon what had started out as a light-hearted lark, I asked him what the near future held in store in regards to travelling. 'Well, I fly back to Paris tomorrow. My girlfriend and I need to figure out what we're going to do. We're both writers, but we're not making enough money to survive.' Suspended as I was in a similar situation, I relayed an ounce of sympathy across the table. It was all I could spare.

'It can only be compared to teleportation. That's the best way to describe flying. The element of fun is extracted from the process of getting around.' I nodded in earnest, telling him that I needed to reach KL as well, although I feared that every single bus, train and plane ticket had been booked up well in advance owing to the upcoming Chinese New Year celebrations. 'It's best to see how landscapes change at ground level. Anybody can hop on planes here, there and everywhere. It takes a different kind of person to travel overland because they have so much more to deal with.' Life's most flamboyant trials are conceived to be toppled.

When I fitfully mentioned that I'd been offered the opportunity to work on a movie in Oz, Quentin swanked off at a tangent, asking me what movie I'd last seen. 'The Tourist,' I guffawed. Abolishing a pause in my speech, he jumped in, Americanised: 'You ever catch Johnny Depp in *Dead Man*? Now that's a cool film. It's directed by Jim Jarmusch; Neil Young provides the music.' Magically marrying talk of the movie with our previous conversational thread, Quentin waxed lyrical about the scene in which Depp's character is on a train and various landscapes can be seen rushing behind, through the window. 'It's so surreal. Just like flying,' he remarked. He went on to ask if I'd heard of Werner Herzog. My head shook itself before I found time to properly process the name. 'He's a German director. My favourite. You might know one of the movies he produced. It's called *Grizzly Man* and it's devastating.' All it took was those two words for me to start reading from the same page, a fellow fan of the documentary. Although much of it had been shot by Timothy Treadwell as he ingratiated himself with nature at its grizzliest, Herzog had conscientiously pieced together all elements to form a consumable and moving whole. 'He's such a maverick, Herzog,' Quentin laughed, sweeping back his hair with one hand, pushing back his chunky specs with the other. I suddenly glimpsed the art-loving bohemian in him. Stalking similarly offbeat tracts, he refocused his concentration on Johnny Depp's career. 'You ever seen *Lost in La Mancha*, a documentary about the making of another movie?' My smile said it all. 'It's a mini-masterpiece,' I beamed. 'Shame the big stars only play small parts. Still, it's splendid to see Depp in there. Even his wife,

Vanessa Paradis, pops up at one point.' Talk of Terry Gilliam subsequently hurtled into the fray. He was the director of the movie upon which the documentary cleverly focused. 'Gilliam's greatest work is *Brazil*. No question. I love its satirical ambience, its unnerving interpretation of a future that's already arrived,' Quentin divulged, a rise in his otherwise soft voice reflecting his passion. I knew the film well: it starred none other than Michael Palin, an actor and travel documentary-maker I'd held in high regard for longer than I cared to recall. 'Gilliam's such a visionary film-maker,' I offered, sensing that the intensity of our chat was doomed to curtail as Quentin closed his laptop with a view to skedaddling. The frightful shadows beneath his eyes suggested that he'd scored little sleep since hightailing his way over from PNP. Failing that, it was the poorly filtered light playing tricks. Whatever, it didn't matter. I needed to head out as well. There were places I wanted to be, people I needed to see. So it was 'au revoir' from him, and 'goodbye' from me. At least so-to-speak.

~

I'D NEVER SEEN RAIN LIKE IT. Relentlessly crashing to earth with untold malice, there couldn't have been a dry eye in any house. The Kampong Glam drains simply couldn't shoulder the blow, unwilling to embrace the deluge, their network of subterranean conduits already full. There was nowhere for the water to go, so it pooled. The street was literally awash, the paved road floundering two feet under. The grey skies promised nothing but more of the same. Opposite 'Sleepy Sam's Guesthouse', a camera specialist struggled to nudge open his door for business... not that he'd be lapping up any passing trade until the heavens gave it a rest. If nothing else, the downpour was a sight to behold, bug-sized water droplets ricocheting off rustling palm fronds. Sultan Mosque at the end of the road remained indifferent; the governor of Bussorah Street since the Malay-Muslim community laid down its foundations, it had seen it all before. It was January, and rain, rain, and then more rain was expected.

I'd been cooped inside all day. It was time to make a dash for it. My stomach hated me for not keeping it busy. My underworked digestive tract was equally as upset, bored out of its inactive body with nothing to do. Although trace elements of breakfast continued to ease their way through the system, the toast and fruit combo hadn't been filling enough. It was time to hit Liang Seah Street, a couple of blocks away. Momentarily teetering in Sam's creepy doorway, I thrust out my right arm, far enough for it to undercut the building's protective eaves. I could see it was lashing, but I needed to feel the rain, to get a handle on the moisture content. If the worst came to the worst, I'd be able to shelter inside 'Raffles Hospital', maybe even 'Park View Square', the latter building ranking as one of Singapore's strangest structures given its Gothic presence. It looks like it belongs in a Tim Burton movie. Gotham City clearly missed out.

Why oh why hadn't I bought an umbrella? It's an essential part of a person's Singapore Survival Kit, yet I'd been living in hope that the weather might improve. My optimism had even propelled me through a particularly evil thunderstorm whilst I'd been walking alongside the river, inland from Robertson Quay. I was surprised at the way land use altered so uncompromisingly, Clarke Quay's bars and restaurants giving way to Robertson Quay's luxury penthouse suites, a dizzying community of bland apartment blocks disgracing Kim Seng Park with their overbearing, Communist-styled ugliness.

Back on Liang Seah Street, I sat myself down and ordered a wholesome soup of appetite-appeasing proportions. In spite of presiding over an open sewer, the roadside restaurant couldn't be faulted. Even the likes of Gordon Ramsey could have learnt a thing or two about teamwork, for the place ran like clockwork. No sooner had I ambled up to a server, my order was taken, I was seated, and my food was delivered within the space of ninety seconds. Fond of favouring unpretentious eateries, I was gobsmacked. What's more, the row of five cooks appeared to be having a blast, enjoying the act of producing dishes as much as customers enjoyed consuming them. Good-natured banter liberally flew between the woks and the plastic tables around which people were eating. Efficiency was paramount. Priding itself on its fantastic customer service, there was little wonder that my stomach felt compelled to persuade my feet to meet it halfway along the street at specific times each day.

Chinese New Year was almost upon the city, as it was the world at large. Lavish banners bearing Chinese script flapped up a musical storm in Chinatown. Below such banners, rows of women frantically packed dried food. Perfect for parties, the food would be presented on platters in the run-up to the much-anticipated return of the rabbit.

As much as I wanted to hang back in the 'Pore, it was time to leave. I just didn't know by which means I'd be able to get into Malaysia. I'd been told that it would be near-impossible to book a bus ticket out of the country. Remembering that Jeremy at the guesthouse was a font of travel-related knowledge, I bustled back to 'Sleepy Sam's' after sweeping my way along Orchard Road one final time, almost tripping in shock when I saw the heavily-secured Royal Thai Embassy midway along its mile-long stretch. On the wall, in front of two helmeted guards, banners insisted that people 'Believe in Thailand'. Adding intrigue to temptation, fleets of double-decker buses sported adverts for 'Air Asia' flights. 'Chiang Mai... just a nap away!' screamed the most prominent, turning my head if not my heart. Although the 'Land of Smiles' remained one of my favourite countries, I'd seen much of what it had to offer on two previous journeys. Malaysia, on the other foot, remained something of a mystery. That in mind, a ticket to Melaka would suit me down to the sea.

'Sorry, man. You need to get yourself to The Golden Mile. We don't actually sell tickets here; we just dispense advice.' For once, Jeremy was on the defence, his unusually curt answers proving he was preoccupied with a Japanese lady and her young daughter, stranded amidst check-in formalities. Taking my cue, I ventured to the door. It had just begun to rain again - and when I say 'rain', I mean 'pour'. The striking of ten p.m. was nigh, at which time the majority of travel agencies would customarily unhook phones and slam closed shutters to announce the end of another exhausting working day. Feeling guilty for intruding, I meekly backtracked to the desk to ask if I could borrow Jezza's umbrella. 'Sure, Steve! Why not? Everybody else does.' I couldn't tell if he was being kind or contemptuous. Grabbing the ready-soaked instrument of salvation, I didn't hang around to find out. The Japanese girl had spilt her drink; Jeremy had other things to worry about.

Standing on the threshold between comfortable familiarity and freezing distress, I looked to the skies for confirmation that what I was about to do was destined to do me few favours, if any. But what choice did I have?

~

I HAD TEN TRAVEL AGENCIES TO GO AT, but only one shot in each. Luckily, they were lined up beside one another. Inside The Golden Mile Complex, hundreds of people huddled, many of them taking metaphorical pews at tables, eating out the thunderstorm. Starting at one end of the line, I ducked inside each agency, asking about prices for bus tickets to Melaka, Malaysia. The first man I asked refused to entertain me at point blank range. 'Busy,' he said, denying me even a sincere glance in the eye. Sceptical, I sauntered around the back of his desk, in a position to do so since the agency teetered on the edge of the building. Clocking my move, he hastened to cover his computer-based tracks. He was too slow. It was blatantly obvious he'd been playing cards on his PC instead of working. He wasn't bothered, though, cockily swivelling on his seat, laughing.

Not one single ticket to Melaka was available from any of the next four agencies that I entered. Midway along the line, I paused for reflection, staring out at the semi-submerged state of Beach Road, thankful that I wasn't caught in the rain, but anxious that I could be stranded in Singapore until the residual traces of the celebrations had been erased from memory. The sixth agency I stumbled into granted me a tenuous ray of hope, confirming that one ticket to Melaka was indeed available... at the grossly inflated price of thirty-five dollars. Choking at the cost, I trailed away in shock, having expected to pick up a ticket for less than twenty dollars. Crushingly, only one other agency had a ticket for sale, charging the frankly ridiculous price of fifty-five dollars. Thus, my decision had been made. I rushed back to scoop up the cheapest ticket, not expecting to be faced with a crisis in-the-making. A man had just sat down at the desk. Though he was talking in 'Singlish', I intercepted the gist of the conversation. The word 'Melaka' tripped off his tongue with alarming regularity. It was obvious he wanted to go: badly. But not as badly as me. I considered distracting him somehow so I could ram a request in edgeways, but the agency employee was engaged in an intense bartering war as the wannabe customer vainly attempted to lower the price to thirty dollars. It wasn't a market stall: there was no way that any form of bargaining was going to come to pass. Disgruntled at failing in his mission to snag a bargain, he charged away from the desk in a huff, granting me a chance to intervene. Wasting no time in slapping three ten-dollar notes atop a cache of one-dollar bills on the overworked desk, I begged for the agency's last ticket to Melaka. If I got stuck in Singapore, there would be no telling how much more money I might blow.

I couldn't sleep. Anxiety had consumed me, and now regurgitation had taken hold. A nightmare provoked me to stir in a cold sweat, holding me hostage until dawn. Deep down, I was terrified of being held up at the border. Ever since the debacle at Surabaya Airport when I'd been refused entry into Indonesia on grounds that I didn't have a return flight ticket to present, I'd been conscious that I consistently seemed to fall foul of bad luck upon entering and leaving countries. Because the border crossing between Singapore and Malaysia can be awkward if you're seen to be suspicious, I wondered what I might be able to do in advance to ease my subsequent passage through Immigration. A self-certified insomniac, I rolled out of bed earlier than the birds nesting in the musty guesthouse loft. Shame I'd forgotten that I was on the top bunk and it was a three-foot drop to the floor. Such is life, and potential death. It was a good thing I was leaving in any case; 'Sleepy Sam's' was due to have its so-called 'spring clean' that morning which would involve a thorough scraping-away of general grime. It would also involve the spraying of the entire upper floor, private rooms and dormitory included. No inch would go untouched in the name of freshening the busy-bodied building up.

I was packed and downstairs by half-eight. Lunging forward to relay my door key to Jeremy, the American Guardian of Reception, he made to shake my hand, not expecting to have his palm scarred by the serrated side of the metal in my grip. 'Oh… you're going? I thought you just wanted to shake my hand for some abstract reason. Well don't forget your ten-dollar key deposit.' In truth, the reclamation of such money had totally slipped my mind. I thanked Jeremy for being so honest when he could have posted the cash into his back pocket. Trading in Khaled Hosseini's *A Thousand Splendid Suns* masterwork for Martin Cruz Smith's crime-corrupted novel *Havana Bay*, I bid adieu to the other two members of staff before easing my limbs onto Bussorah Street. Barely a murmur of life could be detected. Shops began to open as I loped east, pining to make contact with Beach Road - one of the city's main arteries - sooner rather than later. Striding up the steps of the nearest overpass, my attention come a cropper as a result of 'The Concourse', one of the most imposing buildings within reach of The Golden Mile Complex, the base of which housed a party of lifeless shops.

I'd been instructed to check-in for my bus at least half an hour prior to departure. I made it in the nick of time, surmising that I might as well spend the loose change a-jingling in my pocket. I only had one remaining note to my name, but I hoped that the ten dollars it was worth would see me through Melaka Sentral upon arriving in the city without any Malaysian currency. Confident that I'd be able to convert the dollars into ringgits at the bus station, I folded and stuffed the note into one of my breast pockets for safekeeping, spying my coach below the slippery concourse. It spelt the end of my life as an honorary Singaporean. Like itinerant wanderer Jack Kerouac knew only too well, the open road beckoned. It was up to me to boldly hit it like I meant it, without backing down.

~

AT NATURE'S MERCY, I EXCEL; I THRIVE; I NEVER FEEL
MORE ALIVE. It was fortunate then that I was on the cusp of
entering Penang National Park, an extensive swathe of
protected land languishing on the north-western corner of the
lush Malaysian island of Penang. Stationed in the coastal
village of Teluk Bahang, it was a short walk to the main
entrance of the park. Even better, it was free to gain access,
the sole charge relating to the canopy walkway which graces
the densely forested interior of the park.

Conspiring to stick as closely to the sea as we could, a
snaking path ushered us towards a couple of pagoda-spirited
rest-stops. A wooden bridge spanned the gap between banks
flanking a stream clamouring to spill its load into the sea. A
commotion was breaking out at the far side, an outbreak of
wild-eyed monkeys snatching bags of nuts from the hands of
passers-by. They weren't stupid, the monkeys. They knew
food when they saw it, even when it was disguised by plastic.
The three monkeys saw no shame in lunging for the naïve
tourists; one monkey even went so far as to slash a man's
wrist in his quest to get some nuts, as though Mr. T had
insisted that he do so via a subliminal message of the most
surreal variety. Their quarry obtained, such monkeys swung
away, leaving the visitors with very little to show for their
money. As it was, they'd purposefully purchased such nuts to
feed to the monkeys; they'd just hoped that a dab of
enjoyment might have surfaced as a result of relaying the
nuts one at a time to the expectant, impatient demons.

A short distance beyond the bridge, the path forked,
knifing our desire for a decision-free morning. Taking what
we hoped would be the route less traversed, we clung to the
coastline, rising and falling with the rocky nature of the
terrain, aiming for Monkey Beach by striking a well-worn
course through thick canopy, between boulders so huge they
wouldn't have looked out of place in *Raiders of The Lost Ark*'s

opening scene. We latched onto rock-anchored stretches of rope whenever caution became a necessity.

Tom from Tokyo led, allowing me to converse freely with a German vagabond called Felix as we skulked through virtually untouched rainforest. It was incredible to think that more than half of the species on earth live in rainforests, yet certain companies remain intent on destroying such sanctuaries for their own commercial gain. Approximately twenty-five per cent of 'ingredients' used in cancer-fighting drugs originate in such environments, hence the urgent need to protect and preserve rainforests. Worryingly, a desolate swathe of Penang National Park had suffered from deforestation, a tract of land on its northern edge showing signs of physical distress. One regiment of trees listened to the ground from an unnaturally horizontal position: slain and uprooted. However, there must have been good reason for such a clearing, for the rest of the park remained intact, its coast-hugging trail asserting minimal damage to the canopy through which it sliced.

The first beach to be reached on the trail fronted a university-affiliated complex of buildings in which marine biologists and oceanographers stayed whilst undertaking research. The self-contained cluster of buildings couldn't be located in a more idyllic setting, a useful jetty extending out from the sand, palm trees aplenty swaying on the doorstep. It wasn't a long hike to Monkey Beach by any means, yet most people larking about on the crescent of sand had rocked up by boat. A legion of BBQ pits suggested it was a popular place to kick back with skewers of sizzling meat to hand. Populated by teen-aged students, the grassy area backing the sand provided ample space for games to be played, a boisterous group of children from Myanmar proving as much by indulging in a frenzied game of 'pass the football'. Whenever the ringleader's chanting perished, it was up to the person left holding the ball to fathom a forfeit, usually in the guise of a silly dance designed to embarrass yet build confidence at the same time. Only a few of the teenagers were too self-conscious to initially participate. The man running the show with a whistle soon persuaded them to engage in the fun-lashed spirit of proceedings before they split for a sack race, then a volleyball match, prior to lunch.

As they indulged in chicken and rice, Felix, Tom and I stripped to the waist. For swimming purposes, I hasten to add. The water was too calm to resist, even though we were worried about the potential to be stung by jellyfish. A Liverpudlian staying at our guesthouse had remarked that stings were common. We took our chances, front-crawling away from the flotsam-sheathed shore as a united front of different nationalities. Encountering jellyfish was one thing; being bitten by a scorpion was another. Terrifyingly, the latter horror had befallen an Australian man with whom we'd chatted the previous evening. He regularly pitted himself against the challenging range of trails in the Teluk Bahang area, confiding the existence of a path which cut clean across to Georgetown, suitable only for the hardiest walkers. It later emerged that the man, who appeared to be in his sixties, hadn't once returned to Oz in twenty-five years, preferring to keep moving. Exceedingly fit for his age, he made a conscious effort to keep himself in shape by walking every day. His physical condition wasn't a concern. His happiness, on the other hand, was. A distressing strain of sadness desecrated his forever-tearing eyes.

After our dip, we uncharacteristically lazed around for half an hour, Tom merrily swinging in a pre-strung hammock for the first time, Felix and I chatting about his job in Vietnam. Whilst in the hammock, Tom got chatting to a family from Kuwait, the mother and daughter shrouded by black burqas. In English, they told Tom that he was the first Japanese person they'd ever met. They subsequently taught him a few pleasantries in Arabic. He returned the favour in his native language. Felix, meanwhile, chatted candidly about his role working for a non-profit organisation that aspired to advise Vietnam on economic matters. Just as we veered into political territory, Tom suggested that we continue hiking. It had already gone three, and we were still nowhere near our destination: Muka Head Lighthouse.

It was all uphill from the beach, a seemingly never-ending path consisting of well-laid steps luring us deeper into the rainforest over partly decomposed leaves and lethal roots. Forty-five minutes later, we wheezed into a fenced compound, disappointed there was no view to greet us. On the upside, it was possible to enter the lighthouse and climb its spiral staircase. Around and around we excitedly stomped. Emerging at the top, sunlight attacked us as though we were vampires, our eyes and patches of exposed skin recoiling from its malicious intent to scorch us out of our minds. Staggering through our collective blindness, we were careful not to tumble over the railing to our deaths. Instead, we steadied ourselves, collecting our thoughts, squinting through antique light that seemed to have suddenly become brighter. Was it heaven we saw before us, or did Penang revel in deceiving? Judging by the breathtaking three-hundred and sixty degree view, I vowed to straddle the fence until further notice, belittled by the interface zone below, unhurried waves unconsciously biting into a primeval land of barking giants, impervious to human nature.

~

'NO CHANGE,' chirruped the driver. I was instantly reminded of a trip I once took from Buffalo to Niagara Falls. The smallest change I had on my being was folded in the

form of a ten-ringgit note: more than two pounds. The cost of
the journey was just over one ringgit. I protested that it was
unfair to sting travellers for not having change, penalising
them for something beyond their control. The driver
remained unmoved, pushing the earphones of his iPod as far
down his ear canals as possible to muffle our incessant
crowing. He handled no money whatsoever; the only thing he
was employed to do was drive. He pointed at a funnel to his
left, under our noses. It was the cue for us to pour in all we
owed. Thus, we posted my note, surrendering more than
enough money to fund a ride to Georgetown, the first British
Straits Settlement to come into being in the late eighteenth
century. An intoxicating city that's undergone a colossal
transformation over the last two centuries, it's incredible to
think that the pivotal trading post started 'life' as a swampy
frontier, but that's history for you.

Having stayed in the north-western corner of the Malaysian
island of Penang for two nights after three days spent
marauding around Melaka, I was ready to move on. It was
difficult to say goodbye to a whole host of newfound friends,
however. Loping away from a quaint guesthouse owned and
overseen by a matronly Chinese lady called Miss Loh, Tom
and I aimed for the main street unapologetically cleaving the
sleepy settlement of Teluk Bahang in half. Even the four dogs
owned by Miss Loh were considerate enough to see us off,
chasing us to the ant-overrun gate as we waved back at Felix,
a man with whom we'd been travelling for five days since
randomly meeting on a bus out of Singapore. A captivating
renegade teetering on middle age, Felix had been living in
Hanoi for the past year, having upped and left Hamburg for
Asia on a long-term basis. He'd outlined the main reasons for
such a drastic relocation over a beer in Melaka. Cruising on
similar wavelengths in terms of how we approached life,
neither one of us was prepared to kowtow to society's

expectations. We decided to stick together whilst travelling further north through Malaysia. Done with the relaxing Heritage City of Melaka, we'd booked a bus ticket to Penang, one of the most popular places to visit in the country. An island of exceptional bounty, Penang can be reached from the mainland either by the spectacularly long Penang Bridge, or by various ferry services, the most frequent shuttling back and forth between Butterworth and Georgetown.

In spite of its natural beauty, Penang harbours a legion of off-putting surprises, mainly in the guise of high-rise apartment blocks which literally put the sprawling city of Georgetown to shame. Fortunately, the wealth of old buildings gracing the heart of Old Georgetown shoot the larger, more modern structures down in a blaze of glory. Such 'classics' are by far and away the most majestic and aesthetically pleasing from an architectural standpoint. Although Georgetown lacks the tranquil charms of Melaka further down the country's west coast, the hustle and bustle of Georgetown certainly ensures that the city's cultural melting-pot sucks visitors into its melee with accommodating gusto.

Once Tom and I had secured a night's lodging at 'Crystal Guesthouse', we pounded our way along Chulia Street in the rough direction of the waterfront, secretly vying to catch a cheap ferry over the strait to see how Butterworth compared. South of the busy terminal, the low-slung yet distinctive silhouette of the Penang Bridge flexed its arm of asphalt with modest expertise, suavely supporting a slow-moving wave of traffic that was evidently going nowhere. A ferry had just docked. The turn-around time was short enough to enable us to hop on-board had we so wished. But then I confronted my senses, arguing with myself that it would only be fitting to hang back in Georgetown given the amount of extraordinary buildings within its arbitrary city limits. It hadn't been designated a World Heritage City by UNESCO in 2008 for nothing. Wrestling logic back over Pengkalan Weld, I drove my legs forward, away from the people-packed ferry, past a den of grubby eateries, hankering after a glimpse of the famous clock tower on Lebuh Light. A commanding sixty-foot structure, as elegant as it is imposing, it took five years to build to commemorate the sixtieth year of Queen Victoria's reign. Unsurprisingly, Georgetown is suffused with reminders of when the British ruled the roost.

Pausing for a concoction of Indian and Malaysian cuisine, Tom caught up as a nut-flecked tray of noodles found its way into my palms. The proud cook kicked a plastic stool towards us, primed to unveil details about the inglorious sadness of a life that had begun in Chennai, India. Surprisingly, we shared a common background in the respect that he'd always suffered from abominable self-doubt owing to a lack of affirmation which had precipitated a lack of direction. Sensing that I empathised because I understood, he confided that he suffered from diabolical mental health. Like me, he'd been trying yet failing to outwit his paranoia for decades, railing against darkness elicited by depression. Roaring in the style of a religious fanatic, he seemed determined to convert me to his way of thinking. Tom, mindlessly gazing at the street life, was dismissed for precisely that reason. 'You listen and you understand,' he said, refusing to break eye contact as he stood to douse his pan in more oil. 'I can see your heart because you look into my soul.' Progressively sickened by the taste of his close-minded fervour, I calmly thanked him for the food and scuttled off, the balanced Buddhist within forgiving him his aggressive desire to shun alternative beliefs.

Aspiring to see more of the waterfront, I instinctively turned my attention to the port. The funnels of a behemothic cruise liner could be seen peeking over the roof of the nearest terminal, yet no access to the jetty could be granted to those without tickets. An aloof security guard warned me as much as I attempted to pass 'Go'. Instead, I led the way around to Padang Kota Lama, an attractive playing field sandwiched between two roads and tucked behind Fort Cornwallis. Such a fort once acted as the administrative centre of the island, built by Francis Light. Evidently an adaptable structure, it was even used by the Sikh Police at one time. Although it's not immediately obvious that the old fort is star-shaped in nature, its high walls and raised cannons go a long way in helping passers-by to imagine how intimidating a sight it must have made to strait-farers in colonial times of yore.

Turning our backs on the football-playing and kite-running children on the neatly-trimmed 'padang', we hopped over the road to see the stone war memorial silently paying tribute to those who'd laid down their lives between 1914 and 1918. The sobering monument enlivened the memory of various relatives. Dogged by a sudden dash of disconsolation, I inched over to the sea wall. Allowing my eyes the luxury of panning along the hotel-ridden coastline, I had to remind myself that my time in Malaysia had all but come to a shuddering climax. The following morning, I was due to take a six-hour bus ride south to Kuala Lumpur, agreeable weather permitting.

~

PRECISELY NINETY-TWO MINUTES after walking out of my guesthouse in Chinatown, I sat down a few yards shy of Gate Eighteen at Kuala Lumpur Airport, primed to return to the UK. Having coped considerably well with a life spent largely 'in transit', I'd mastered the art of streaming through airports unhindered, armed with the silent stealth of a secret agent. For sure, plans sometimes backfired, not least when Immigration collared me, but my passage through LCCT was a bona fide breeze worthy of the history books.

Following a frantic repacking session in my room, I'd stumbled out of my guesthouse consumed by stress, unfamiliar with the layout of KL's city centre. I'd stayed in the grand Malaysian capital over four years beforehand, but much had changed in the interim. Atop impossibly small and bare plots of land, gargantuan construction projects raged in support of the city's evolving, ever-modernising skyline. The last time I'd left the city, I'd done so by a coach bound for Singapore. This time around I needed to find the nearest Light Railway Terminal, unless I was in the mood for shelling out eighty ringgits for a taxi to the 'Air Asia' terminal - which I wasn't. Given that eighty ringgits equated to the best part of twenty pounds, I opted to travel the hard way, even though 'the hard way' wound up being simple to sweeten. It was only a ten minute walk to the nearest train terminal for a start, past an open-backed lorry laden with 'spare' dragon parts ready to be employed in yet another New Year-embracing spectacle. The dragon's lolling head promoted a tongue almost as long as the Penang Bridge over which I'd recently rolled.

The most difficult part of the initial stage in my journey was finding a set of steps in order to gain access to the elevated train line. A ticket to KL Sentral - just one stop away - cost a single ringgit, so I relayed two fifty-cent circles of silver under the counter. A couple of German travellers were waiting to go to KL Sentral, too. I'd seen them the previous evening whilst moseying around, searching for food and presents. Shockingly, the cost of food in Chinatown was expensive: a no-frills plate of white rice topped with an omelette sucked eight ringgits from my pocket without a hint of guilt, even though the menu proclaimed such a plate to be two ringgits cheaper than what I'd been charged. Nowhere else in Malaysia had tax been non-inclusive, so I questioned the gulf in price for want of something more productive to do. 'It's Chinese New Year,' the money-grabbing cashier abruptly remarked. 'Prices are higher for two weeks.' Fair enough, I thought... but it would still have been a commendable gesture to warn customers in advance that their food would beg for more moolah than expected.

There was no time to ascend in the lift to the Skywalk linking the iconic Petronas Towers. I'd barely had time to dash across to an ATM, desperate for a fresh wad of cash to pay for my guesthouse room. Once into KL Sentral, I loped to the Information Counter, keen to discover the easiest and cheapest way to get to the airport. As soon as I'd asked the man how to reach LCCT, a lady butted in. A fellow backpacker with location-specific knowledge tripping off her glossed lips, she told me to head to the basement.

A modern transit point of dazzling proportions, KL Sentral is simple to get around, its spacious interior playing host to myriad shops and restaurants. Luck was clearly on my side, for a boldly-signed coach revved at the foot of the steps. A prominent 'Air Asia' placard dominated the window. I threw my backpack in the hold and clambered aboard, reassured to see an 'Air Asia' flight attendant lounging in the first seat I brushed. Amazed that everything was running so smoothly, I braced myself, unwilling to let my guard down more than I already had in case the coach broke down - or worse. Five minutes later, we spun away from KL Sentral with less than twenty passengers present for the forty-five minute ride. One final glimpse of the distant Petronas Towers was all I could steal, the enlightened zeal of the rising sun's rays deflecting the structure's well-defined vision of a future that had done away with the past sooner than anticipated. The cost of the ride? Just eight ringgits. Spying the lofty flagpole catapulting attention upon Merdeka Square, I suddenly wished that I had more time to explore KL further, to probe its exotic back streets and side alleys deeper. They never failed to surprise. High-flying wisps of cloud promised a day of fine weather at odds with the situation on the east coast, widespread flooding the consequence of freak downpours.

What had started in Kathmandu, at the dawn of the millennium, was about to conclude in Kuala Lumpur. Wondering if people really are the sum of their experiences, I let my thoughts drift, confident I was making the right decision, the best decision, the only decision. After all, a vagabond's vices can just as readily be interpreted as deadly hallmarks of a crisis.

Sweeping away from KL's historical core, the grim sight of characterless apartment blocks sent shivers bucking down my spine, their grandiose designs inspiring terror instead of awe, their tiny windows allowing as little hope to escape as they permitted light to enter. Never before had I been in a position to marvel at the gigantic parcel of land over which the city spread its tentacles. Cursed estates kept schtum beside the highway as the familiar sight of spiritually impoverished houses hit home. Cringing at the gross banality of it all, I advised my conscience to remove both of my wrists from suburban suicide watch. Behind flimsy fences, personal lives were privatised in large and colourful detached houses. They wouldn't have looked out of place on Wisteria Lane. Drive after drive lay flat, lifelessly thinking of Japan, as cars and vans that had started life in the Far East sat out their Sunday morning without so much as a rag-wielding child to smear them. I wondered who lived on such out-of-the-way estates. It went without saying that the owners and tenants of such residences had a frankly disturbing cache of money at their disposal, as confirmed by their pretentious taste.

Already, my mind slogged through feelings inspired by friends and family back home. My thumping heart smashed the window and soared over to my girlfriend as a matter of course. It also beat for a beloved dog: Enzo, the beautiful pet Spinone that had belonged to one of my mum's best friends.

Having suffered from an unhealthily enlarged heart, his owner had agonised over her options before allowing a vet to put him to sleep. The news of Enzo's passing saddened me beyond belief, cajoling me into reflecting upon the extraordinary way in which animals can positively influence and enhance people's lives in a fashion they'll never fathom.

KL continued to reappear in fits and starts, random explosions of housing dotting the landscape between the epicentre of the melting pot and the airport. As the bus sped on, blue taxis bounced by, pre-labelled luggage keeping front seats warm while passengers unconsciously pulled faces from the rear seats, eliciting waves of anxiety, perhaps worried that their flights might desert them. On the far side of the multi-laned expressway, signs for Ipoh lured my stubble-grazed face towards the ghost of a grin. Felix had earlier messaged to say he'd been stranded in Ipoh on his way down to KL from Penang. If only I'd known that he'd been in Chinatown the same time as I'd been bustling between its haze of soup halls and maze of market stalls, dodging rainfall as I raced against time.

Tom, meanwhile, had considered trading in the island of Penang for Langkawi, until reports of extortion filtered through what remained of his common sense. He'd been ripped off too many times during the course of his short tour of Malaysia to surrender his wallet to any further financial misgivings or poor travel-related investments. For all that Langkawi resembled a fully-fledged tropical paradise, Tom had come to blows with his desire to visit on account of dire warnings he'd received from somebody who'd just returned. Unbelievably, the man 'in question' had returned without seeing anything of the island since he couldn't even find a splinter of accommodation. Every hotel, guesthouse and 'homestay' had been pre-booked to the rafters. 'That's the Chinese New Year for you,' the man sobbed. Langkawi remains one of the most popular destinations for Malaysians to visit over the holiday period. 'It's true,' the man continued, now in a better mood. 'Some Malaysians throw every last cent they've earned during the year into their two-week holiday over the New Year period. They work so hard for fifty weeks of the year that blowing money on lavish hotels is justifiable to them.' Understanding and sympathising with his level of discontent, I would have been just as disillusioned if I'd blown over two-hundred ringgits on getting to and from Langkawi without apprehending the opportunity to kick back on its fabled shores.

The spectre of the UK couldn't have been less tropical in nature. The thought of lowering myself beneath its damning thumb made my blood run colder than a thousand Malaysian coaches with their air-conditioners yoked to the sub-zero setting. As much as Britain declared itself to be a liberal country awash with conservative labourers, I wasn't convinced that it was a country in which I'd be able to settle again on a long-term basis. As Felix had said less than forty-eight hours beforehand: 'Life, in all its glory, all its richness, all its poverty, is lived out on the streets in Asia.' Gladdening memories considered, I wanted to be a part of those streets like never before, lusting after horizon-broadening experiences on a daily basis instead of mindlessly toiling for corporate clowns. I sought to chat and debate and laugh with real people in real time without feeling any need to bow before the impersonal evil balancing upon Facebook's increasingly anti-social neck. I needed to look to a future brimming with tantalising positivity and tangible prospects, at risk of turning my back on all that I'd conventionally held dear and believed to be true.

Asia, at large, had consumed me. I'd return the favour if it killed me.

~

VERY LITTLE COMPARES TO THE HEIGHT ADVANTAGE
OFFERED BY PLANES. Distanced from terra firma's dirty
reality, high-fliers are free to dream, to plot, to charge through
time whether they like it or not. Heading in what could only
be construed as a rough north-westerly direction, our
predetermined course would see us soar over India, Pakistan,
Afghanistan, Turkmenistan, Azerbaijan, and Georgia. The
pilot informed us of that much from the flight deck before we
taxied onto the runway. 'Afghanistan?' a woman in front of
me trilled. 'We'll surely get shot down if we fly over there!'
Outright fear preceding her sense of logic, she was adamant
that a surface-to-air missile might be capable of plucking us
out of the sky at thirty-three thousand feet. As dangerous as
the landlocked country is regarded to be, a friend called
Jonny Bealby leads tours into its most mountainous reaches,
highlighting its staggering beauty. A writer and tour operator
par excellence, Jonny's company is known as 'Wild Frontiers',
and he prides himself on taking customers well off the beaten
track in their quest to learn more about lesser-known realms
of our beautiful planet.

Chasing the light, we left Kuala Lumpur at three in the
afternoon, a little later than scheduled. Bracing my body for
the fourteen-hour flight, I'd wisely pocketed my copy of
Coupland's *Eleanor Rigby*, unwilling to fork out for the
handheld entertainment console available to passengers.
Fortunately, my hand luggage weighed less than seven
kilograms, thereby avoiding additional charges. Prepared to
shoulder no risks whatsoever, I'd jammed as much gear as I
could in a small satchel purchased in a New Delhi Bazaar.
Psychologically scarred by the debacle I'd faced at Surabaya
Airport when my backpack had gone AWOL, I was
determined to keep everything of importance and sentimental
value close to my chest.

Having breezed into the airport with three hours to spare before take-off, I'd foolishly waited until the last minute before approaching the gate, neglecting to remind myself that most gates close twenty minutes before the plane's due to hit the skies rumbling. I was too busy buying a chicken wrap to notice that my gate was on the verge of closing. Fellow travellers had already begun trekking out of the terminal, over the tarmac towards the waiting plane. Spying the line of people ascending the twin-set of steps, I rapped my wrap and followed suit, relaying my crumpled boarding pass to a rep a minute before the gate prevented further additions to the flight. Once on-board, I found myself wedged between a Malaysian woman and a Chinese man, neither of whom spoke English. Positioned at the centre of the fuselage, I couldn't have been further away from the nearest window if I'd locked myself in the toilet cubicle at the centre. Deprived of a vision, I watched the flight attendants slog through the motions, pointing to the emergency exits, demonstrating how to put on and inflate life jackets. A child to my left started crying in protest, perhaps disappointed by the lack of enthusiasm displayed by the reddened personnel. In their defence, they did what needed to be done with enough professionalism to rid them of responsibility if the plane took a nosedive. Momentarily engaged in a morbid battle of wills, I wondered if it would be best to crash-land into the sea, the mountains, or the desert.

The stewardesses could only cover their fatigue with so much make-up. One girl's eyes were lowered by lack of sleep to such a degree that she felt the need to excuse herself for being tired whilst on the job, confiding that shift patterns were proving detrimental to sleep patterns when asked if she was okay by a concerned gent who'd noticed her eyelids meet in the middle whilst undertaking final safety checks. I was reminded of what Sarah had said about her time as a flight attendant, and how Chronic Fatigue Syndrome had come to affect her, full-blown burn-out syndrome often experienced by folk toiling on the front line of the aviation industry.

As we dipped through turbulence, my trust in the crew bloomed. The central section of the fuselage dared to shake itself free from its bondage, the rattling of various fixing points focusing my attention on the apparent flimsiness of our suddenly vulnerable means of high-speed conveyance. Tuning my ears to circumstantial evidence, it sounded like the engines had drifted to sleep and that we were descending. Not plummeting; simply falling. I could no longer hear air rushing over the wings. A disturbing silence pounded both of my eardrums, seizing my composure, mutilating it beyond recognition into panic. Sea, mountains, or desert, I wondered. I craned my neck left and then right, attempting to ascertain the kind of landscape over which we were screaming. A bleeping drone belatedly warned people to return to their seats in order to belt up. Scenic excursions to the toilet would have to wait. I squirmed in consternation, potentially strapped to my death-seat. My curved spine hated me for taking long-haul flights, yelping its loudest grievance from the fourth vertebrae. It had been fractured five years earlier in an accident. I felt its pain. By Buddha, did I feel it.

Rolling with all that the tempestuous skies had to throw at us, we eventually arced over European airspace, mentally mapping our futures as we collectively imagined who or what might be waiting for us at Stansted. Beginning our descent some two-hundred miles from the airport, a multitude of young children began to cry, wondering why their ears were suddenly hurting so much, nonplussed by the unbearable pain brought about by the change in air pressure. Although I resisted crying, I felt like joining their ranks, duly rubbing my earlobes, vying to calm their passions.

Constantly craving fresh experiences, I had no intention of succumbing to a work-orientated lifestyle of woe. Whether I was squaring up to The Fantastic Four in Canada, suffering from altitude sickness in the Himalayas, rubbing shoulders with Hollywood heavyweights in Thailand, reeling from food poisoning in Morocco, being threatened with detention in Montenegro, sending myself to Hel and back in Poland, doing as the locals don't in the USA by walking everywhere, treading carefully in the landmine-littered mountains of Bosnia, penetrating Vietnam's boundaries in the company of illegally smuggled snakes, stumbling upon gypsy markets in Romania, living on borrowed time in Northern Ireland, teaching in Turkey, clubbing in Latvia, living in Mexico, kipping down with the homeless in Denmark, losing my bearings in Italy, being moved to tears by Cambodia's recent history, sharing random rooms with relative strangers, or getting blatantly ripped-off more times than I cared to remember, I remained receptive to all that a life in transit could fling my way. Rarely feeling more at 'home' than when of no fixed abode, I stalked an otherworldly avatar as a walking contradiction in terms.

The landing was smooth. The only disappointment came at the carousel. Waiting for eternity to come and go and then return, a German man jockeyed for the best position, ducking his head through gaps at certain points along the length of the slow-turning Conveyor of Hope. A Polish man subsequently muscled his hips between us for bad measure. The latest addition to the line-up appeared not to know what his luggage looked like, for he proceeded to pick up then replace four suitcases. None of them belonged to him. I'd made a point of racing to Immigration, conscious that dishonest bones in some folk can intermittently tempt them to steal 'excess baggage'. Forty-five minutes after the carousel began running in circles, my backpack ascended from the bowels and plonked itself in sight. It had never looked so battle-scarred or road-weary. We'd come a long way together since falling for Nepal in 2000. Grabbing it by its straps before it undertook a lap of honour, I staggered back. Slipping out of my grasp, my baggage acted like dead weight, the floor slapping its face. Stooping to retrieve it, the palm of my right hand touched base with the underside of my left wrist. It detected something I'd not felt for more than ten years. Like Kerouac and Ginsberg, the ragged yet poetic beat inspired. Rooted by a re-evaluated life throbbing through enlarged and enlightened veins, I'd finally found a pulse.

EPILOGUE

Driffield, England
July 1, 2011

READ, LISTEN, RESPOND. Obey the order of orders by giving more than you take. If there's something of a constrictive persuasion clipping your heels, walk, and keep walking, and don't ever look back. The end is the beginning if there's light beyond the black.

The world can turn on its axis in an instant. As I type this, swaying between the first and second half of 2011 with Springsteen on the radio, I'm conscious that each passing day coyly persuades one and all to take outlandish chances. This memoir-ridden travelogue represents a snapshot of a season's window of opportunity, reflecting how I felt at the time. Though unforeseen circumstances have significantly altered the course of my life since returning to the UK, I didn't feel inclined to tamper with the truth in the form of the original text's bare bones. Had I shadily edited my writing, I would have done the integrity of my emotional journey a gross disservice. Succinctly shoving affairs into perspective, it's only right to reveal that my girlfriend and I 'let go' of one another at the end of June, sadly yet selflessly parting ways to fortify our respective futures.

Retreading familiar territory in Yorkshire, it was imperative that I confronted a shocking epiphany: long-haul travel doesn't always change a person for the better. On the upside, it tempts folk to be brutally honest. The truth of any given situation becomes more outstanding when viewed through experienced eyes; ergo, the act of travelling has a 'Magic Eye' effect, enabling transient souls to literally peek between the lines that repel interpretations of reality from elusive spiritual planes.

In the shadow of a week's decompression in France, I trudged to Beverley Job Centre. There, sweating beneath Orwellian lights, I was made to feel personally responsible for the Global Economic Crisis. 'What kind of job are you looking for?' I was asked. 'Anything!' I shrieked in desperation. I was then forced to fill in a detailed questionnaire to prove that I was British, my extended absence abroad branding a certain Mr. Rudd a 'Systematic Deserter'. The 'Ethnic Origin' tick box stumped me. I wondered if I'd be able to get away with acknowledging my ancient African heritage. In spite of knowing who I was, and where I was from, being a 'Citizen of the World' was no longer an option.

Early on in my travels, I'd commented upon a blind boy clocked crawling along the gangway of a train. I'd described the state of his eyesight as 'compromised' when, in fact, it had been 'obliterated'. To elaborate, the blind boy saw more than I ever had. Gingerly patting my pockets, he taught me a vital lesson: if you shed your blinkers, the world opens up. Fresh opportunities can then whip into reach. Eliminate money, and what have you got? Life in its rawest form… as it once was, and as it should be. So much depends on personal perspective, expectations, context. As an example, I rushed to see David Hockney's 'Bigger Trees Near Warter', temporarily hung in Hull. A lifelong fan of the artist's work, I sloped away from the painting into a burgundy curtain of disappointment, the monstrous scope of the work somehow overshadowed by the fine detail displayed in a nebulous 'Night School' original.

I vowed to work in whatever capacity I could. All the while, I knew something wasn't right. Money was too much of an issue. Crying for a haircut upon hitting London, I asked how much it would cost to have my head shaved in a salon near Covent Garden. The proprietor said it would be cheaper to dart around the corner to the nearest barbers. Neglecting to ascertain the price in advance, I sat and smiled as an insult to Cockney Rhyming Slang bounced off the mirror. Two minutes later, my heart lurched. 'That'll be thirteen pounds and fifty pence, please.' My wallet lamped the floor. Later, in St. Pancras Station, my jaw dislocated itself at the price of coffee and tickets. I couldn't believe that it cost more to travel between London and Hull than it had to rail thousands of miles around the subcontinent. That reminded me: on Elephanta Island, I'd climbed a tree, only to be reprimanded by a cave-guarding official. 'What do you think you're doing?' he barked. 'I don't think I'm doing anything,' I replied. 'I know what I'm doing; I'm communing with nature.' His bushwhacked eyebrows crumpled hysterically. 'Not here you're not,' he affirmed. 'But two negatives make a positive!' I amicably protested. 'You're in India!' he shot back. In spirit, I was still there.

Pound signs, or lack of, served notice not only to my relationship, but also a number of friendships. In the wider world, Simon and Sheetha returned to London shortly after I resettled in England. A week later, they were winging their way to Rio, anticipating fresh adventures in South America. In the Far East, Tom bore the brunt of nuclear fallout as disaster crippled Tokyo.

Some coincidences are 'conveniently coincidental' to suspicious degrees. For a start, I'd randomly encountered Fabienne in four different cities. Before first talking to her in Agra, I'd seen her in Udaipur. I subsequently bumped into her in Varanasi and Kolkata, days and miles apart. When she confessed that she was bound for Melbourne, I wasn't surprised. At the time, I was also poised to touch down in the Australian city. However, I ultimately missed Fabienne's 'message'; fate prodded me in a different direction too soon. I pondered some more about the nature of chance, reflecting upon how I'd met a man at the Grand Canyon before stumbling into him again in Seattle, and how Steph Greenstreet, a student I'd befriended over breakfast in Frankfurt was best friends with an Essex girl I became attached to in Thailand. Strangely, at the same table in Germany's aloof capital of finance, I met a writer and model from Sydney: Taylor Schon. Three years later, I was shocked to discover he was friends with a woman (a former 'FHM' editor called Georgia) who'd once worked with one of my closest boyhood pals (photographer Chris Manson) in Dubai. Such thoughts forced me to rip apart the substance surrounding the concept of destiny. To what extent had my return to the UK been based on a conscious decision fuelled by what my head and heart had suggested I do? Once upon a time, I was convinced we were masters of our own destinies. As of now, I'm not sure.

Though practicalities duly ruptured the influential bond shared with Sarah, I refused to regard anything as regrettable. I'd once flown all the way to Mexico just to tell a girl I loved her. My Sarah-bound flight had been propelled by an added shot of emotional momentum. Pity the gravity of reality progressively punctured our dazzling demonstration of mutual support in action. Amidst the debasing murk of society's smokescreen, I lost focus, retreating into myself as the pressure to provide without relevant means hammered my self-esteem as much as it did my bank account. It was nobody's fault; it was merely circumstantial.

In the past, when faced with an emotional crisis, I would have been tempted to flit, keen to ignore the situation's severity. I might have spontaneously booked a flight to see a friend in Sedona, an uncle in Calgary, or a shaman in Outer Mongolia, in spite of wanting to walk 'El Camino' before investing a month in Dharavi. The temptation to bolt edged into my consciousness by way of tabled magazines and timeless gossip. But I had to break the cycle. I couldn't keep running. I'd learnt that people don't necessarily have to lose themselves in order to find themselves.

Regardless, I reopened my Atlas, closed my eyes, and pointed.